Germany and Europe in the
Era of the Two World Wars

Germany and Europe in the Era of the Two World Wars

Essays in Honor of
ORON JAMES HALE

Edited by
F. X. J. Homer
and
Larry D. Wilcox

University Press of Virginia
Charlottesville

THE UNIVERSITY PRESS OF VIRGINIA
Copyright © 1986 by the Rector and Visitors
of the University of Virginia

First published 1986

Frontispiece:
Oron James Hale on the occasion of his retirement, 20 May 1972.

Library of Congress Cataloging-in-Publication Data
Main entry under title:

Germany and Europe in the era of the two world wars.

Bibliography: p.   86-10201
    1. Germany—History—20th century—Addresses,
essays, lectures. 2. Germany—Foreign relations—
Europe—Addresses, essays, lectures. 3. Europe—
Foreign relations—Germany—Addresses, essays, lectures.
4. Hale, Oron J. (Oron James)—Addresses, essays,
lectures. I. Hale, Oron J. (Oron James) II. Homer,
F. X. J., 1941–   . III. Wilcox, Larry D., 1942–
DD235.G47   1986   943.08   85-13405
ISBN O-8139-1077-3

Printed in the United States of America

Contents

Preface

O RON JAMES HALE, *a Virginia gentleman from the state of Washington via the University of Pennsylvania, devoted nearly half a century to the historical profession in this country. His academic career at the University of Virginia (1929–1972) spanned the period from the beginning of the Great Depression to the academic depression of the 1970s. In between he served as both soldier and diplomat, most notably in the military government of Bavaria from 1950 to 1952. He received various awards from the historical profession, the United States government, and the Federal Republic of Germany. He somehow found time to complete four substantial monographs, as well as numerous reviews and articles in a wide variety of journals. He shepherded at least sixteen aspiring young historians through Ph.D's and countless more through M.A.'s at the University of Virginia. Until the boom times of the mid-1960s, he made up most of the modern European section of the history department at the University of Virginia. Those of us who arrived in Charlottesville during those boom times frequently heard Professor Hale's colleagues remark that it would take at least three good historians to replace him when he retired. One need only look at the impressive current roster of modern German and European historians at the University of Virignia to conclude that this may have been an understatement.*

Professor Hale's teaching and scholarship reflected a broadly based approach to historical research and writing, as illustrated by his publications. Through his own teaching, scholarship, and service, he consciously witnessed against the narrow specialization overtaking the historical profession by the end of his academic career. His career illustrates the successful practice of what we should all aspire to, the golden mean between distinguished scholarship and teaching and service to the larger community within which scholars work.

Since Oron Hale's career, academic and public, interacted most closely with the development of Germany, it does seem appropriate that he be honored with a festschrift. The tradition of former students presenting scholarly essays in honor of their academic mentor in such a volume is one deeply rooted in the culture of German universities. Though hardly a sufficient offering of the gratitude of Oron James Hale's many students, it is in this spirit that we present the following collection of essays.

The editors of this volume began making contact with Professor Hale's former graduate students some years ago about their reactions to a festschrift in his honor. All who responded to our inquiry offered enthusiastic encouragement; many offered scholarly contributions for possible inclusion. After careful consideration of Professor Hale's own scholarly emphases and the nature of the proffered contributions, we agreed that the proper focus for any festschrift honoring Professor Hale should be Germany and its relations with Europe in this century, particularly the period framed by the two world wars. All of the substantive contributions accepted by the editors for inclusion in this volume are original scholarly essays related to our chosen theme. These eight contributions are bracketed by a biographical essay composed by Professor Enno Kraehe, a colleague and friend of Professor Hale at the University of Virginia, and a Hale bibliography compiled by Ms. Marie Donaghay. Sadly, one of our colleagues in this venture, Professor James Mumper, died before the publication of this volume. His essay had been completed before his death and the editors have added only a few revisions without changing any of its substance.

The editors of this volume have accumulated many debts along the way beyond those due the other, and very patient, contributors to this volume. A number of former Hale associates have tendered valuable assistance to several authors of essays, in particular Mr. Robert Wolfe of the National Archives, who helped clarify points about Professor Hale's career and events in his own former posting with the U.S. Army in Heidelberg. Many individuals have also provided support for the necessary publication costs of this volume, both former students and former colleagues of Professor Hale at Virginia. We are also grateful for institutional assistance from Emory and Henry College.

No such endeavor reaches fruition without the untiring assistance of the departmental secretaries who help decipher illegible scrawls and umlauts in order to provide the publisher with a usable manuscript. Lucille Endsley, senior history department secretary at the University of Toledo, helped hold up the Toledo end of this project throughout the entire process, typing enough German history, and German words, to make her contemplate retirement. Her colleague, Paula Ashton, though a latecomer to this project, has already received her initiation into the world of umlauts. Mary Lynn Duris assisted in the preparation of our index. At the University of Scranton, editor Homer received more help than he can really afford on his professional salary from Nancy Birrane, former history department secretary, and her diligent successor, Elizabeth Caputo. The critical task of typing the entire manuscript into a word processor was ably carried out by Patricia Jolley and Barbara Quinn. Thomas L. Scott, S.J., generously took time away from his own projects to proofread the manuscript.

Mr. Walker Cowen, Director of the University Press of Virginia, and our editor, Mr. Gerald Trett, have guided, very gently, two novices through the wondrous world of scholarly publishing. Of course, as always in such projects, the editors bear the final and full responsibility for the product of our long journey.

F. X. J. HOMER
University of Scranton

LARRY D. WILCOX
University of Toledo

Germany and Europe in the Era of the Two World Wars

I

Oron James Hale and the Twentieth Century

ENNO E. KRAEHE

ORON JAMES HALE has been more than an outstanding teacher at the University of Virginia. As the author of four major books, officer in military intelligence during World War II, official interrogator of high-ranking Nazi officials, United States commissioner for the state of Bavaria after the war, director of the mammoth project to preserve German war documents on microfilm, a founder of the Conference Group for Central European history, and, not least, the venerated mentor of the authors contributing to this volume, Professor Hale is a national and international figure whose career reflects the course of world history in the twentieth century.[1]

Hale is the scion of generations of venturesome pioneers who landed in New England in the seventeenth century, reached St. Louis in the 1830s, and then moved on further west, his grandfather settling in the Washington territory in the 1880s. His father, William Robert Hale, married Frances Putnam, who gave him two sons, Estell William, born in 1900, and Oron James, born on 29 July 1902 in Goldendale, Washington—safely within the new century. As a boy Oron so disliked this exotic name that a sympathetic aunt resolved to call him Pat, an appellation that soon virtually replaced the original for all but legal and literary purposes. Pat's first brush with world history was a slight one: his withdrawal from high school for two years during World War I because his help was needed on the family ranch. In 1919 he made up the deficiency and then enrolled at the University of Washington, where he pursued a prelaw program. In those days the staple of such programs was English constitutional history, which young Hale studied with profound interest under Henry Steven Lucas. Oliver Huntington Richardson in political science was another powerful influence.

Without taking a bachelor's degree—another commonplace of the time—he entered law school at Washington in 1923, to all appearances bound for a career in a small-town western law firm. During the year, however, he was stricken with appendicitis and peritonitis, which combined to keep him from his studies too long for him to make up the work that year. There was time, however, to return to the College of Arts and Sciences, where he acquired the bachelor's degree after all, as well as a renewed passion for history and a determination to pursue the subject in graduate school. Through Lucas's influence he was admitted to the University of Pennsylvania, probably without making any other applications.

Unlike many students who left Washington and traveled to the eastern schools on sheep trains, Hale luxuriated in a Pullman for three days. The comforts did not last past the Philadelphia station, however. It was 23 September 1926, the day of the first Dempsey-Tunney fight in a town already jammed with visitors to the Philadelphia world's fair. Finding no hotel room, he asked directions to the campus itself and then could not find it. The greenhorn, it seems, was looking for the kind of bucolic atmosphere and spacious lawns that he had known out west, not the red bricks of an urban school. He was on the campus without knowing it, but at least he found lodgings.

At Pennsylvania he studied mainly with Edward P. Cheyney, the medievalist, and William Ezra Lingelbach, the professor of modern European history, attending their lectures, reading their papers, and teaching their preceptorials, which he later described as more rowdy than scintillating. The summers of 1927 and 1928 he was able to spend in Paris, Munich, and Berlin doing research on a dissertation relating to European diplomacy and the press in the years 1904–6. His suitcases bulging with notes, he returned in September 1928 for his final year and to the amenities permitted by the George Leib Harrison fellowship, which paid the handsome stipend of $1000, enough to meet expenses without teaching and to finance the summer of 1929 writing his dissertation while working on the ranch in Washington. This was all very well but not so important as his courtship of a young journalist, Annette Van Winkle, whom he married on 7 August of that year, the dissertation not quite finished.

In the meantime the wheels most vital to a budding academic career were in motion. A colleague of Lingelbach's heard about Hale and alerted his friend of Oxford days, the historian String-fellow Barr, at the University of Virginia, who consulted the department chairman, or rather the assistant chairman, Dumas Malone, who did the work. A department of only four members was stretched very thin and badly needed someone to bolster the entire range of European courses. Oron Hale, with medieval and English history from Cheyney and Modern Europe from Lingelbach seemed a promising prospect.

Only after his retirement did he confess that the young hopeful of 1929 did not know then where the University of Virginia was located; he soon found out, however, and in the spring boarded a train to Charlottesville for an interview. He received the typical Virginia treatment: informal discussion in the Colonnade Club with members of the department, a talk with the president, Edwin A. Alderman, and luncheon at the home of Dumas and Elizabeth Malone. Returning to Philadelphia that night, he began that period of anxious waiting and repeated reassessment of performance that is common to all applicants. Two weeks later the offer came, and Hale accepted it. An opening at Princeton was also a possibility at the time, but he did not pursue it because another Lingelbach student in the same field was already there: Raymond J. Sontag, who in fact was to have a career similar to his at Princeton and Berkeley.

The academic year of 1929-30 continued the excitement and strenuous activity. There were, first of all, three courses at advanced and graduate levels: Medieval Civilization, Tudor and Stuart England, and Europe since 1814, a strenuous program for anybody, much more a beginner, but that is the brutal way of the profession. In December, Hale presented his first paper to the American Historical Association, meeting that year in Durham, N.C. In a session on "Diplomatic Episodes of the Later Era," the intrepid doctoral candidate argued that after the fall of the French foreign minister Theophile Delcassé, the French press, which had brought him down, led Germany to expect a rapprochement with her neighbor, which of course was a mistaken view of actual French policy.[2] The meeting also involved an official banquet for which tickets needed to be purchased in advance. Forgetting his new marital status, the young scholar, as in years past, bought only one and later found that it was too late to undo the damage; Anne dined privately with friends and no doubt had a better meal than he. Then there was the uncompleted dissertation, the key to all else, but by dint of exhausting late nights familiar to all doctoral candidates who accept employment without the degree, he finished at last, receiving the coveted diploma in May 1930. The big disappointment of the year, however, was the sudden departure of the man Lingelbach had painted as a counsellor and companion above all others: Dumas Malone, who was called to Washington, D.C. by his old teacher, Allen Johnson, to join him in editing the *Dictionary of American Biography*. Hale's disappointment was great, but it was to be reversed in the end.

The titular chairman of the department when Hale began was Richard Heath Dabney, a formidable man who, like many of his generation, had received his graduate training in the famous universities of Germany. Barr and, after him, Cary Johnson were the actual managers in the 1930s. Hale, meanwhile, published his dissertation under the title *Germany and the Diplomatic Revolution 1904-1906* (Philadelphia, 1931). This study cannot be called a pioneering work, but it was one of several that took a new direction in the study of diplomacy. The publication of Sidney Bradshaw Fay's *The Origins of the World War* (2 volumes, New York, 1928) and Bernadotte E. Schmitt's *The Coming of the War* (2 volumes, New York, 1930) seemed to exhaust the possibilities of scholarship based mainly on diplomatic dispatches, at least on this subject, and Fay himself mentioned the "poisoning of public opinion" as a cause of the war. There followed a spate of public opinion studies, notable among which were Hale's book and E. Malcolm Carroll's *French Public Opinion and Foreign Affairs, 1870–1914,* both published in 1931.[3]

Hale dealt with both the influence of the press on governments and the use the latter made of the press during the formative period of the Entente Cordiale and the First Moroccan Crisis, a development that he was one of the first to characterize, with some exaggeration, as a diplomatic revolution. Thus, the emphasis was not on public opinion as such but on its manipulation, sometimes with unpredictable results, as when the skeptical French remained unmoved by Francophile overtures coming out of England. Of special importance was the role of a hostile press in the fall of Delcassé as previously argued in his Durham paper. Though criticizing some matters of style and a few debatable conclusions, the reviews were mostly favorable, but none more so than that of the committee which awarded the book the George Louis Beer prize of the American Historical Association for the best book on diplomatic history that year.[4]

With such credentials Hale received a grant for the year 1932-33 from the Social Science Research Council to pursue further research in Europe on diplomacy and the press. The timing was exciting for one who, having studied revolution from afar, now spotted one coming in Germany and was itching to be on the scene. And indeed he was, arriving, via the Library of Congress and the British Museum, in Berlin in January 1933 to witness the marching of Brown Shirts, violence in the streets, and finally the actual appointment of Hitler as chancellor on 30 January. The next few months were not easy for research but fascinating all the same. In early May he and Anne bought a car and motored to Prague, Vienna, and finally to Munich, where Dabney chanced to be seeking out his haunts of student days. A convivial tour of the beer gardens followed.

At the end of the summer the Hales returned to the America of depression and New Deal. At the university salaries were successively cut but never in devastating amounts. Besides, for someone of Hale's growing reputation the losses could be recouped by visiting assignments elsewhere: at Duke, where he taught in the summers of 1934, 1938, and 1939, and the University of Missouri in the summer of 1937. In Charlottesville in the rest of the year parties at the Colonnade Club continued as did dinners in private homes, usually in formal dress. Students by tradition dressed as gentlemen, always appearing in class in jacket and tie. Although the young westerner took surprisingly well to this style of life, his innate dignified mien comporting easily with the image of a Virginia gentleman, he was grateful all the same that a change was but a rifle shot away in the beautiful meadows and woodlands surrounding Charlottesville and in the Blue Ridge Mountains. There, over the years, he found his happy hunting grounds and formed strong attachments to successive generations of retrievers and pointers that passed through the Hale household. How could a red brick university compete with this?

In the history department, meanwhile, Thomas Perkins Abernethy became Malone's replacement in 1930. When Stringfellow Barr left in 1937 for the University of Chicago, Hale took over the undergraduate program, most importantly the course on Europe since 1500 (B1 and B2). It was not easy to follow the dazzling and original Barr, who went on to develop the Great Books programs at Chicago and later at St. John's College, but Hale, with his rare combination of dignity and wit and an exciting familiarity with recent events, was triumphant in his own way and taught the course till his retirement in 1972. The Medieval Civilization, on the other hand, he surrendered to Charles Julian Bishko, who joined the department in 1938. About the same time Dabney retired as chairman, to be succeeded by Cary Johnson, another brilliant teacher, whom Hale greatly admired.

In 1940 the materials gathered in the Hitler year and perspired over for the rest of the decade finally came to flower in the publication of another book, *Publicity and Diplomacy 1890-1914 with Special Reference to England and Germany* (New York). This work continued Hale's interest in how the press was deliberately used by interest groups to affect government policy and how the latter in turn used the organs of publicity to influence public opinion. Though recognized today as "the best book on the subject in any language,"[5] and admired at the time for the technical mastery displayed in it, its immediate reception was equivocal, partly by reason of Hale's unpopular (even if defensible) contention that an irresponsible press might be more dangerous to peace than secret diplomacy. The author, moreover, wrote in the spirit of the revisionist interpretation of World War I and believed that Britain's entry in 1914 had been a "tragic blunder"—hardly what the British and many Americans wanted to be told in 1940.[6] The timing was poor in another way, for the Germans, who might have praised the work, were almost cut off from American publishing at the time; they never did review Hale's work and after the war eventually became more critical of their country's action in 1914 than he had been. This issue remains controversial, but the major theme of the book, the linkage between the press and government policy, remains a lasting contribution to the field.

Soon the United States was in the war, and it was inevitable that the man with the itch to witness events at first hand should enter the service. First, however, there was one last duty in academe: serving in 1942 as director of the university's widely known Institute of Public Affairs, a summertime series of round tables and lectures that brought students and townspeople together with visiting dignitaries—most notably, during Hale's term, Assistant Secretary of State Dean Acheson. Shortly thereafter the history professor joined the military intelligence section of the War Department General Staff, rising to the rank of lieutenant-colonel by the end of the war, and adding to his historical perspective stores of information about Germany that prepared him for perhaps his most intimate contact with the great events of his day.

This encounter occurred in the summer of 1945, when he was called to represent the intelligence section on a small commission of experts assigned to interrogate a number of high-ranking Nazi politicos and military leaders then in the custody of the allies. Unlike some similar missions, which were to assemble evidence for the war-crimes trials, this one was simply to gather intelligence at the highest level regarding not only the German conduct of the war but also the impact of our own performance as experienced on the other side. The mission was headed by George Shuster, president of Hunter College and the author of several well-known books on Germany; most of the other members likewise came from a variety of academic backgrounds.

The interrogations took place in an obscure spa in Luxembourg, called Mondorf-les-Bains, where the prisoners were being held in a modest resort hotel surrounded by three rings of electrified barbed wire but camouflaged to look like a detention camp for ordinary prisoners of war, not the likes of Hermann Goering, once next to Hitler in the Nazi hierarchy; the foreign minister, Joachim von Ribbentrop; Wilhelm Keitel, Hitler's personal military advisor; Alfred Rosenberg, the so-called party philosopher; Franz von Papen, the minister who had engineered Hitler's appointment as chancellor; Admiral Karl Doenitz, the commander of the German navy; and many others of similar importance—some forty in all. Not many second-class hotels ever had guests of such distinction all at once, Hale observed.[7]

In their interviewing rooms on the second floor the commissioners divided the work on the basis of professional interest and expertise, Shuster, Hale, and the Stanford political scientist John Brown Mason concentrating on political and related military issues. Among Hale's subjects in this capacity were Ribbentrop and Goering. The former he found to be too shattered and incoherent to be of much use. Goering, on the other hand was witty, keen of mind, endowed with a good memory, and—ever the egotist enjoying the limelight—eager to cooperate. Indeed, when other visitors came to the compound, he was inclined to sulk if they did not ask for him. Most of the prisoners, now absolved of their oaths, were relatively informative so long as their personal roles were not under examination. And some in fact, like General Adolf Heusinger, who became a lifelong friend of Hale's, were anti-Nazi. Of special interest to Hale were the half dozen or so journalists such as Wilhelm Weiss, editor of the party newspaper, the *Völkischer Beobachter,* Paul K. Schmidt, chief of the Press Division of Ribbentrop's foreign office, and most importantly, Max

Amann, head of the so-called Eher Verlag, the firm that in devious ways had gradually taken over the independent newspapers and publishing firms, often without public awareness that the firms had changed hands. Almost twenty years later Amann's testimony was to become the cornerstone of Hale's next book.

Hale was the principal interrogator in some twenty-two cases extending over about four weeks in July and August. While most of the commissioners then returned to the United States, he stayed on another ninety days to collate the reports prepared on each of the interviews and prepare a comprehensive summary of the whole. This he submitted on 20 December.[8] In the meantime, the historical division of the Department of the Army had undertaken a far larger operation, which required that before deactivation every unit, staff, or agency must submit, along with its official records, a narrative history of its activities and accomplishments. When Hale returned to Washington in late December 1945, these histories were beginning to pour in, many of them ineptly written. To edit, synthesize, and evaluate this mass of material the call went out to reassign those in the service who appeared most qualified for such work. In this way Hale's tour of duty was unexpectedly extended for six months as he became chief of the section established to review the ever-rising piles of manuscripts. It was, he observed, "one of the biggest mass production jobs of book reviewing" ever undertaken, the one assignment in the army that he was glad to leave.[9] This he did in time to teach in the summer session at the University of North Carolina in 1946, after which he returned at last to the familiar contours of the Blue Ridge Mountains and the intimate scale of the academical village, as Mr. Jefferson liked to call his university.

The immediate postwar years were relatively serene. On his return, Hale was promoted to full professor and found himself in great demand as a speaker. Classes were larger than before, owing to the influx of former soldiers under the G.I. Bill of Rights, but Virginia remained relatively small compared to the average state university. Then events abroad again intruded. As civilian authority replaced military occupation in Germany,

John J. McCloy in 1949 became the United States High
Commissioner and appointed as state commissioner (landeskommissar) for Bavaria George Shuster, who immediately
asked Hale to sign on as his deputy. By that time the Korean
War had broken out, and Hale, still an active reservist, was
pondering whether his next post would be in Korea or the
Pentagon. Under the circumstances it was easy indeed to opt
for Munich.

During this transitional period in Bavaria, Hale's principal
responsibility was to supervise a program for replacing military
government at the local level with American civilians, usually
young Foreign Service officers, whose duties were to administer the occupation law, to give aid and friendly counsel (rather
than orders), and to encourage a democratic spirit at the grass
roots.[10] When Shuster resigned after a year, McCloy elevated
the deputy, thereby plunging Hale into the manifold political
problems of Bavaria. One was a dispute over the future of
Hitler's famous compound on Mount Kehlstein outside of
Berchtesgaden. In their zeal to stamp out all vestiges of Nazism,
the Americans demanded its total demolition. Certain Bavarian
interests, however, wished to keep at least some structures, like
Hitler's teahouse perched on the mountain top, as a source of
tourist revenue, for in the entire region this was the only such
scenic outlook accessible by paved roads rather than cable car.
Hale, perhaps in his appreciation of the amenities available on
the Blue Ridge, pressed for a compromise: most of the compound should be razed, but the teahouse (usually referred to
mistakenly as the Eagle's Nest) the access roads, and the eleva-
tors would remain, in return for assurances that the scenic spot
would only be commercialized, not developed into a Nazi
shrine. This practical solution was adopted—to the satisfaction
of thousands of spellbound tourists, including Oron J. Hale.[11]

A more important issue, one with worldwide implications,
was the disposition of Jewish properties for which no heirs
could be found. Given the circumstances of the disappearance
of so many Jewish claimants, the world in general, including the
inchoate new German government, supported the principle
that such "heirless" properties were not subject to the usual laws

of inheritance but should be restituted to the Jewish community as a collective whole. The trouble was with the practical execution in individual cases; elsewhere in Germany the dockets were filled for years to come, no one knowing what the total claims would come to in the end. For this reason the Bavarian government balked at recognizing the principle itself. Hale's charge was to force a change. Again he proposed a compromise: the desired legislation should assure the Jews of a minimum total they would receive in return for their acceptance of a maximum limit on their claims against Bavaria. Within these limits whole classes of cases could be settled and the interminable case-by-case litigation avoided. A bill to this effect was finally adopted.

In the above cases Hale was essentially a mediator; but on another front he had to act in peremptory fashion to execute American policy. As Soviet-American relations deteriorated and Germany became the central prize in the Cold War, a rebuilding of American forces in Bavaria, as in Germany generally, was underway. There was as yet no German army, and the United States had only one division in Bavaria, the state with the longest iron-curtain frontier: that is to say, along the Russian zones of Germany and Austria and the Czech border as well. With an expansion of five divisions planned, it was Hale's responsibility to requisition land for camps and firing ranges and to commandeer former German army barracks, many of which already housed refugees only recently resettled from Eastern Europe. The eviction of these victims of twentieth-century brutality was probably his saddest duty. The operation was part of the great reversal in grand strategy by which the western allies restored sovereignty to their zones in exchange for a German military contribution. As Hale later described it, the problem was the ironic one of how to convert a military occupation into a military alliance.

With the restoration of sovereignty to the German Federal Republic, as the successor regime has since been called, the office of landeskommissar was abolished, and again Hale returned to his academic duties in Charlottesville, gaining an even larger following among the students with his first-hand knowledge of world events and an endless fund of memorable anecdotes. Who would not be amused to hear about the mayor of Munich, who protested American efforts to chlorinate the water supply as something akin to "placing a brassiere on the Venus de Milo"? Or about the American private who, on hearing from the elderly Prince Hohenlohe that he was indeed a prince but would not become a king, replied: "What's the matter, aint'cha got no ambition?" Nor should one overlook the poor French soldier vainly calling for help as he drowned in the Main River. Observing his struggles, one Bavarian farmer said to another: "It's a pity the lad did not speak German; I wonder what he was trying to say."[12] Life back home, however, was more than recounting amusing stories. From 1955 to 1962 Hale served as department chairman, presiding over the early stages of expanding student enrollments, increased and more diversified staffing of the faculty, and a redoubled emphasis on graduate training as the nation began to cope with the "war-baby" generation then coming of age—college age, at any rate.

Partly in this connection the president of the university at the time, Colgate W. Darden, was determined to interest the Thomas Jefferson Memorial Foundation (established in 1923 to maintain Monticello as a national treasure) in extending its largesse to graduate fellowships and a special professorship in history. In the summer of 1957 he turned to Hale as a historical expert to assist a local banker named William Hildreth in negotiating with the trustees in New York. The protracted and intricate operation was successful, resulting in the appointment of Dumas Malone as the first holder of the Thomas Jefferson Memorial Foundation chair and later the creation of numerous fellowships in history and government. Since Malone was then at Columbia University, it was Hale's place to gain the approval of the history department and as chairman to hire his old friend, who had hired *him* exactly thirty years earlier.

Another project that occupied the former landeskommissar was the formation of a section for European history within the framework of the Southern Historical Association. Europeanists had been moderately active in this body since its founding in 1934, serving on its committees and organizing sessions in their fields, but there were seldom enough of the latter to fill the time available. To make the program more attractive and in other ways to promote the cause of European history in the South, a rising young scholar at Tulane, the enterprising John L. Snell, concluded that a more formal structure was necessary. To this end he persuaded Hale and two other veterans, J. Wesley Hoffman (University of Tennessee) and Carl H. Pegg (University of North Carolina), to join him in inviting a number of their colleagues to discuss the prospects at the approaching SHA meeting in Columbia, South Carolina, in November. The group so convened prepared the way for the first meeting of the section the following year.[13]

Although Hale was more an elder statesman lending his prestige than a prime mover, he was a fixture in the group from the beginning, appearing on numerous programs over the years and in 1958-59 serving as the chairman of the section. As the featured speaker at the meeting in Little Rock in 1964, he redeemed the least palatable luncheon in the section's history with an engrossing address entitled "Europe 1900–1914: Was It Morning Light, High Noon, or Evening Twilight?" His answer was that in general the period truly began the twentieth century; only in international relations was it the denouement of the nineteenth—a thesis that was to become the core of his last book, *The Great Illusion 1900–1914* (New York, 1971).[14]

Meanwhile, outside the university Oron J. Hale became involved in his biggest project yet, the microfilming of vast stores of German government documents that the allied armies had captured at the end of the war. Hale's interest in these papers went back to the days of the interrogation project. On a routine mission in 1945 to interview several ministerial officials, he found them at work in an abandoned powder plant near Cassel sorting out millions of documents. Conducted to one of the buildings by an American lieutenant, Klemens von Klemperer (who was also to become a distinguished historian), Hale was dumbfounded at the mass of the collection: hundreds of packing crates piled close together in stacks over seven feet high. Unfortunately, this mass did not include the records of the German Foreign Office from 1867 on, which he had tried in vain to examine when preparing his books on diplomacy, but it hardly mattered: the diplomatic documents, then stored in Marburg, were of similar dimension, hardly lending themselves to a quick scanning and an afternoon's notetaking. Indeed, when they were later hauled to Berlin as one way of demonstrating the Western Powers' interest in establishing a new central administration for Germany, they filled sixteen freight cars to overflowing. Not long afterwards, however, when the former German capital came under siege by the Russians, the records were moved again, this time as the reverse side of the legendary air lift, whose planes would otherwise have returned empty. In this way the valuable cargo was removed from danger and came to rest at Whaddon Hall in Buckinghamshire, England, where it was then sifted, edited, and published by teams of American, British, and French scholars, working over the years in relative peace and security. The chief American editor from 1948 to 1959 was the historian Paul R. Sweet.[15]

Meanwhile, there remained in Germany, at several collecting centers, millions of other documents, measured literally in tons and truckloads, that could only be handled by an international division of labor. By agreement, the British took the naval records, the French the materials dealing with the occupation of their country, and the Americans the military archives, the Nazi party files, and all ministerial records not needed by the occupation authorities. The latter included the highly sensitive Nazi party membership lists which remained in Berlin. Parts of the American share went to Maxwell Field and the Library of Congress, but the bulk of it went first to the basement of the Pentagon and later to an unused torpedo plant in Alexandria, Virginia, where it was combined with even larger masses of American army records and some Italian and Soviet materials to form the World War II Records Center. In all, the depository contained over 20,000 linear feet of German documents alone, the equivalent of some four miles. The whole mass was unsorted and unsifted, and because still classified as confidential, generally inaccessible to scholars. As a reserve officer with high security clearance, however, Hale was able to spend some of his summers to rummage through the material, sometimes on his own and at times while on active reserve duty.[16]

Meanwhile, as the Cold War intensified and Germany became an ally, the pressure mounted to return the records. The moral right of a country to possess the documentation of its past was widely recognized, and the Germans further argued plausibly that without the records it would be difficult to educate the public about the crimes of National Socialism. Besides, given the political urgency of propitiating Germany, few officials in Washington considered the documents a major issue. Scholars, on the other hand, were concerned, not only by the prospect of losing such a windfall, material of the kind that governments normally do not declassify so soon after the events, but also by the possibility that, in exclusively German hands, the documents might be doctored for publication as had been the case with some works regarding World War I. Especially opposed to returning the records were Jewish scholars and leaders, who feared that the documentary evidence for the horrors of gas chambers and concentration camps, far from being exposed, would be suppressed and perhaps disappear forever. When the Records Center early in 1955 did in fact routinely return, unexamined by anybody, the records of the Bavarian state police, their alarm became acute, and a group headed by Hans Kohn of Smith College, George W. Hallgarten, a free-lance scholar and authority on imperialism, and Sidney Wallach, a Jewish publicist and founder of *Commentary* magazine, cast about for ways to block the operation.[17]

Such was the situation when Hale arrived at Harvard that year to teach summer school. Another visitor there, as it happened, was Hans Kohn, who briefed him on the situation. Reginald Phelps, a Harvard professor of German, was also brought into these preliminary talks. That fall, at a meeting in Washington, D.C., arranged by the deputy librarian of Congress, Verner Clapp, a broader group, which included Kohn, Hallgarten, Wallach, and Fritz T. Epstein, then a bibliographer at the Library of Congress, launched the American Committee for the Study of War Documents. Phelps was the first chairman. Its goals were, first, to have the documents declassified to permit free scholarly access, and then to microfilm them so that copies would remain in this country regardless of the fate of the originals. Filming on such a scale was unprecedented, but in the political atmosphere then prevailing it was doubtless a more realistic goal than Kohn's and Hallgarten's original idea of simply blocking the return of the documents till they could be studied here. What Hale's role in this decision was cannot be documented, but he would certainly have favored common sense.

Whether microfilming was indeed common sense or not remained to be seen, of course, for still unsolved were the problems of raising money and inducing military and State Department officials to budge from an ingrained disinclination to rush into declassifying documents, no matter whose they were. For both purposes Hale's experience was crucial. For funding he turned to his friend and immediate superior of Bavarian days, John J. McCloy, who was now on the boards of both the Ford Foundation and the Chase Manhattan Bank. With a grant from the former the committee was on its way, its task much simplified by the willingness of Boyd Shafer, executive secretary of the American Historical Association, to administer this money and any other subsequently raised.[18] Hale's connections in army intelligence and the army historical division were likewise effective, and the declassification, steadily attended by monitoring and trouble shooting on his part, plowed through the morass of the Intelligence Division of the General Staff, which had to give clearance, and the Office of the Adjutant General, which had custody of the records in Alexandria. As a colleague later said of him, "He was the ideal person to carry this off, and he did so regularly with that combination of grace and firmness which made him successful without causing hard feelings among those government officials who had been talked into changing their policies."[19] The Department of the Army also obligingly provided, at least for the first few years, the required film, cameras, and operators. Later the National Archives donated this support and, as well, published guides to the collection and made film copies available to scholars at no charge.

In the summer of 1956 the operation in Alexandria began,

under the supervision of a subcommittee on microfilming headed by E. Malcolm Carroll of Duke University, later by Fritz Epstein. The officer immediately in charge was Gerhard L. Weinberg, a leading expert on Hitler's foreign policy. The next year the Committee on War Documents, with Oron J. Hale as its new chairman, became an official committee of the American Historical Association, which thus lent the weight of the entire profession to the continuing promotional efforts.[20] Still, the latter was too unwieldy and too diverse in its interests effectively to bombard the State Department, the National Archives, the Defense Department, and private foundations with resolutions by the historical experts most affected, specialists in German history. It was specifically to rally this constituency behind the committee that Hale joined Walter Dorn of Columbia University, S. Harrison Thompson of the University of Colorado, and Hans Kohn in sending invitations to key people to attend an organizational meeting at the annual convention of the American Historical Association in 1957.

Hale's efforts coincided with a similar campaign launched by R. John Rath of the University of Texas to form a society to promote Habsburg studies in the United States. The result could have been a struggle reenacting the original *kleindeutsch-grossdeutsch* controversy of the nineteenth century, but with a wisdom that the rulers of Germany and Austria had rarely displayed, Hale and Rath decided to join forces and bring their constituents together during the AHA meeting, which was held in New York in December. Hale brought to the meeting a constitutional sketch that he had drafted for a so-called Conference Group for Central European History. With a few minor amendments this, as well as the proposed name, were adopted. Hans Kohn was elected the first chairman, William O. Shanahan of Notre Dame vice-chairman, and Oron J. Hale secretary-treasurer. The first standing committee was also created then, the Committee to Promote Studies of the Habsburg Monarchy, with Rath as chairman.[21]

The business meetings of the Conference Group for many years were dominated by progress reports by the War Documents Committee, proposals from the director, Weinberg, and resolutions directed to appropriate agencies. Since then the organization has expanded well beyond its initial concern and is now a diversified scholarly society that sponsors two learned journals, the *Austrian History Yearbook* (founded in 1960 as a newsletter, becoming a bona fide journal in 1965) and *Central European History,* founded in 1967. The group also awards prizes, sponsors a session each year at the meeting of the AHA, and holds an annual *Bierabend,* an occasion for shoptalk and *Plauderei.* As a founder, Oron Hale was elected chairman of the group in 1964 and served on the first board of editors of *Central European History.* Even he has been amazed at the hardy growth of his offspring.

Throughout this period his main worry was funding for the war documents, for the original Ford grant covered just one year. Again Hale's unique situation and experience proved important. Probably nobody but a professor at Virginia could have persuaded the old Dominion Foundation, which normally focused its interest on Virginia history, to make an exception of the German documents (they were after all *stored* in Virginia), and even its support, when forthcoming, was limited to one year. Hale, with the assistance of Boyd Shafer, next approached the Eli Lilly Foundation, which likewise agreed to finance another year but no more. The much-traveled history professor then turned back to his friend on the board of the Ford Foundation, John McCloy. Though sympathetic, the latter was more circumspect this time, fearing that the foundation might construe his repeated pleas on behalf of the documents as somehow connected with the Chase Manhattan Bank's business dealings in Germany. Accordingly, he advised Hale to make one more request but for a two-year funding period and with the understanding that half the money would be raised elsewhere as evidence that no conflict of interest on McCloy's part was involved.

The key this time was another acquaintance of the days in Munich, Frank Altschul, a prominent investment banker, philanthropist, and noted bibliophile. One of his contributions was a special grant of $5,000 to carry out filming at the Record Center in Berlin, where the membership lists of the Nazi party

are stored. Mr. Altschul also provided a vital introduction to
Dr. Thomas Parran, the president of the Avalon Foundation,
who in the end made available the critical matching half of the
projected grant.[22] "Well, I think this is a very good idea," He
told Hale, "if McCloy and Altschul are behind it."[23]

Thus was obtained the $60,000 that enabled the Committee
to complete the project in 1962 after filming over twelve
million pages. The originals were in course returned to Germany and are for the most part stored in Koblenz, where the
guide lists developed by the American Committee are still in
use. The filming and publication of guides continues, since
1968 financed by the National Archives and under the direction of Robert Wolfe, a member of the AHA team, whom
the National Archives took over along with the project. Even
so, the Adjutant General's Office continued for years to come to
ask Hale's permission before returning records to Germany.[24]

During the years of the war documents project Hale continued to teach full time, direct graduate students, and carry out
his duties as chairman of the history department. At the same
time he struggled to protect a few hours each week to pursue his
own research and writing. Ever since his interviews with Max
Amann and the other journalists, he had been impatient to use
this material for a book on Hitler's press policy and its place in
creating the dictatorship. Much other material on the subject
was in the war documents themselves, but as long as that
project continued, there was little time to exploit these advantages. By 1962, however, the work was nearly done, and Hale
felt free to accept a year's appointment to the prestigious
Institute for Advanced Study at Princeton University, at the
same time resigning as department chairman at Virginia. The
first product of this sudden liberation was *The Captive Press in
the Third Reich*, (Princeton, 1964), which won the Polk award
in journalism that year as well as enthusiastic reviews. A German edition was published by Droste Verlag in 1965 and
enjoyed a wider sale than the American version. The reviews in
general noted the departure from sweeping surveys of the Nazi
regime common at the time in favor of a treatment in depth of a
single but fundamental facet of the Nazi regime.[25] Such mod-

esty was in sharp contrast, for example, to the approach of William L. Shirer, who in Hale's company took one look at the Record Center, realized a comprehensive book based on original sources was impossible, but went ahead anyway with his *Rise and Fall of the Third Reich* (New York, 1960), a celebrated book in its day but soon outdated by the monographs based on original sources, many of them derived from the microfilmed documents.

During the year at the institute Hale was also able to make a good start on what is perhaps his best known work, occupying as it does a place in the distinguished series, *The Rise of Modern Europe,* edited by William L. Langer, a longtime friend and president of the AHA during some of the delicate negotiations to fund the war documents. Hale's contribution, published in 1971 under the title *The Great Illusion 1900–1914,* is a broad general history of the period leading up to World War I. Almost at the inception of the series in the 1930s the topic had been assigned to the renowned expert on this period, Sidney Bradshaw Fay, but the pressure of other duties over the years and later the infirmities of age convinced Fay that it must be reassigned, and he generously passed his incomplete manuscript on to Hale.

The new author found the drafts valuable but, as he noted in the preface, not such that they could be integrated with his own work. The title was also a problem. *The Great Illusion* was Fay's choice going back to the 1930s, a time of obsession with a war that had shattered the nineteenth century's faith in progress. Thirty years later, however, the period seemed more complex, and Hale himself believed that it should not be viewed as the denouement of the nineteenth century but rather as the seed time of grand developments, like relativity and quantum theory, which are peculiarly twentieth century in character. Accordingly, he cast about for alternatives but in the end decided to keep the original, probably less out of conviction—and this is personal conjecture based on Hale's character—than the feeling that to do otherwise would be somehow disloyal to Fay.[26]

Returning to Charlottesville in 1963, Hale happily found the chairmanship in the capable hands of Edward Younger and himself free to work on the volume for Langer. In 1965 he was appointed to the William W. Corcoran Professorship of history, a chair that had just been established with funds that Mr. Corcoran (also the benefactor of the Corcoran Gallery in Washington, D.C.) had originally, before the turn of the century, given to endow the whole department, or school, as it was called then.

The honor of the chair and the excitement provided by the challenge of the Langer series were soon overwhelmed by gloom, when Anne Hale was stricken with cancer and died in the summer of 1968. During the long months of agony Oron was in constant attendance, affording the local community an inspiring example of devotion which extended many months beyond death. To this personal grief, moreover, was added another sorrow: dismay at the changes taking place at the university. Burgeoning enrollments and the disappearance of jackets and ties were no problems, and the admittance of women was a positive gain. The raucous and disruptive political demonstrations, however, the declining academic standards and grade inflation, the earnest arrogance of the junior faculty, and some outright acts of vandalism—these were not only alien to the institution that he had known but were as well an attack on universal principles of truth, civility, and scholarship. Nevertheless, he carried on with his manuscript and his duties as classroom teacher, director of graduate students, and conscientious committeeman.

By this time he had been on the scene long enough to qualify (he was amused at this notion) for membership on the "names" committee, the body charged with combing the past for the names of deserving local celebrities to adorn new buildings and all the other monuments that abound in an academic community. More importantly, he continued to defend his principles, attending countless faculty meetings to defend the ROTC, foreign languages, required courses, the grading system, or whatever other traditional value was under assault. While some of the elders threw up their hands and retreated into their studies, it must be said that enough of them, like Hale, stayed to fight it out—and for the most part prevailed. As he himself observed, it was easier for his generation to postpone the cocktail hour than for the younger men to keep their wives and children holding supper past six o'clock. As a result, the University of Virginia weathered those turbulent times better than most, generally introducing constructive reforms while, in true Jeffersonian style, avoiding the worst excesses.

Oron Hale meanwhile was overcoming his own personal sorrow. In the spring of 1969, in ceremonies at the German embassy in Washington, D.C., he was awarded, for his services to German history, the Commander's Cross of the Order of Merit of the German Federal Republic, one of the country's highest honors and unusual in its way, for as the recipient once observed, "You don't ordinarily give a high decoration to somebody who's occupied your country."[27] Then, only a few weeks later, he received his university's most coveted honor, the Thomas Jefferson Award, conferred annually "for advancing, through his character, work, and personal example the ideals and objectives for which Jefferson founded the University." Among the many accolades in the formal citation was President Edgar Shannon's observation that "it is not given to every historian to make history as well as to write it and preserve its records."[28] The following year was also rewarding, bringing the decorated historian a new wife, Virginia Zehmer, the widow of an old friend and bridge partner. They were married in July 1970 and the next month embarked on a wedding trip to the Soviet Union, mainly to Moscow, where the International Congress of Historical Sciences was holding its quinquennial meeting. The trip included Hungary and Poland as well as many provinces of the USSR. As Oron was not on the program, he had time to make a honeymoon of it and this time remembered always to obtain *two* tickets to everything. To add spice to the adventure, Virginia had had no time to renew her passport as Mrs. Hale and so traveled under her former name — to the amusement more of their travel companions than of the desk clerks along the way, who hardly noticed.

Back home in Charlottesville, the Hales settled first in her house, later in his. In 1971, as noted above, *The Great Illusion* was published by Harper and Row, generating mostly favorable reviews. In eight chapters on demography, property relationships, technology, philosophy, science, reform movements, and almost a pioneering treatment of the relationship between art and politics the author convincingly demonstrates his thesis that the twentieth century began something new. Nevertheless, it is probably the three chapters on diplomacy and war that are most original, resisting as they do the strongly anti-German current so popular at the time, even—or most of all—in Germany, and achieving a mature synthesis between this extreme and Hale's earlier revisionist views of World War I.[29]

However that may be, the book was a fitting climax to a long and varied career and perhaps a factor in the author's decision to retire in 1972, one year short of the institutional requirement. Hale himself later attributed this step to his personal sorrows and dissatisfaction with the politicized atmosphere at the university, and what better authority could there be? Still, a man of his caliber would never have withdrawn, with a manuscript half finished, dissertations in his charge dangling in midair, and students shunning his classes because of a generation gap. No, he retired in style, and a winner he remains today, recovering from a stroke in 1973, keeping abreast of his field, refurbishing the gravesites of his New England ancestors, and again attending an ailing spouse—all in good spirit and with the vigor one might expect of an old rancher and huntsman.

Notes

[1] This informal account is based mainly on the transcript of a series of interviews that Mr. Hale gave to Mr. Charles Moran in 1976, as corroborated (or corrected) by standard reference sources, a few personal interviews, and Hale's own writings, which are listed in the bibliography to this volume. The transcript is on deposit in the Manuscripts Division of the University of Virginia Library. A definitive investigation has not been possible, but I have avoided many errors through the interest, sharp memories, and other assistance provided by the following: Dumas Malone, Emmett B. Ford, Jr., and Raymond Bice, all of the University of Virginia; Reginald Phelps, Harvard

University; R. John Rath, University of Minnesota; Gerhard L. Weinberg, University of North Carolina; Paul R. Sweet, Michigan State University; Klemens von Klemperer, Smith College; Robert Wolfe, National Archives; and the Honorable Kenneth Hechler, former congressman from West Virginia. For submitting letters of reminiscence I am further indebted to Dr. James Edgar, U.S. Army; Professor Eugene L. Rasor, Emory and Henry College; Professor Roland V. Layton, Jr., Hiram College; Dr. T. Daniel Shumate, Jr., George Mason University; and Professor Emeritus Joseph Reither, New York University—all former students of Mr. Hale. My thanks—and I am sure Pat's as well—go out to all.

[2] Abstract of the meeting by Henry E. Bourne in *American Historical Review*, 35 (1929), 489. The convention, which also held sessions in Chapel Hill, attracted 593 historians, who warmly praised the hospitality extended to them.

[3] Interestingly, Carroll had appeared on the same session with Hale at the meeting in Durham.

[4] Reviews by Johannes Ziekursch in *Historische Zeitschrift*, 146 (1932), 644 f., and J. V. Fuller in *American Historical Review*, 37 (1931), 330 f.; and a review article by Jonathan Scott, "The Press and Foreign Policy," in *Journal of Modern History*, 3 (1931), 627–38, which examines Hale's and Carroll's works and five others.

[5] Dwight E. Lee, *Europe's Crucial Years: The Diplomatic Background of World War I, 1902–1914* (Hanover, N.H., 1974), p. 449.

[6] Cf. reviews by E. Malcolm Carroll, *Journal of Modern History*, 13 (1941), 258 f., and Pauline M. Anderson, *American Historical Review*, 46 (1942), 640–42.

[7] On the Shuster mission see, besides the Hale transcript, George Shuster, *The Ground I Walked On* (New York, 1961), pp. 222–29.

[8] "Report on Historical Interrogations of German Prisoners of War and Detained Persons," 20 December 1945, on deposit in the National Archives, with the papers of the War Department Historical Commission; reprinted in Robert Wolfe, ed. *Captured Germans and Related Records: A National Archives Conference* (Athens, Ohio, 1974) following p. 172. The conference referred to took place in 1968 with Hale presiding at one of the sessions. I am indebted to Mr. Wolfe, who is also the chief, Modern Military Headquarters Branch of the National Archives, for making the original available to me.

[9] Hale transcript.

[10] Ibid. and statement by Emmett B. Ford, Jr., at the time one of the resident officers under Hale, currently an administrator of research at the University of Virginia.

[11] This and following from Hale transcript.

[12] My memory, assisted by Dr. James Edgar in a letter of 17 January 1983.

[13] Enno E. Kraehe, "The Origins of the European History Section," *European History Newsletter,* 14, no. 1 (Spring 1977), 2 f.

[14] Abstract in *Journal of Southern History,* 31 (1965), 53 f. The evaluation of the meal, however, though widely shared, is my own.

[15] Letter from Sweet, 15 August 1983.

[16] Hale transcript and Oron J. Hale, "World War II Documents and Interrogations," *Social Science,* 47, no. 2 (Spring 1972), 77–79.

[17] Hale transcript amplified by Gerhard L. Weinberg in a letter of 3 June 1983, for this and following.

[18] The American Historical Association also administered a related project at Whaddon Hall, the microfilming of pre-1918 documents, which were not scheduled for publication. The director was Howard Ehrmann of the University of Michigan.

[19] Weinberg to Kraehe as in n. 17 above.

[20] Hale succeeded another Lingelbach student, Lynn M. Case of the University of Pennsylvania, in this office.

[21] Rath to Chairman Peter Paret, 11 December 1981 (copy to me), on the occasion of Rath's retirement from the Habsburg Committee.

[22] In 1969 the Avalon Foundation was merged with the Old Dominion Foundation and renamed the Andrew W. Mellon Foundation.

[23] Hale transcript.

[24] Ibid.

[25] E.g., reviews by Frederick G. Heymann, *Journal of Modern History,* 36 (1964), 480 f.; and Harold J. Gordon, *American Historical Review,* 70 (1964), 453–55.

[26] Based in part on my personal recollection.

[27] Hale transcript.

[28] Text of citation in the Records of the President's Office, University Archives, Manuscripts Division, University Library. It was written by Dumas Malone, the chairman of the Thomas Jefferson Award Committee that year.

[29] See, for example, the reviews by Joachim Remak, *American Historical Review 47* (1972), 780–81; and Charles F. Delzell, *Virginia Quarterly Review 47* (1971), 282–85. *The Times Literary Supplement,* 27 August, 1971, p. 1026, criticized Hale's treatment of diplomacy as "old fashioned," but today, thirteen years later, opinion on the whole vindicates the latter.

II

A Survey of Recent Historiography on Pre–World War I Germany and England with Special Reference to Anglo-German Relations

EUGENE L. RASOR

PROFESSOR ORON JAMES HALE established a foundation from which the last quarter century of the historiography of Anglo-German relations before World War I might be surveyed. His two books on pre–World War I diplomacy, *Germany and the Diplomatic Revolution* (1931) and *Publicity and Diplomacy* (1940) have been widely cited and praised by many.[1] This review of the literature attempts to complement his comprehensive bibliographical essay (pp. 315–55) in *The Great Illusion, 1900–1914* (1971), volume eighteen of the prestigious *Rise of Modern Europe* series.[2] This essay will, however, concentrate on that longer period from 1870 until 1914, when Great Britain and Germany appeared the most powerful and highly advanced industrialized countries in the world. In 1870 their relations were normal and each served as the other's best trading partner. Great Britain acquiesced when Prussia defeated France in the Franco-Prussian War of 1870–71 and to the subsequent unification of Germany, notwithstanding the resultant major upset in the continental balance of power. By the end of the period, Europe had divided into two armed camps with Germany leading one side, the Triple Alliance, and Great Britain joining the other, the Triple Entente. In the fatal

July 1914 crisis, Great Britain did not remain neutral, as German Chancellor Theobald von Bethmann Hollweg gambled, but joined the war in support of her allies, France and Russia.

By the nineteenth century, Great Britain had evolved deliberately into a unified, politically sophisticated nation that led the world in imperialism and in the process and extent of industrialization. During this period timely political reforms had ensured relative domestic stability. The British colonial empire contributed to the enormous financial resources that supported the most powerful navy in the world. Germany, by contrast, achieved unified, nation-state status only late in the century and had its constitutional system, which has been called "the Prussian Monarchical Civil Service State," imposed from above, primarily at the instigation of its first chancellor, Prince Otto von Bismarck. Simultaneously, in Germany the process of industrialization proceeded rapidly, perhaps too rapidly, because political and social maturity lagged behind advances in economics and industrialization. Prussian-led Germany was a land power with the most powerful army in the world. The German potential for expansion in the commercial, industrial, military, naval, and colonial spheres would be exploited by Germany's new leaders in the later nineteenth and early twentieth centuries.

Scholarly interest remains high in the subject of Anglo-German relations before World War I. Much of the most important scholarship in German has been translated or summarized in English.[3] In addition, an identifiable network of mostly British, German, and American historians has formed in recent decades, for example, the Anglo-German Group of Historians and the German Historical Institute of London. A series of conferences on social history has been sponsored by the Social Science Research Council (especially at the University of East Anglia, Norwich), and other international symposiums and conferences have been held in both England and Germany.[4]

The volume and emphases of the most recent scholarship lead initially to the subject of German history where there has been continuing and controversial evolution of interpretations. Innovators and revisionists have abandoned or modified traditional fields, techniques, and approaches usually associated with the followers of the nineteenth-century German historian Leopold von Ranke. Rankeans concentrated on political history, diplomatic relations, and foreign affairs, "history from above." Some subsequent historians have adopted and incorporated new social science methodologies and socioeconomic concepts with greater emphases on structures and functions, all applied to the study of history, what some have called "history from below." Two historians, both natives of Germany but separated by three decades of time and World War II, have led the way in this transformation of German historiography.

An obscure young historian, Eckart Kehr, who died at age thirty-three during a visit to the United States in 1933, has been credited with the earliest and most far-reaching revisionist historical views. The orthodox Rankean school stressed the *Primat der Aussenpolitik,* the primacy of foreign affairs, in governmental and political decision making. Using new approaches and methodology, Kehr reversed the emphasis, stressing instead the *Primat der Innenpolitik,* the primary importance of internal affairs and policies. He focused his analysis on the period of the Second Reich, especially the Wilhelmine era (1888–1918), but few of his contemporaries in Germany followed his lead. His writings lay dormant for almost thirty years until their rediscovery after World War II. A quarter century later, in our own day, Kehr's emphasis on the primacy of domestic politics has almost become the new orthodoxy. Wolfgang Mommsen, in a key analysis of the domestic factors influencing German foreign policy before World War I, concluded that Kehr's "opinion that foreign policies are primarily determined by social and economic structures, and in particular by the social and political interests of the ruling elites, is shared by a great majority of historians." American historians have evaluated Kehr's significance in even stronger terms. For example, Gordon Craig, in his introduction to the English edition of Kehr's essays, labeled him "the father of German historical revisionism" and argued that "the influence of Eckart Kehr has become perhaps the strongest reforming force in German historiography and one that has been largely responsible for curing the myopia that affected its vision of the past."[5]

Meanwhile the historiography of modern Germany, and indeed of most of Europe, has been affected by the dramatic impact of the Fritz Fischer "revolution," the reactions to it, and the implications and consequences of it, especially, but not only, in Germany in the 1960s. That impact has been broad and deep. A substantial number of books and articles discussed in this survey have assessed its significance: "ignited a scholarly controversy of unparalleled intensity," "no postwar historian has been more influential," *"Die Fischer-Kontroverse,"* "the acerbic Fischer Debate," and "the new synthesis."[6] Fischer, professor of history at Hamburg University, and his students and disciples have resurrected several highly sensitive and controversial matters in the German past: the *Kriegsschuldlüge,* or "war guilt lie," the question of German war aims before and during World War I, the "grasping" for world power, and the implications of "continuity" in German history.[7]

The notorious and pervasive war guilt question was first "answered" by Article 231 of the Treaty of Versailles of June 1919: the moral judgment that Germany and the Central Powers were guilty of causing World War I. The punitive articles followed. That political verdict of the victorious peacemakers would be superseded by the emphasis of interwar revisionist historians on collective guilt of all of the participants. Even Prime Minister David Lloyd George of Great Britain concluded that "the nations slithered over the brink into the boiling cauldron of war."[8] A 1967 semiofficial German version declared, with seeming finality, "The allegation that Germany and her allies alone were to blame for the First World War (Art. 231 of the Versailles Treaty) has, in the meantime, been refuted by the findings of international historical research."[9]

In two key studies of the origins of World War I in the 1940s, the American Bernadotte Schmitt and the Italian Luigi Albertini still emphasized primary German war guilt. Another American writing in the 1950s, Hans W. Gatzke, introduced several new points, for example, the role of pressure groups, links between domestic politics and annexationism, and the continuity of German imperialism. Curiously, such studies attracted little notice in Germany.[10] In 1960, however, Fritz Fischer revived the sole German guilt thesis, basing his conclusions upon more solid and original documentation, particularly newly available sources gleaned from archives in East Germany. Fischer focused on German war aims and concluded that they were formulated by a broad contingent of civilian and military leaders of all persuasions; they were imperialistic and annexationist in nature; they were based on illusions; they demonstrated "continuity" in German history because there were similarities in foreign policies and internal structures, for example, between the Second and Third reichs; and they indicated that there were no significant differences among German leaders such as Bismarck, Bethmann Hollweg, and Adolf Hitler. Although he personally discounted the role of individuals and personalities, Fischer in effect claimed there were no "good" Germans and "bad" Germans. A number of Fischer's students and disciples have developed and expanded upon these ideas during the 1960s, among the most prominent Imanuel Geiss, Dirk Stegmann, and Peter-Christian Witt.[11]

The reaction in Germany was immediate, hostile, and in some cases, political and unprofessional; Fischer opened old wounds. He was persecuted and attacked by officials and peers who argued that he had resorted to "national masochism" (Giselher Wirsing) and "self-deprecation of German historical consciousness" (Gerhard A. Ritter).[12] The academic polemics, led by Ritter, Egmont Zechlin, Fischer's colleague at Hamburg, and Andreas Hillgruber centered on the interpretation of key documents, for example, an incriminating list of war aims, dated 9 September 1914, and on personalities, especially Chancellor Bethmann Hollweg. Hillgruber objected to the implications of continuity in twentieth-century German foreign policies. German historical development, he insisted, did not represent an uninterrupted stream; the aggressive, expansionist—and racist—villain remained General Erich Ludendorff, not Bethmann Hollweg, whose objectives were limited to "semihegemony."[13]

The scholarly literature generated by this controversy has been enormous and uneven, but a number of judicious, sensible, and careful analyses have appeared. They seem to agree that the Fischer thesis, with modifications, coincides with the acceptable interpretations of German foreign policy before 1914. For example, Richard J. Evans has concluded, in an important review essay of recent studies of Germany "from Hitler to Bismarck," that the parallels and links between the Second and Third Reichs are "too striking to ignore."[14]

The Fischer debate has stimulated further, and more critical, study of the Second Reich. A number of perspectives and approaches have utilized new sources and methods of analysis. Earlier studies, beyond those of Eckart Kehr, by Thorstein Veblen, Gordon A. Craig, Ralf Dahrendorf, and others have been revived and reevaluated.[15] Kehr previously had impressed Charles A. Beard, Alfred Vagts, Hajo Holborn, and Hans Rosenberg. Pauline R. Anderson, author of *The Background of Anti-English Feeling in Germany 1890–1902* (1939), thanked Kehr for "inestimable help" and dedicated her book to him. She also helped translate and edit an English edition of Kehr's most important study, *Schlachtflottenbau und Parteipolitik,* four decades after it first appeared, in the University of Chicago series *Classic European Historians.*[16]

During the late 1960s "post-Fischer" historians emerged, including among them a school variously described as "Kehrites," "the New Orthodoxy," and "the radical-liberal Max Weberian structuralists." Led by Hans-Ulrich Wehler and Volcker R. Berghahn, this group of younger scholars also looked to Kehr, but they have adopted innovative methodologies and ideas while conducting a more systematic analysis of the German Empire that stresses the *Primat der Innenpolitik.* For example, Kehr had researched the social and financial bases of the elaborate propaganda complex and agitation created by Admiral Alfred von Tirpitz, founder of the German battle fleet, who solicited aid from shipbuilders and subsidized newspapers as Bismarck had done earlier.[17] Kehr thereby demonstrated the importance of domestic considerations in explaining foreign, military, naval, and colonial policies, as Fritz Fischer would do thirty years later with better documentation. The conclusions of the followers of Kehr have emphasized a number of other key points: anachronistic elites formulating *Sammlungspolitik,* that is, the politics of rallying together certain rightist elements such as Junkers and heavy industrialists in order to create diversions from the process of democratization; alleviation of the problems of industrialization and modernization by a "conservative revolution" or "belated modernization"; and organized intervention by the traditional or neofeudal hierarchy to distract the populace from domestic difficulties. These scholars label such tactics "Bonapartism," "social imperialism," and "the radicalization of the Right" in which conscious manipulation involved "negative" or "secondary integration" through glorifying the monarchy, militarism, navalism, and colonialism, or portraying certain minorities such as Jews, Catholics, socialists, Africans, Poles, and even Bavarians as subversives and thus dangerous to the security and stability of the German Empire.[18]

The juxtaposition of domestic political concerns and governmental decision making in the realm of foreign and colonial policies in Germany and other European powers in the nineteenth and twentieth centuries has become the focus of a series of studies by the "humanistic Marxist" historian from Princeton University, Arno J. Mayer. Mayer, whose sweeping interpretations and theses are particularly challenging, has provoked considerable reaction in his effort to apply the concept of *Primat der Innenpolitik* to all of the European states participating in World War I. In an article on the origins of the war he presented his "new considerations": dysfunctions in the international system, domestic dysfunctions experienced by all European powers, and "the inextricable interplay" between them.[19] Elsewhere Mayer has concluded that in times of instability, both internal and external, "this all pervasive politicization is proof that international relations, including war, have become an extension and tool of domestic politics."[20]

At first Mayer was universally dismissed; then a few admitted that his thesis might apply to Germany only; and, finally, some admitted that there may be validity in its application to Italy, France, Russia, and even Great Britain. For example, in the last case the interpretation might be that the British politicians Lloyd George and F. E. Smith, representing a "new elite" or "haute bourgeoisie," including ambitious lawyers, looked to relieving domestic upheavals, such as civil war in Ireland, militant suffragettes, and syndicalist labor agitation, by encouraging adventures abroad. Mayer has not only cast his net in an expanding geographical and international arena, but also has projected the debate on origins and causes of World War I ahead in time, linking the Bolshevik Revolution in Russia and peacemaking during the Versailles Settlement of World War I to the origins and causes of the Cold War.[21]

The views represented by Kehr and Fischer have come to represent a new orthodoxy in German historiography that has recently come under attack from even younger historians. Lacking an identifiable mentor, those critics have not yet won sufficient notoriety to acquire a recognizable name. They have been variously characterized as "Gramscian," "neo-Marxian," "New Left," and "Young Turks." They include younger historians of Germany, many of them British, for example, Geoff Eley, David Blackbourn, and Richard J. Evans. They accuse the "New Orthodoxy" school of being too doctrinaire, deterministic, simplistic, and historicist; of making excessive use of social science models; and of overemphasizing structure and continuity. The Kehrite definition of social history, these critics claim, is merely the social history of politics, which Kehrites depict as "Manichean dualism" of the forces of modernization vs. the forces of reaction. Neo-Marxians have introduced the wider and deeper bases of German society—the masses, or "the Other Germany"—and a "broadening of the political nation." They focus on the "life situation" of what they call the authentic and indigenous working class. They distinguish between members of the organized socialist party and the "true" workers, between rural and urban *Mittelstand,* and between the "old" and "new" Rights. They point to new forms and methods of politics and activism, a political populism both more complex and less structured, and both more diverse and less tangible. They conclude that change, not continuity, created the "preconditions for fascism." In short, this group of critics challenges the orthodoxy of the Kehr-Fischer perspective from the left by "uncovering popular initiatives for illiberal policies in Imperial Germany." They present as models the Annales school of French sociologists and historians and Edward P. Thompson's *The Making of the English Working Class* (1963).[22]

The traditionalists and conservatives have not remained completely silent, as illustrated by two examples of prominent and articulate traditionalists in the United States, Gordon Craig and Georg G. Iggers. Craig rejects the claim of continuity in German history and used the platform of the 1982 Presidential Address of the American Historical Association to express concern about the current imbalance of too much interest in domestic influence on foreign policy and neglect of the study of diplomacy. Iggers has also lamented the demise of classical German historicism.[23]

Perhaps the traditionalists and those who prefer "pure" political and diplomatic approaches and the *Primat der Aussenpolitik* feel stifled by the new vocabulary and historical terminology. The use of social science jargon and doctrinaire phraseology have made communication and mutual understanding extremely difficult. How can those schooled in such concepts as "Blood and Iron," "encirclement," "the Bismarckian System," and "the army as a state-within-a-state" communicate with those whose explanations are in terms of "socialist polycracy," "feudalization of the bourgeoisie," and *"Mittelstand," "Mitteleuropa,"* and *"Mittelafrika"*?[24] Nevertheless, the organic nature of the historiographical process has persisted. A leading American historian, Konrad H. Jarausch, has assessed the status of the interpretations of this period of German history as a "stalemate which offers a bewildering variety of theories and qualifications, but no clear-cut answers . . . a new consensus is nowhere in sight."[25]

Consideration of the role of personalities and their influence on events has been an approach consciously avoided by the structuralist, neo-Marxian, and socioeconomic historians who have been leading the German historiographical revolution of recent decades. However, the volume and extent of the studies on individuals and leaders require some mention here. Among the Germans, the most popular personality remains Bismarck, who has been demythologized, dubbed a "White Revolutionary" and instigator of "Bonapartism," in a recent monumental biography.[26] Kaiser Wilhelm II, whom the contemporary British Foreign office dubbed "His Impulsive Majesty" and, more recently, called "Imperial Germany's Albatross," has been the subject of considerable attention, including an international conference in 1979 "held . . . in the bedroom of the Kaiser's villa on the island of Corfu . . . in a faintly ridiculous act of self-indulgence entirely appropriate to its subject." Participants unsuccessfully attempted to salvage some of the older thesis of the "personal rule" of Wilhelm. Criticisms of the conference papers labeled this "history as the butler saw it," "a mishmash of pseudo-psychoanalytic banalities," and "a disgrace." The assessment that the Kaiser was tactless, unpredictable, incompetent, perhaps psychopathic, and a pawn for "bosom" male friends apparently will prevail.[27] Fritz Fischer was also responsible for projecting Chancellor Bethmann Hollweg into new historical and biographical prominence. Few leaders have been characterized in such a variety of ways: gambler, "Machiavellian in sheep's clothing," and megalomaniac; depicted as either innocent, unscrupulous, mediocre, or puzzling; and even presented as a seemingly honorable man pulled down by the ubiquitous and ever-victorious militarists.[28] Predictably, the "old school" éminence grise of the German Foreign Office, Baron Friederich von Holstein, has been rehabilitated and transformed from evil genius, recluse, and man of mystery into an ambitious anglophile and brilliant conversationalist as a result of the publication of four volumes of papers and a major biography. Nevertheless, Holstein seems to have been displaced in interest among scholars by Prince Philipp Eulenburg-Hertefeld, a member of the "Liebenberg Circle," called a "Chancellor-maker," deemed influential but not a "Rasputin," and involved in a sensational homosexual scandal.[29] Admiral Tirpitz's star has set. The studies of him and his much-trumpeted naval theories, for example, "risk fleet," "danger zone," and "alliance value," generally have concluded that all was fallacious, that there was neither a naval war plan nor a role for the High Seas Fleet when the war broke out, and that Tirpitz was a self-serving obstructionist and a bureaucratic megalomaniac.[30] Two significant diaries have also surfaced, those of Kurt Riezler, conservative journalist and aide to Bethmann Hollweg, and Admiral George A. von Müller, chief of the Naval Cabinet.[31]

Eckart Kehr and Fritz Fischer, as well as their followers and critics, have also influenced the development of the historiography of other European nations. Though German historians have taken the initiative, similar but less extensive, if not less heated, controversy has characterized the historiography of Great Britain and some other states. Indeed, one major publisher has devised a series on individual European states and the approach of World War I incorporating the Kehr-Fischer thesis. There are volumes on Germany (Volcker R. Berghahn), Great Britain (Zara S. Steiner), Italy (Richard Bosworth), France (J. F. N. Kieger) and Russia (D. C. B. Lieven).[32]

For reasons of scholarship, and because there has been less vulgar sensationalism, the British side of Anglo-German relations before World War I has attracted less attention than the extensive analyses of the "German question" and "German problem." The British were never directly associated with the swastika, the Holocaust, euthanasia, and medical experimentation, or with the search for precursors of those horrors. Historians of Great Britain have pursued more mundane issues such as political transformation.

Arno Mayer has revived some of the debate over the Elie Halévy and George Dangerfield theses about the "strange death" of liberal England, "killed" by syndicalists, suffragettes, and Irish nationalists during the two or three years before 1914. Robert J. Scally, Bernard Semmel, Avner Offer, and Geoffrey R. Searle, in various ways, have introduced a British variation of "social imperialism" to describe a hybrid array of ideas, strategies, and coalitions, for example, issues such as the Ulster question, foreign trade, overseas investment, domestic welfare, tax reforms, right-wing opposition, and the Radical wing of the Liberal party. Lloyd George has been the individual leader most closely linked to all of this. Paul Kennedy, discussed more below, has insisted that primacy of internal politics is not as applicable in this case. The liberal government before World War I included no reactionary forces or "neo-feudal" elements and the establishment believed war would cause revolution, not prevent it.[33]

Among governmental leaders of Great Britain, not counting Lloyd George, who has attracted the major attention, already mentioned, the focus has been on the Foreign Office. Most historians agree that no "British Holstein" or éminence grise existed. Fewer agree about respective roles of Sir Edward Grey, the foreign secretary after 1905, and his advisers, dubbed a "Clique of mandarins" and "determined Germanophobes." Grey has been depicted as distracted by personal problems, "insular," and seen as a pawn of sinister and selfish machinations of such advisers as William Tyrrell and Eyre Crowe. Keith M. Wilson's detailed analysis of the famous Eyre Crowe memorandum of 1 January 1907 and its thesis, which was skillfully and persuasively tilted against Germany, is not convincing to Paul Kennedy, Zara Steiner, and George W. Monger. Elsewhere some historians argue, for example, Keith Wilson and Philip Taylor, that the British, unlike the German and French governments, took no initiatives to "educate" the public and that Grey and the Foreign Office fostered ignorance and evaded efforts to "open" and "democratize" the department. Such deficiencies would be ameliorated only after 1914.[34]

In the study of Anglo-German relations, traditional and revisionist methodologies and approaches have coexisted. Some historians persist in maintaining the worst of the old ways and thereby confirm the accusations of critics. Especially irritating is Dwight E. Lee who seems obsessed with personalities, including the mother-in-law of German chancellor Bernhard von Bülow, yet he curiously excludes mention of Tirpitz and the younger Helmuth von Moltke.[35] At the other extreme stands Judith M. Hughes, who has converted to the psychoanalytic interpretation of history. Hughes is "puzzled" because British and German leaders at the summit in the late nineteenth and early twentieth centuries, Bismarck, William Gladstone, and their respective "heirs," including Holstein, the kaiser,

Joseph Chamberlain, and Arthur James Balfour, often nego-
tiated but were incomprehensible to one another. They "spoke
past each other" and there was a "crisscross of discourse." She
claims that because of "dissonant tempers" deeply rooted in the
childhoods of these leaders and the fact of contrasting experiences of maternal care, the British were perplexed with the
Germans and the Germans were distrustful of the British. Since
there was no resolution, she notes, war ensued. The evidence
for these conclusions remains highly speculative and questionable.[36]

Between such extreme approaches can be found many more
balanced and valuable studies of Anglo-German relations. Certainly the most prolific scholar in this field has been Paul M.
Kennedy, who has recently moved from the University of East
Anglia to Yale. Kennedy has produced a number of major
works that attempt to apply Kehr-Fischer theses and approaches to Anglo-German relations, as well as more generally
to the diplomacy of the last century or so. Perhaps the most
ambitious of these is *The Rise of the Anglo-German Antagonism,
1860–1914* in which the orientation is explicitly structuralist.
Thirteen of its twenty-two chapters deal with economic, religious, cultural, social, and imperial factors. Specific chapter
titles reflect his emphasis: "The Press, Pressure Groups and
Public Opinion," "Discourse—The Weakening of Liberalism?" (in which he concludes that most German Anglophiles
and British Germanophiles were liberals and that their numbers
decreased), and "The Impulse and Orchestration of Patri-
otism." In his massive study of over 600 pages, Kennedy
defines the "primacy of domestic politics" as the background of
social, economic, ideological, and domestic-political factors
that influenced, and in some cases dictated, the course of
foreign, military, naval, and colonial policies, most notably the
decision to go to war in 1914.[37] In reviewing this book for the
Journal of Modern History, Professor David Kaiser of Carnegie-
Mellon University called it "the most important work on the
origins of World War I to have appeared in English in many
years."[38] The prolific Kennedy has produced other related
studies: *The Realities behind Diplomacy: Background Influences on*

British External Policy, 1865–1980 (1981) and *Strategy and Diplomacy, 1870–1945* (1984); and has edited (with J. A. Moses) *The War Plans of the Great Powers, 1880–1914* (1979) (foreword by Fritz Fischer) and (with Anthony Nicholls) *Nationalist and Racialist Movements in Britain and Germany before 1914* (1981).

The role of Anglo-German economic competition in contributing to faltering relations (specifically, how, in Anglo-German commercial activities, each side saw the other as a potential market, trading partner, underhanded competitor, or a threat to dominance, if not existence) has also been reconsidered. With variations, each resorted to protectionist measures, but Kennedy has stressed two trends in global economic relations before World War I: the absolute rise in production, trade, and prosperity and the relative decline of British and rise of German indices. The British establishment must have been very anxious about this loss of commercial supremacy.[39]

Nonetheless, Anglo-German diplomatic relations remained good during the Bismarckian era when Germany industrialized and acquired an empire, formal and informal. Under Kaiser Wilhelm II, however, a "new course" and "grasping" for world power, or weltpolitik, raised Anglo-German tensions. The Germans claimed loudly that they were being encircled. The British initially bragged of "Splendid Isolation" but later, after the Anglo-Boer War, began to take on commitments and "moral obligations" to France and Russia, the other two members of the Triple Entente. Theories about the particular year of the crucial and irrevocable turning point in Anglo-German relations abound. Examples include 1884, 1894, 1902, 1904, 1909, 1911, and 1912. Most historians seem to agree that the final two years before the war, 1912–14, evoked hopes of détente. Slow progress was evident in some minor matters, such as the Berlin to Baghdad railway issue and the possible disposition of Portuguese colonies. As Oron Hale has demonstrated, and others have confirmed, official Anglo-German diplomatic, colonial, and intergovernmental policies were never in serious conflict. The press in particular, however, exploited petty bickering, exaggerated nationalism, pervasive spy and invasion scares, as well as a number of increasingly serious international crises, such as Agadir in 1911, to exacerbate Anglo-German antagonisms.[40]

The subject of European imperialism in the late nineteenth and early twentieth centuries, including German and British, has also continued to generate extensive debate. The early general theories of Rudyard Kipling, J. A. Hobson, and Lenin still provoke comment though traditional diplomatic historians, such as William L. Langer, have dominated the field with more descriptive and less theoretical studies. In the postwar period activity in the study of imperialism has revived, particularly among economic historians. John Gallagher and Ronald E. Robinson raised new, or at least rephrased, questions about the motives for Victorian imperialism in Africa. In the process they stressed continuity and posited alternative forms of imperialism—formal, informal, semiformal. Their study, even though limited to British adventures in Africa, sparked new debates that still continue over the initiatives for the revived imperialism of the late nineteenth century. Were European colonial offices planning and executing, or were they reluctantly reacting to dynamic events in Africa or Asia? Social Darwinist speculations about survival of some empires led to conflicting claims. For example, both "Cape to Cairo" and *"Mittelafrika,"* respectively British and German imperial dreams, were geographically impossible to fulfill.[41] Anglo-German rivalry over colonies, empire, and international trade precipitated several serious crises, but all were eventually resolved. Therefore, Anglo-German colonial conflict was not a major contributing factor to World War I.[42]

Not surprisingly, the Kehr-Fischer approach has been adapted by some historians in search of explanations for "the New Imperialism" of European great powers after 1870. Hans-Ulrich Wehler in Germany and Bernard Semmel in Great Britain, among others, have emphasized the model of "social imperialism," a manifestation of changes in social structure, political fragmentation, and rapid industrialization. It has been claimed that Bismarck, the kaiser, Prime Minister Benjamin Disraeli, and Joseph Chamberlain launched foreign adventures as a means of creating internal political consensus.[43] As might be expected, Geoff Eley has attacked the concept of social imperialism as a simplistic device to obscure the real dynamics of conservative radicalization.[44]

The "conversion," motivations, and intentions of Bismarck when Germany suddenly blundered into colonization in the 1880s have stirred much speculation. The best general study of Bismarck's imperial policies remains that by Wehler, but H. P. Meritt, in a study of German East African policies, has described Bismarck as an "eclectic opportunist" who among other things desired to embarrass Gladstone and undermine the Anglophile German crown prince Frederick. Paul Kennedy concludes that "the number of birds which Bismarck sought to kill with this one stone is truly remarkable, even for him."[45]

For years almost the only good general studies of German colonialism were the works of Mary E. Townsend. Though still useful, these have now been superseded by newer works influenced heavily by the changes in German historiography spawned by the Fischer revolution. Historians now focus more on the interrelationship of imperial with domestic policies. Some, in both Germanies, have followed Hans-Ulrich Wehler's even "more broadly conceived sociological approach to the domestic causes of imperialism."[46] Such studies tend to follow closely—some argue too closely—dominant social science explanatory models. Many of the newer studies of German imperialism also emphasize critical perspectives of official policies. Imperial Germany has been accused of "genocide," gross and inhuman brutality, incompetence, and "totalitarian extremism," especially in South-West Africa. The most serious accusations against German colonial policies relate to the suppression of rebellions of the Hereros, Nama, and Hottentot tribes in Africa in the early years of the twentieth century. Some even claim the current apartheid policy of South Africa has its roots in earlier German African policies.[47]

If imperial conflicts proved a less disruptive factor in Anglo-German relations than many contemporaries were led to believe, the naval competition of the two powers constituted a much more serious problem, perhaps, as Oron Hale em-

phasized in his work, the very root of the problem.[48] Great
Britain had enjoyed extraordinary naval predominance
throughout the nineteenth century, unchallenged at least since
the battle of Trafalgar of 1805. Thus, in British historiography
naval studies have always overshadowed military ones. Older
studies, such as those by E. L. Woodward and A. J. Marder,
have been supplemented, if not superseded, by better-
documented studies.[49] In this area also, Paul Kennedy has
attempted to apply newer methodologies and insights to his
study of Anglo-German relations.[50] There have even been
attempts to connect British naval policies to domestic
concerns.[51]

Some in Great Britain apparently believed that the continuation of naval and imperial hegemony was Britain's strategic and geopolitical, if not religious, destiny in the nineteenth
century. The Royal Navy did, however, suffer from some very
real deficiencies. Members of the British Admiralty, like so
many other sailors around the turn of the century, were much
influenced by the American naval strategist Alfred T. Mahan.
They, therefore, based their war plans on past experiences,
which involved preparing for a close blockade, planning amphibious invasions, and focusing on the battleship as the proper
British war vehicle. The very un-English submarine was ignored. Even more seriously, the state of British naval and
military intelligence before the war was pathetic, and cooperation between the army and navy never really developed. Great
Britain would fight the real war in ways opposite from prior
planning and preparation.[52]

One major influence on British naval planning would be the
beginning of the German naval buildup in the 1890s, an
extensive, and expensive, plan for a battleship High Seas Fleet
encouraged by the new kaiser and executed by Admiral Alfred
von Tirpitz. The latter's theories, which remained unchanged
despite alterations elsewhere, were based on concepts now
assessed as fallacious, needlessly provocative, "irrational," and
"plausible rather than convincing." Tirpitz persevered on his
course in the face of rational, financial, and political arguments,
and even after a shift of emphasis back to the German army, the

real first line of defense for Imperial Germany. Nonetheless, this naval competition ensured that the British would fight on the side of Germany's enemies, the French and Russians. Upon the outbreak of war, the German battle fleet, which had cost so much in money and English estrangement, sat idle. Tirpitz, some claim, was only concerned about his bureaucratic empire. Historical assessments still lay the heaviest responsibility for Anglo-German tension on Tirpitz and his master, Wilhelm II, who loved so to play with his new fleet.[53]

Not surprisingly, however, the influence of both Eckart Kehr and Fritz Fischer has been significant on studies of the German navy before 1914. This was, of course, the very focus of Kehr's major work. Generally, more recent studies document how well the emerging naval officers corps and developing naval policies reflected Wilhelmine society and its stresses and, therefore, place rather less emphasis on their negative impact on Anglo-German relations. At least this is the tentative conclusion one can draw from research reports such as the volume of essays sponsored by the *Militärgeschichtliches Forschungsamt* on naval politics in Imperial Germany.[54] Holger Herwig, in particular, has emphasized the feudalization of middle class naval officers: "Thus, even though it prided itself on being a national Reich institution, the naval officer corps in time became no less a 'feudal' body within a rapidly changing industrial society than the Prussian army. It also became a mirror, or microcosm, of the Wilhelmian class society with its growing antagonisms that ultimately split and paralyzed German society as a whole."[55]

Thus, we come full circle to the final tragedy of pre-1914 Anglo-German relations, the July 1914 crisis. Naturally, this summer crisis continues to evoke much scholarly comment and controversy, some of it influenced by the Kehr-Fischer revolution, most notably the works of Arno J. Mayer discussed earlier in this essay. Though this is hardly the appropriate place for an extended survey of this enormous literature, it should be at least noted that the recent focuses of research have reflected Fischer's critical treatment of Bethmann Hollweg's role in the crisis and the influence of the idea of "preventive war" in Germany. The real and psychological pressures on German leaders have been analyzed and dissected, including such factors as their fear of encirclement and the "Copenhagen complex," that is, the fear that Britain would initiate a surprise and devastating invasion of Germany. All German leaders seemed to have militarist and navalist compulsions, according to most critical observers, and they also reflected other characteristics: "national paranoia," a "syndrome of the inevitability of war," a pronounced "fatalism," as well as a "chronic paralysis." More concretely, German leaders, and especially Bethmann Hollweg, harbored fears about the continued military and geographic expansion of Russia. Bethmann Hollweg expressed, for example, considerable alarm and exasperation when he learned of the secret British-Russian naval negotiations in the summer of 1914. Other incidents have attracted considerable historical notice, most notably Bethmann Hollweg's "leap in the dark," and the kaiser's marginal note, "now or never," on the report of the Sarajevo assassination. One naval historian has even found an early German contingency plan, dating from 1897, for the invasion of Belgium and Holland, providing additional support for those who emphasize the role of "preventive war" in German thinking.[56] Yet other historians, using intelligence sources now available, have attempted to modify Fischer's theses by pointing to evidence that military plans were not as thorough as often claimed and to the lack of evidence for the argument that Moltke and his advisors had already decided, by at least the winter of 1912–13, to launch a preventive war to break the French and Russian encirclement of Germany.[57]

In Great Britain, much has been made of the deadlock, hesitations, and indecisiveness of the cabinet during the July crisis. Some questions have been answered; for example, Grey did repeatedly warn the German government that Great Britain could not and would not remain neutral during a major continental war; yet some Germans, including Bethmann Hollweg, acted on the assumption that the British would not participate in a continental war. It remains much less clear whether the indecision-decision sequence of the British cabinet during the first days of August was motivated by a desire to hide internal, including Irish, problems, by purely political considerations, or by a sense of obligation, moral or otherwise, to external commitments. Most likely it was some combination of these and other pressures on the men who had to deal with the crisis.[58]

In sum, then, the Kehr-Fischer revolution in pre-1914 historiography, especially of Germany and Anglo-German relations, has added substantial and significant insights to our understanding of this crucial period, insights still being digested by a new, if depleted, generation of European historians on both sides of the Atlantic. In particular, it is now impossible to discuss the origins of the Great War without reference to the domestic conditions and politics of the great powers involved, as interwar historians frequently did. This may not be as revolutionary an insight as some argue, but it is one that historians and politicians ignore at their peril. Though "the humanitarian belief that a general war among Europeans was really unthinkable" may have been spreading within "enlightened" circles, European governments not only wore "the outmoded garments of the nineteenth century" in their international relationships, but in their domestic relationships as well.[59] "Dawning light, rich in promise for a fair day, never became high noon because of the failures and miscalculations of Europe's political and military leaders," failures and miscalculations that reflected in some significant ways, the influence of domestic forces on foreign policies. Though this may not necessarily equal *Primat der Innenpolitik,* it most certainly no longer equals *Primat der Aussenpolitik.*

Notes

[1] Oron J. Hale, *Germany and the Diplomatic Revolution: A Study in Diplomacy and the Press, 1904–1906* (Philadelphia, 1931; reprint 1971); and *Publicity and Diplomacy: With Special Reference to England and Germany, 1890–1914* (New York, 1940; reprint 1964).

[2] Oron J. Hale, *The Great Illusion, 1900–1914* (New York, 1971), especially pp. 347–55.

[3] Important examples would include the works of Eckart Kehr, Fritz Fischer, and Gerhard Ritter: Kehr, *Schlachtflottenbau und Parteipolitik, 1894–1901* (Berlin, 1930; reprint 1965), and *Der Primat der Innenpolitik,* (Berlin, 1965); Fischer, *Griff nach der Weltmacht* (Düsseldorf, 1961), *Krieg der Illusionen* (Düsseldorf, 1969), and *Weltmacht oder Niedergang* (Frankfurt a.M., 1965; 2d ed. 1969); Ritter, *Der Schlieffenplan* (Munich, 1956), and *Staatskunst und Kriegshandwerk,* 4 vols. (Munich, 1954–68). All of these have now been translated into English. Two excellent summaries worthy of mention here at the beginning are Volcker R. Berghahn, *Germany and the Approach of War in 1914* (New York, 1973); and Zara S. Steiner, *Britain and the Origins of the First World War* (New York, 1977).

[4] "Conference Report," *Social History,* 6 (January 1979), 103–9; Richard J. Evans, "From Hitler to Bismarck: 'Third Reich' and *Kaiserreich* in Recent Historiography," part 2, *Historical Journal,* 26 (December 1983), 1018.

[5] Wolfgang J. Mommsen, "Domestic Factors in German Foreign Policy before 1914," *Central European History,* 6 (March 1973), 4–5; Eckart Kehr, *Economic Interest, Militarism, and Foreign Policy: Essays on German History,* edited by Gordon A. Craig (Berkeley and Los Angeles, 1977), p. ix. Craig's edition provides translations of the Kehr essays, though in different arrangement, reprinted in Germany as *Der Primat Der Innenpolitik: Gesammelte Aufsätze zur preussischdeutschen Sozialgeschichte im 19. und 20. Jahrhundert,* edited by Hans-Ulrich Wehler (Berlin, 1965; 2d ed. 1970). James J. Sheehan presented a long review of the latter in *Central European History,* 1 (June 1968), 166–174. On Kehr's brief career, see also Peter Gay, ed., *Historians at Work,* 4 vols. (New York, 1972–75), IV, 69–86; and George Iggers, *New Directions in European Historiography* (Middletown, Conn., 1975), pp. 95–122.

[6] David Blackbourn, *Class, Religion, and Local Politics in Wilhelmine Germany: The Centre Party in Württemberg before 1914* (New Haven, 1980), p. vii; Geoff Eley, *Reshaping the German Right: Radical Nationalism and Political Change after Bismarck* (New Haven, 1980), pp. 1–2; Michael R. Gordon, "Domestic Conflict and the Origins of the First World War: The British and German Cases," *Journal of Modern History,* 46 (1974), 191–226; Isabel V. Hull, *The Entourage of Kaiser Wilhelm II, 1888–1918* (New York, 1982), p. 1; David French, *British Economic and Strategic Planning, 1905–1915* (Boston, 1982), p. 4; David E. Kaiser, "Germany and the Origins of the First World War," *Journal of Modern History,* 55 (September 1983), 442–43; and Berghahn, *Approach,* p. 73. A useful survey of the early reverberations of the Kehr-Fischer revolution on the historical views of Imperial Germany can be found in James J. Sheehan's "Germany, 1890–1918: A Survey of Recent Research," *Central European History,* 1 (December 1968),

345–72. Sheehan's own work, *German Liberalism in the Nineteenth Century* (Chicago, 1978) has attracted critical review from Geoff Eley in "James Sheehan and the German Liberals: A Critical Appreciation," *Central European History,* 14 (September 1981), 273–88. Obviously, this essay can hardly do justice to the full range of works on all aspects of German history in the nineteenth century. Those desiring more complete coverage should consult the major journals in the field, among which *Central European History* provides the most thoughtful commentaries on recent trends with regular bibliographical essays such as Sheehan's in the first volume and others more recently, for example: James C. Hunt, "The Bourgeois Middle in German Politics: 1871–1933: Recent Literature," 11 (March 1978), 83–106; Richard Breitman, "Negative Integration and Parliamentary Politics: Literature on German Social Democracy, 1890–1933," 13 (June 1980), 175–97; and Holger H. Herwig, "Andreas Hillgruber: Historian of 'Grossmachtpolitik' 1871–1945," 15 (June 1982), 186–98.

[7] The English editions of his works are: *Germany's Aims in the First World War* (New York, 1967); *War of Illusions* (New York, 1975); *World Power or Decline* (New York, 1974). See also his essay in H. W. Koch, ed., *The Origins of the First World War* (New York, 1972), pp. 79–145, one of several collective volumes that summarize interpretations of the origins of World War I.

[8] Koch, *Origins,* p. 22. Interwar revisionists included Harry Elmer Barnes, *The Genesis of the World War* (New York, 1926); and Sidney B. Fay, *The Origins of the World War,* 2 vols. (New York, 1930; reprint 1966).

[9] Walter Hubatsch et. al., eds., *The German Question* (New York, 1967), p. 16.

[10] Bernadotte E. Schmitt, *The Coming of the War, 1914,* 2 vols. (New York, 1930; reprint 1966); Luigi Albertini, *The Origins of the War of 1914,* 3 vols. (New York, 1952–57); and Hans W. Gatzke, *Germany's Drive to the West: A Study of Germany's War Aims during World War I* (Baltimore, 1950; reprint 1963).

[11] Imanuel Geiss, ed., *July 1914* (New York, 1967; reprint 1974); Dirk Stegmann, *Die Erben Bismarcks* (Cologne, 1970); Dirk Stegmann, Berndt-Jürgen Wendt, and Peter-Christian Witt, eds., *Industrielle Gesellschaft und Politisches System: Festschrift für Fritz Fischer* (Bonn, 1978); Hartmut Pogge von Strandmann and Imanuel Geiss, *Die Erforderlichkeit des Unmöglichen Deutschland am Vorabend des ersten Weltkrieges* (Frankfurt a.M., 1965).

[12] Georg Iggers, *New Directions,* pp. 90–122; Otto Pflanze, "Another Crisis among Germany Historians? Helmut Böhme's *Deutschlands Weg Zur Grossmacht," Journal of Modern History,* 40 (March 1968), 118–29; Abraham J. Peck, *Radicals and Reactionaries: The Crisis of Conservatism in Wilhelmine Germany* (Washington, D.C., 1978), pp. v and 107–63; and Geiss, *July 1914,* pp. 9–13.

[13] Perhaps the most convenient source is Koch, *Origins,* which contains three essays from the perspective of Gerhard Ritter, who died in 1967: Egmont Zechlin, pp. 145–256, Karl-Heinz Janssen, pp. 257–85, and Klaus Epstein, pp. 286–306. Ritter himself devoted much of vol. 3 of his *The Sword and the Scepter: The Problem of Militarism in Germany,* 4 vols. (Coral Gables, Fl., 1969–73), to a detailed refutation of Fritz Fischer. See, among other sources, Georg G. Iggers, *The German Conception of History* (New York, 1968), pp. 229–68; L. L. Farrar, *Arrogance and Anxiety* (Iowa City, 1981), p. 149; Wolfgang J. Mommsen, "The Debate on German War Aims," *Journal of Contemporary History,* 1 (July 1966), 47–72; and Hans Medick, "Review Essay: H. U. Wehler, *Bismarck und der Imperialismus,* 1969," *History and Theory,* 10 (1971), 228–39.

[14] Richard J. Evans, "From Hitler to Bismarck: 'Third Reich' and *Kaiserreich* in Recent Historiography," part 1, *Historical Journal,* 26 (June 1983), 485–97 and part 2, *HJ,* 26 (December 1983), 999–1020. Reflections of the Fischer controversy can be found in Gerald D. Feldman, ed., *German Imperialism, 1914–1918* (New York, 1972); J. C. G. Röhl, ed., *1914: Delusion or Design?* (New York, 1973); John A. Moses, *The Politics of Illusion: The Fischer Controversy in German Historiography* (London, 1975); A. J. P. Taylor, "Fritz Fischer and His School," *Journal of Modern History,* 47 (1975), 120–24; Samuel R. Williamson, Jr., ed., *The Origins of a Tragedy: July 1914* (St. Louis, 1981); and Christopher J. Bartlett, *The Global Conflict, 1880–1970* (London, 1984).

[15] Thorstein Veblen, *Imperial Germany and the Industrial Revolution* (New York, 1915); Gordon A. Craig, *The Politics of the Prussian Army, 1640–1945* (New York, 1955; reprint 1964); Ralf Dahrendorf, *Society and Democracy in Germany* (New York, 1967); Ludwig Dehio, *Germany and World Politics in the Twentieth Century* (New York, 1959); Hans Rosenberg, *Grosse Depression und Bismarckzeit* (Berlin, 1967); Henry C. Meyer, *"Mitteleuropa" in German Thought and Action, 1815–1945* (The Hague, 1955); and George W. Hallgarten, *Imperialismus vor 1914,* 2 vols. (Munich, 1963).

[16] Pauline R. Anderson, *The Background of Anti-English Feeling in Germany, 1890–1902* (Washington, D.C., 1939; reprint 1969); Eckart Kehr, *Battleship Building and Party Politics in Germany, 1894–1901,* edited and

translated by Pauline R. Anderson and Eugene N. Anderson (Chicago, 1975); Arthur Lloyd Skop, "The Primacy of Domestic Politics: Eckart Kehr and the Intellectual Development of Charles Beard," *History and Theory,* 13 (1974), 119–31.

[17] See particularly his *Battleship Building and Party Politics in Germany, 1894–1901,* and two essays in *Economic Interest, Militarism, and Foreign Policy:* "The German Fleet in the Eighteen Nineties and the Politico-Military Dualism in the Empire" and "The Social and Financial Foundations of Tirpitz's Naval Propaganda."

[18] Important examples beyond those already cited would include: Hans-Ulrich Wehler, *Bismarck und der Imperialismus* (Cologne, 1969) and *Das deutsche Kaiserreich, 1871–1918* (Göttingen, 1973; 2d ed. 1975, 3d ed. 1977); Volcker Berghahn, *Der Tirpitz-Plan* (Düsseldorf, 1971); Klaus Saul, *Staat, Industrie, Arbeiterbewegung im Kaiserreich* (Düsseldorf, 1974); Peter-Christian Witt, *Die Finanzpolitik des Deutschen Reiches von 1903–1913* (Hamburg, 1970); Hans-Jürgen Puhle, *Agrarische Interessenpolitik und Preussischer Konservativismus im Wilhelminischen Reich, 1893–1914* (Hanover, 1967). Good examples of recent views in English can be found in Richard J. Evans, ed., *Society and Politics in Wilhelmine Germany* (New York, 1978) and Roger Fletcher, *Revisionism and Empire* (London, 1984). See also two recent essays by leading American historians of Germany: Theodore S. Hamerow, "Guilt, Redemption, and Writing German History," *American Historical Review,* 88 (February 1983), 53–72; and Konrad H. Jarausch, "Illiberalism and Beyond: German History in Search of a Paradigm," *Journal of Modern History,* 55 (June 1983), 268–84.

[19] Arno J. Mayer, "Domestic Origins of the First World War," in Leonard Kreiger and Fritz Stern, eds., *The Responsibility of Power: Historical Essays in Honor of Hajo Holborn* (Garden City, N.Y., 1967), p. 288.

[20] Arno J. Mayer, "Internal Causes and Purposes of War in Europe, 1870–1956: A Research Assignment," *Journal of Modern History,* 41 (September 1969), 303.

[21] Mayer, "Causes," 291–303; "Domestic Origins," 286–300; *Political Origins of the New Diplomacy, 1917–1918* (New Haven, 1959; reprint 1970); *Politics and Diplomacy of Peacemaking: Containment and Counterrevolution at Versailles, 1918–1919* (New York, 1967); and *The Persistence of the Old Regime* (New York, 1981). See also: Donald Lammers, "Arno Mayer and the British Decision for War: 1914," *Journal of British Studies,* 12 (May 1973), 137–65; Peter Loewenberg, "Arno Mayer's 'Internal Causes and Purposes of War in Europe, 1870–1956,': An Inadequate Model of Human Behavior,

National Conflict and Historical Change," *Journal of Modern History,* 42 (December 1970), 628–36; Robert James Scally, *The Origins of the Lloyd George Coalition* (Princeton, 1975), pp. 16–28; and Gordon, "Domestic Conflict," 191–226.

[22] See, in addition to the works of Eley, Blackbourn, and Evans already cited, the following: David Blackbourn and Geoff Eley, *Mythen deutscher Geschichtsschreibung* (Frankfurt a.M., 1980); Geoff Eley and Keith Neild, "Why Does Social History Ignore Politics?" *Social History,* 5 (May 1980), 249–71; Geoff Eley, "Reading Gramsci in English," *European History Quarterly,* 14 (October 1984), 441–78; and Mary Nolan, *Social Democracy and Society: Working Class Radicalism in Düsseldorf, 1890–1920* (New York, 1981). Eley and Blackbourn have elaborated their post-Fischer arguments in a long introduction to the revised and expanded English edition of *Mythen,* especially the emphasis on prewar radical and popular nationalism as an important part of the background to National Socialism *(The Peculiarities of German History: Bourgeois Society and Politics in Nineteenth Century Germany* [New York, 1984], 1–35). See also Philip Rees, ed., *Fascism and Pre-Fascism in Europe, 1890–1945* (Totowa, N.J., 1984).

[23] Gordon A. Craig, "The Historian and the Study of International Relations: Presidential Address, December 1982," *American Historical Review,* 88 (February 1983), 1–11; Georg Iggers, *New Directions,* pp. 80–122, and *German Conception.* Eggers has revised *New Directions* (New York, 1984).

[24] Reflections of this problem can be found in nearly all of the previous citations, but Leonard Krieger reviews a few of the more traditional studies in "German History in the Grand Manner," *American Historical Review,* 84 (October 1979), 1007–17. See also Jacques Droz, "In Search of Prussia: A Review Article," *Journal of Modern History,* 55 (March 1983), 71–77.

[25] Jarausch, "Illiberalism and Beyond," 268–69, 282.

[26] Lothar Gall, *Bismarck: Der Weisse Revolutionär* (Frankfurt a.M., 1980). Hans-Ulrich Wehler, *Bismarck und der Imperialismus,* is another major study of the master at work. Examples of works in English might include not only the popular biography by Edward Crankshaw, *Bismarck* (New York, 1981), but some interesting periodical literature such as Alan Mitchell, "Bonapartism as a Model for Bismarck's Politics," *Journal of Modern History,* 49 (June 1977), 181–99; and Henry A. Kissinger, "The White Revolutionary: Reflections on Bismarck," *Daedalus,* 97 (Summer 1968), 888–924. The master's diplomacy has received less favorable than usual treatment in George F. Kennan, *The Decline of Bismarck's European Order: Franco-Russian Relations, 1875–1890* (Princeton, 1979).

[27] The conference papers are in J. C. G. Röhl and Nicolaus Sombart, eds., *Wilhelm II, New Interpretations: The Corfu Papers* (Cambridge, 1982). See especially the papers of Lamar Cecil (pp. 91–119), Paul M. Kennedy (pp. 143–68), and Isabel V. Hull (pp. 193–220). The standard biography of Wilhelm II in English has an Afterword in the revised edition to accommodate new interpretations: Michael Balfour, *The Kaiser and His Times* (New York, 1964, 1972), pp. 525–31. General coverage can also be found in a number of other works: Erick Eyck, *Das Persönliche Regiment Wilhelms II* (Zurich, 1948); *Deutschland im Zeitalter des Imperialismus, 1890–1914* (Frankfurt a.M., 1972; rev. 1982); and Hull, *Entourage*, pp. 6–75. The post-Bismarckian period is still generally seen as a time of incompetent and militarist-dominated leadership by many historians, such as J. C. G. Röhl, *Germany without Bismarck* (Berkeley and Los Angeles, 1967), J. Alden Nichols, *Germany after Bismarck* (New York, 1958; reprint 1968); and Ekkehard-Tega P. W. Wilke, *Political Decadence in Imperial Germany* (Urbana, Ill., 1976). A number of studies focus, as Oron Hale did, on the *Daily Telegraph* interview of 28 October 1908 as an important element in the decline of Wilhelm's leadership; for example, Geoff Eley applies the new historiography to this crisis in *Reshaping the German Right*, pp. 279–90.

[28] The best single study is probably Konrad Jarausch, *The Enigmatic Chancellor: Bethmann Hollweg and the Hubris of Imperial Germany* (New Haven, 1973), but many other historians have joined the debate within the context of their own works, many of which have been mentioned already, for example, Gerhard Ritter in vol. 3 of *Sword and Scepter*, partly a response to Fischer's treatment of Bethmann Hollweg in both *War Aims* and *War of Illusions*. See also Wayne C. Thompson, *In the Eye of the Storm: Kurt Riezler and the Crises of Modern Germany* (Iowa City, 1980).

[29] Wilke, *Decadence*, pp. 62–80; Norman Rich, *Friedrich von Holstein*, 2 vols. (New York, 1965); Norman Rich and M. H. Fisher, eds., *The Holstein Papers*, 4 vols. (New York, 1955–63); and J. C. G. Röhl; "Review of *Friedrich von Holstein*, by Norman Rich," *Historical Journal*, 9 (1966), 379–88. On Eulenburg see Hans W. Burmeister, *Prince Philipp Eulenburg-Hertefeld, 1847–1921* (Wiesbaden, 1981).

[30] See, for example, Berghahn's *Der Tirpitz-Plan*, as well as other recent studies on naval policies discussed below.

[31] The first diary, that of Kurt Riezler, who later came to the United States to teach, has been edited by Karl Dietrich Erdmann as *Tagebücher, Aufsätze, Dokumente* (Göttingen, 1972). See also the Thompson biography noted above. The second diary is that of Admiral von Müller, edited by Walter Görlitz as *The Kaiser and His Court* (New York, 1959; reprint 1964). On this

see the review by J. C. G. Röhl, "Admiral von Müller and the Approach of War, 1911–1914," *Historical Journal*, 4 (December 1969), 651–73.

[32] The *Making of the Twentieth Century* series, published by Macmillan and St. Martin's; review of Richard Bosworth, *Italy and the Approach of the First World War* in *History Today*, 33 (October 1983), 56–57.

[33] The standard general work is R. C. K. Ensor, *England, 1870–1914* (Oxford, 1936). The classic interpretations are George Dangerfield, *The Strange Death of Liberal England, 1910–1914* (New York, 1935; reprint 1961); and Elie Halévy, *A History of the English People in the Nineteenth Century*, vol. 6, *The Rule of Democracy, 1905–1914* (New York, 1929; reprint 1961). Examples of work by those named in the text are: Bernard Semmel, *Imperialism and Social Reform: English Social-Imperial Thought, 1895–1914* (New York, 1960; reprint 1968); Scally, *Origins of the Lloyd George Coalition;* Avner Offer, "Empire and Social Reform: British Overseas Investment and Domestic Politics, 1908–1914," *Historical Journal*, 26 (March 1983), 119–38; and G. R. Searle, "The Edwardian Liberal Party and Business," *English Historical Review*, 98 (January 1983), 28–60. Perhaps the following illustrate the variety of the work being done within the last decade or so: Martin Pugh, *The Making of Modern British Politics, 1867–1939* (New York, 1982), esp. pp. 93–160, provides an introduction; Robert Rhodes James, *The British Revolution*, 2 vols. (London, 1976–77); Patrick Joyce, *Work, Society, and Politics* (New Brunswick, N.J., 1980); Peter Clarke, *Liberals and Social Democrats* (New York, 1978); A. J. A. Morris, ed., *Edwardian Radicalism, 1900–1914* (Boston, 1974); Stephen E. Koss, ed., *The Pro-Boers* (Chicago, 1973); Bruce K. Murray, *The People's Budget, 1909–1910* (New York, 1980); Patricia Jalland, *The Liberals and Ireland: The Ulster Question in British Politics to 1914* (New York, 1980); Donald Read, *England, 1868–1914: The Age of Urban Democracy* (London, 1979); and David Morgan, *Suffragists and Liberals* (Oxford, 1975). The standard guide to the literature of this period is the massive *Bibliography of British History, 1851–1914* (Oxford, 1976) edited by H. J. Hanham. Several journals, most notably *Historical Journal* and *Journal of Modern History*, provide regular composite reviews of current literature, for example: Alastair Reid, "Labour and Society in Modern Britain," *HJ*, 25 (June 1982), 489–500; and Sheldon Rothblatt, "Some Recent Writings in British Political History," *JMH*, 55 (September 1983), 484–99.

[34] Keith M. Wilson, "The Question of Anti-Germanism at the British Foreign Office before the First World War," *Canadian Journal of History*, 18 (April 1983), 23–42; "The Foreign Office and the 'Education' of Public Opinion before the First World War," *Historical Journal*, 26 (June 1983), 403–11; and "Sir Eyre Crowe on the Origins of the Crowe Memorandum of

1 January 1907," *Bulletin of the Institute of Historical Research,* 56 (November 1983), 238–41. In addition, see Zara Steiner, *Origins,* pp. 4, 42–45, 171–250, and *The Foreign Office and Foreign Policy 1898–1914* (New York, 1970); Philip Taylor's essay in David Dilks, ed., *Retreat from Power,* vol. 1 (New York, 1982), pp. 42–63; several relevant essays in F. H. Hinsley, ed., *British Foreign Policy under Sir Edward Grey* (New York, 1977); Keith Robbins, *Sir Edward Grey* (London, 1971); Michael G. Ekstein, "Sir Edward Grey and Imperial Germany in 1914," *Journal of Contemporary History,* 6 (1971) 121–31; Kenneth Bourne, *The Foreign Policy of Victorian England* (New York, 1970); A. J. A. Morris, *Radicalism against War, 1906–1914* (Totowa, N.J., 1972); and Howard Weinroth, "Norman Angell and the *Great Illusion:* An Episode in Pre-1914 Pacifism," *Historical Journal,* 17 (September 1974), 551–74. The most thorough study of British foreign policy around the turn of the century is probably Cedric J. Lowe and M. L. Dockrill, *The Mirage of Power,* 3 vols. (Boston, 1972). A useful review of some of the recent literature is Bernard Porter, "British Foreign Policy in the Nineteenth Century," *Historical Journal,* 23 (March 1980), 193–202.

[35] Dwight E. Lee, *Europe's Crucial Years: The Diplomatic Background of World War I, 1902–1914* (Hanover, N.H., 1974).

[36] Judith M. Hughes, *Emotion and High Politics: Personal Relations at the Summit in Late Nineteenth Century Britain and Germany* (Berkeley and Los Angeles, 1982).

[37] Paul M. Kennedy, *The Rise of the Anglo-German Antagonism, 1860–1914* (Boston, 1980), p. xi.

[38] *Journal of Modern History,* 55 (December 1982), 804–6.

[39] Kennedy, *Antagonism,* p. 306. Several standard traditional studies of Anglo-German relations, in addition to Hale's studies, have been reprinted: R. J. S. Hoffman, *The Anglo-German Trade Rivalry, 1875–1914* (Philadelphia, 1933; reprint 1964); and Raymond J. Sontag, *Germany and England: Background of Conflict, 1848–1894* (New York, 1938; reprint 1969). Neither has stood the test of time as well as Hale's *Publicity and Diplomacy.* More recent views are illustrated by the essays in Paul Kluke and Peter Alter, eds., *Aspekte der deutsch-britischen Beziehungen in Laufe der Jahrhunderte* (Stuttgart, 1978). Examples of economic studies are D. C. M. Platt, *Finance, Trade, and Politics in British Foreign Policy, 1815–1914* (New York, 1968); and Derek H. Aldcroft, ed., *The Development of British Industry and Foreign Competition, 1875–1914* (Toronto, 1968).

[40] See especially Oron J. Hale's *Diplomatic Revolution* and *Publicity and Diplomacy*. Examples of relevant recent studies are: Lamar Cecil, *The German Diplomatic Service, 1871–1914* (Princeton, 1976); Stephen E. Koss, *Lord Haldane* (New York, 1969), and *The Rise and Fall of the Political Press in Britain*, vol. 1, *The Nineteenth Century* (Chapel Hill, N.C., 1981); Alan J. Lee, *The Origins of the Popular Press in England, 1855–1914* (Totowa, N.J., 1976); Karsten Schroder, *Parlament und Aussenpolitik in England, 1911–1914* (Frankfurt, a.M., 1974); Charles E. McClelland, *The German Historians and England* (New York, 1971). The periodical literature is even more extensive, but the following might serve as illustrations: Eleanor L. Turk, "The Press of Imperial Germany: A New Role for a Traditional Resource," *Central European History,* 10 (December 1977), 329–37; H. W. Koch, "The Anglo-German Alliance Negotiations: Missed Opportunity or Myth?" *History,* 54 (October 1969), 378–92; Keith M. Wilson, "The Agadir Crisis, The Mansion House Speech, and the Double-Edgedness of Agreements," *Historical Journal,* 15 (September 1972), 513–32; Richard Langhorne, "Anglo-German Negotiations concerning the Future of the Portuguese Colonies, 1911–1914," *Historical Journal,* 16 (June 1973), 361–87; M. E. Humble, "The Breakdown of Consensus: British Writers and Anglo-German Relations, 1900–1920," *Journal of European Studies,* 7 (March 1977), 41–68; and David French, "Spy Fever in Britain, 1900–1915," *Historical Journal,* 21 (June 1978), 355–70.

[41] The classics are J. A. Hobson, *Imperialism: A Study* (London, 1902; reprint 1965); and V. I. Lenin, *Imperialism: The Highest Stage of Capitalism* (London, 1916; reprint 1939), but see also the more objective historical studies of D. K. Fieldhouse, *The Theory of Capitalist Imperialism* (New York, 1967) and *Colonialism, 1870–1945* (New York, 1981); and Richard Koebner and Helmut D. Schmidt, *Imperialism: The Story and Significance of a Political Word, 1840–1960* (Cambridge, 1982), as well as the widely discussed Ronald Robinson and John Gallagher, *Africa and the Victorians: The Official Mind of Imperialism* (New York, 1961; reprint 1968). The controversy is illustrated in William Roger Louis, ed., *The Robinson and Gallagher Controversy* (New York, 1976). See also Prosser Gifford and William Roger Louis, eds., *Britain and Germany in Africa: Imperial Rivalry and Colonial Rule* (New Haven, 1967); Christopher J. Bartlett, ed., *Britain Pre-eminent* (London, 1969); Winfried Baumgart, *Imperialism* (Oxford, 1982); and H. John Field, *Toward a Programme of Imperial Life* (Westport, Conn., 1982). The debate over the economic aspects of British imperialism can best be followed in the periodical literature, some examples of which are: D. C. Platt, "The Imperialism of Free Trade: Some Reservations," *Economic History Review,* 2d ser., 21 (August 1968), 296–306; Eric Stokes, "Late Nineteenth Century Colonial Expansion and the Attack on the Theory of Economic Imperialism: A Case of Mistaken Identity," *Historical Journal,* 12 (1969), 285–301, and "Uneconomic Im-

perialism," *Historical Journal,* 18 (June 1975), 409–16; and David McLean, "Finance and 'Informal Empire' before the First World War," *Economic History Review,* 2d ser., 29 (May 1976), 291–305.

⁴² Examples of "peaceful" resolution of colonial conflicts are discussed by Paul M. Kennedy, *The Samoan Tangle: A Study of Anglo-German-American Relations, 1878–1900* (New York, 1974); Miriam Hood, *Gunboat Diplomacy, 1895–1905: Great Power Pressure in Venezuela* (London, 1975); and A. E. Ekoko, "British Naval Policy in the South Atlantic, 1879–1914," *Mariner's Mirror,* 66 (August 1980), 209–23.

⁴³ Wehler's *Bismarck und Imperialismus;* and Semmel's *Imperialism and Social Reform.* See also Woodruff D. Smith, *European Imperialism in the Nineteenth and Twentieth Centuries* (Chicago, 1982), especially, pp. 85–108.

⁴⁴ Geoff Eley, "Defining Social Imperialism: Use and Abuse of an Idea," *Social History,* 3 (October 1976), 265–90, and "Social Imperialism in Germany: Reformist Synthesis or Reactionary Slight of Hand?" in Joachim Radku and Imanuel Geiss, eds., *Imperialismus im 20. Jahrhundert: Gedenkschrift für George W. F. Hallgarten* (Munich, 1976). See also Paul M. Kennedy, "German Colonial Expansion: Has 'Manupulated Social Imperialism' Been Antedated?" *Past and Present,* 54 (February 1972), 134–41.

⁴⁵ In addition to Kennedy's article noted above, see his "Bismarck's Imperialism: The Case of Samoa, 1880–1890," *Historical Journal,* 15 (June 1972), 261–83; H. P. Merit, "Bismarck and the German Interest in East Africa, 1884–1885," *Historical Journal,* 21 (March 1978), 97–116; Woodruff D. Smith, "The Ideology of German Colonialism, 1840–1906," *Journal of Modern History,* 46 (December 1974), 641–62; Gifford and Louis, eds., *Britain and Germany,* essays by Louis (3–46), Henry A. Turner (47–82), and Helmut Bley (607–630). Two older studies have been reprinted: William O. Aydelotte, *Bismarck and British Colonial Policy* (Philadelphia, 1937; reprint 1974); and A. J. P. Taylor, *Germany's First Bid for Colonies* (New York, 1938; reprint 1970).

⁴⁶ See Woodruff D. Smith, "German Imperialism after Wehler: Two Perspectives," *Central European History,* 12 (December 1979), 387–91, in which he reviews Klaus J. Bade, *Friedrich Fabri und der Imperialismus in der Bismarckzeit—Depression—Expansion* (Freiburg, 1975) and Fritz Klein, ed., *Studien zum deutschen Imperialismus vor 1914* (Berlin, 1976), the latter illustrating East German interpretations. Townsend's standard work from the interwar period has been reprinted: *The Rise and Fall of Germany's Colonial Empire, 1884–1918* (New York, 1930; reprint 1966). In addition to the Gifford and Louis collective volume and Wehler's key interpretation of

Bismarck's imperialism: Winfried Baumgart, *Deutschland im Zeitalter des Imperialismus, 1890–1914* 4th ed. (Stuttgart, 1982); Lewis Gann and Peter Duignan, eds., *Colonialism in Africa*, 5 vols. (Cambridge, 1969–75); Woodruff D. Smith, *German Colonialism* (Chapel Hill, N.C., 1978); Wolfgang J. Mommsen, *Imperialismustheorien: Ein Überblick über die neueren Imperialismusinterpretationen* (Göttingen, 1977) and Helmuth Stoecker, ed., *German Imperialism in Africa* (Hamden, Conn., 1985). Hans-Ulrich Wehler has also compiled a *Bibliographie zum Imperialismus* (Göttingen, 1977).

[47] Helmut Bley, *South-West Africa under German Rule, 1894–1914* (London, 1971); Jon M. Bridgman, *The Revolt of the Hereros* (Berkeley and Los Angeles, 1981); Bridgman and David E. Clarke, *German Africa* (Stanford, 1965); John H. Wellington, *South West Africa and Its Human Issues* (New York, 1967), pp. 158–73, 204–22; Horst Drechsler, *"Let Us Die Fighting"* (New York, 1980); William R. Louis, *Great Britain and Germany's Lost Colonies, 1914–1919* (New York, 1967); Lewis H. Gann, *The Rulers of German Africa, 1884–1914* (Berlin, 1970); Kenneth MacKenzie, "Some British Reactions to German Colonial Methods, 1885–1907," *Historical Journal*, 17 (March 1974), 165–75; Hartmut Pogge von Strandmann, "The German Role in Africa and German Imperialism: A Review Article," *African Affairs*, 69 (October 1970), 381–89.

[48] See especially his *The Great Illusion*, pp. 230–40, 260–67.

[49] E. L. Woodward, *Great Britain and the German Navy* (New York, 1935); A. J. Marder, *The Anatomy of British Sea Power* (New York, 1940); A. J. Marder, *From Dreadnought to Scapa Flow*, 5 vols. (New York, 1961–70).

[50] Paul M. Kennedy, *The Rise and Fall of British Naval Mastery* (New York, 1976); "The Development of German Naval Operations Plans against England, 1896–1914," *English Historical Review*, 89 (January 1974), 48–76, as well as *Antagonism*, pp. 403–22. For other examples see Jonathan Steinberg, "The Copenhagen Complex," *Journal of Contemporary History*, 1 (1966), 23–46, and "The Nouvelle of 1908: Necessities and Choices in the Anglo-German Naval Arms Race," *Transactions of the Royal Historical Society*, 5th ser., 21 (1971), 25–43; Richard Langhorne, "The Naval Question in Anglo-German Relations, 1912–1914," *Historical Journal*, 14 (June 1971), 359–70; Paul Haggie, "The Royal Navy and War Planning in the Fisher Era," *Journal of Contemporary History*, 8 (1973), 113–31. A more general study is provided by Peter Padfield, *The Great Naval Race* (New York, 1974).

[51] In addition to Kennedy's *Rise and Fall*, pp. 205–39, see W. Mark Hamilton, "The 'New Navalism' and the British Navy League, 1895–1914," *Mariner's Mirror*, 64 (February 1978), 37–44; and Howard Weinroth,

"Left-Wing Opposition to Naval Armaments in Britain before 1914," *Journal of Contemporary History*, 6 (1971), 93–120.

[52] See, for example, the recent study of Nicholas P. Hiley, "The Failure of British Espionage against Germany, 1907–1914," *Historical Journal*, 26 (December 1983), 867–89.

[53] In addition to Berghahn's *Der Tirpitz-Plan*, the best general studies are Jonathan Steinberg, *Yesterday's Deterrent: Tirpitz and the Birth of the German Battle Fleet* (New York, 1965); Holger H. Herwig, *"Luxury" Fleet: The Imperial German Navy, 1888–1918* (London, 1980); and Robert J. Art, *The Influence of Foreign Policy on Seapower: New Weapons and "Weltpolitik" in Wilhelmian Germany* (London, 1973).

[54] Herbert Schottelius and Wilhelm Diest, eds., *Marine und Marinepolitik im Kaiserlichen Deutschland, 1871–1914* (Düsseldorf, 1972). See also W. Diest, *Flottenpolitik und Flottenpropaganda* (Stuttgart, 1976).

[55] *The German Naval Officers Corps: A Social and Political History, 1890–1918* (Oxford, 1973), p. x. See as well his essay "Feudalization of the Bourgeoisie: The Role of the Nobility in the German Naval Officers Corps, 1890–1918," *The Historian*, 38 (February 1978), 268–80.

[56] Jonathan Steinberg, "A German Plan for the Invasion of Holland and Belgium, 1897," *Historical Journal*, 6 (1963), 107–19. Imanuel Geiss's important two-volume selection of documents, *Julikrise und Kriegsausbruch, 1914* (Hanover, 1963–64) reflects the Fischer interpretation, as do so many other volumes published on the final crisis in the last two decades. See also L. L. Farrar, *The Short-War Illusion* (Santa Barbara, Calif., 1973); and Konrad Jarausch, "The Illusion of Limited War: Chancellor Bethmann Hollweg's Calculated Risk, July 1914," *Central European History*, 2 (March 1969), 48–76.

[57] See the excellent article by Ulrich Trumpener, "War Premeditated? German Intelligence Operations in July 1914," *Central European History*, 9 (March 1976), 58–85.

[58] In addition to Zara Steiner's *Britain and the Origins of the First World War*, noted earlier, see examples of the debate as reflected in the periodical literature: P. H. S. Hatton, "Britain and Germany in 1914," *Past and Present*, no. 36 (April 1967), 138–53; D. C. M. Watt, "The British Reactions to the Assassination at Sarajevo," *European Studies Reviews*, 1 (July 1971), 233–47; Michael G. Ekstein, "Some Notes on Sir Edward Grey's Policy in July 1914," *Historical Journal*, 15 (June 1972), 321–24; and Keith M. Wilson, "The

British Cabinet's Decision for War, 2 August 1914," *British Journal of International Studies,* 1 (July 1975), 148–59.

[59] This quote, and the following one, are, of course, from Oron J. Hale, *The Great Illusion,* p. 314. See also his essay on the same theme: "Europe 1914: Was it Morning Light, High Noon, or Evening Twilight?" *Virginia Quarterly Review,* 61 (Summer 1965), 358–69.

III

The Führer's Faith:
Hitler's Sacred Cosmos

F. X. J. HOMER

THE USE OF religious imagery in describing the nature and appeal of National Socialism has long been commonplace among historians of the Third Reich. In his standard work *The German Dictatorship,* K. D. Bracher characterized Hitler's movement as "a religio-psychological phenomenon."[1] George Mosse has portrayed Nazism as the culmination of a "political religion" that developed around the cult of German nationalism in the nineteenth and twentieth centuries.[2] R. G. L. Waite, in the course of his psychohistorical study of Hitler, pointed to the latter's perception of himself as a messianic figure.[3] More recently James Rhodes has even suggested a parallel between the Nazis and the millenarian fanatics found in early and medieval Christianity.[4] In these instances, however, the term *religious,* when applied to aspects of the Nazi movement, has been generally employed metaphorically. Here, in this study, which will focus upon Hitler himself, the concept of religion will be used in a more literal sense.

Any suggestion of an association between Adolf Hitler and religion will no doubt seem unlikely, if not offensive. Let it be clearly understood, therefore, that *religion* is here used in its most generic context, and not with reference to any particular church or sect. In broad sociological terms religion can be defined as the process by which men establish for themselves a "sacred cosmos." According to Peter Berger, author of *The Sacred Canopy:* "By sacred is meant here a quality of mysterious and awesome power, other than man and yet related to him, which is believed to reside in certain objects of experience. This quality may be attributed to natural or artificial objects, to

animals, or to men, or to the objectivations of human culture.
. . . The quality may finally be embodied in sacred beings, from
highly localized spirits to the great cosmic divinities. The latter,
in turn, may be transformed into ultimate forces or principles
ruling the cosmos, no longer conceived of in personal terms but
still endowed with the status of sacredness."[5] Religion, thus
defined, represents a system designed to provide a comprehensive explanation of both observable and unobservable reality, as
well as a basis for all relationships between man and the world
about him.

Such a system also serves to protect its holder from what is
the opposite category to the sacred, which is chaos. "The sacred
cosmos emerges out of chaos and continues to confront the
latter as its terrible contrary . . . The sacred cosmos, which
transcends and includes man in its ordering of reality, thus
provides man's ultimate shield against the terror of anomy. To
be in a 'right' relationship with the sacred cosmos is to be
protected against the nightmare threats of chaos. To fall out of
such a 'right' relationship is to be abandoned on the edge of the
abyss of meaninglessness."[6] One theologian, Professor Gary
Lease, who has studied Nazism from a religious perspective,
has described this function of religion as "totalitarian," that is, it
represents an absolute framework within which an individual
incorporates and interprets all human experience.[7]

While keeping this conception of religion in mind, let us turn
to a consideration of Adolf Hitler's views on religion. The
authors of two standard works dealing with the relationship
between Nazism and the Christian churches in Germany both
argue that Hitler himself was indifferent to religious matters.
Ernst Helmreich says he was "fundamentally not a religious
man";[8] while J. S. Conway believes he was "basically indifferent
to all theological questions."[9] This judgment, based upon
Hitler's condemnation of sectarian disputes in *Mein Kampf*,
where Catholicism and Protestantism are pronounced to be
"equally valuable pillars for the existence of our people,"[10] is
predicated upon an identification of religion with traditional
Christianity. Moreover, the image of indifference on Hitler's
part is simply not compatible with evidence elsewhere, par-

ticularly in Hitler's table talk, his recorded conversations between 1941 and 1944 where the Führer returned again and
again to the subject of religion, displaying often a significant
intensity of feeling.

To be sure, all of Hitler's writings and speeches present
historians with a welter of inconsistencies and contradictions.
In every instance Hitler was directing his words at some audience, whether it was while dictating *Mein Kampf,* speaking
before a mass assembly, or soliloquizing for the benefit of his
inner circle. More often than not the substance of his statements
was designed to fit the expectations—and prejudices—of his
audience. Nonetheless, the wartime table talk shows Hitler at
his most candid, providing a unique "window into Hitler's
mind."[11] In these conversations the Führer displayed a contempt for Christianity, which he dismissed as "the invention of
sick brains."[12] Expanding on this indictment, he declared that
"the heaviest blow that ever struck humanity was the coming of
Christianity. Bolshevism is Christianity's illegitimate child."[13]
Hitler regarded Christ, not as the Son of God, but simply as a
popular leader whose teachings were distorted by his Jewish
disciples, in particular St. Paul.[14]

These denunciations of Christianity in Hitler's private conversations contrast with his frequent and cynical use of Christian allusions in his public rhetoric where, for example, in one of
his early speeches in 1922, he linked his anti-semitism explicitly
to his own alleged faith in Christ: "My feeling as a Christian
points me to my Lord and Savior as a fighter. It points me to the
man who once in loneliness, surrounded only by a few followers, recognized these Jews for what they were and sum-
moned men to fight against them and who, God's truth! was
greatest not as sufferer but as fighter . . . How terrific was His
fight for the world against the Jewish poison. To-day, after two
thousand years, with deepest emotion I recognize more pro-
foundly than ever before in the fact that it was for this that He
had to shed His blood upon the Cross."[15] Similar references to
Christian traditions and practices can be found in his public
speeches throughout his career.[16]

This dichotomy between Hitler's public and private stance

toward Christianity can in part be explained by practical political concerns; it also reflects a distinction Hitler himself made
between Christianity (and Catholicism in particular) as an
institution, in which he found a good deal to admire, and
Christianity as a religious *doctrine,* which he regarded as a failed
faith. Organizationally, Hitler saw the Catholic church as "a
magnificent edifice."[17] In *Mein Kampf* he praised the "inexo-
rable fanaticism" (always a term he used admiringly) with
which Christianity had defended itself over the centuries.[18]
Speaking before members of the Nazi press corps at the Brown
House in Munich in June 1930, Hitler was reported by one of
his gauleiters to have declared: "The Nazi party was to be built
upon the model of the Catholic Church. Upon a broad pedi-
ment of preachers and 'political pastors' living and working
among the people, the structure should ascend the leadership
pyramid of the party from the county leaders over the Gauleiter
to the senators and ultimately to the Fuehrer-Pope."[19]

Such borrowings from Catholic or Christian structure were,
of course, religious only in the most superficial and shallowest
of senses. Hitler rejected the doctrines of Christianity as "the
peak of absurdity,"[20] and he ruled out any possibility of an
accommodation between National Socialism and the Christian
faith, the obstacle being, in his words, Christianity itself.[21] At
the same time, however, Hitler consistently maintained his
belief in the need for some sort of faith that would provide him
and others with a definition of reality functioning as the kind of
"sacred cosmos" discussed above.

Such a concept of faith *(Glaube)* can be seen as religious in a
fundamental sense, and it was undoubtedly regarded as highly
important by Hitler himself. In the absence of faith, he said,
"man will lose all sense of proportion and, once he considers
himself to be lord of the universe, it will be the end of everything."[22] Years earlier in *Mein Kampf* he had stressed the same
point: "Take away from present mankind its religious-
dogmatic principles . . . by abolishing religious education and
without replacing it by something equivalent, and the result
facing you will be a grave shock to the foundation of mankind's
existence. One may therefore state that not only does man live

to serve higher ideals but that, conversely, those higher ideals also provide the presupposition of his existence as man."[23] In his table talk Hitler explicitly emphasized the importance of a belief in a supreme being which, as he put it, gives men "the opportunity to concretize the feeling they have of supernatural realities."[24]

What then were these "higher ideals," these "supernatural realities," by which the Führer believed life should be guided? Hitler saw man as inherently subject to the laws of nature. "True piety," he once said, "is the characteristic of the being who is aware of his weakness and ignorance. . . . It is a fact that we're feeble creatures and that a creative force exists. To seek to deny it is folly. In that case it is better to believe something false than not to believe anything at all."[25] The crude, racist Social Darwinism that lay at the core of Hitler's thinking was in effect elevated to the level of religious doctrine, a sacred cosmos involving a divinely ordained struggle for existence in which "men dispossess one another, and one perceives that at the end of it all, it is always the stronger who triumphs."[26]

Hitler once remarked to Otto Wagener, a Nazi party chieftain, that the source of religion sprang from an impulse *(Trieb)* in man by which he is led to comply with the demands of nature.[27] The latter, according to Hitler in his table talk, acted providentially: "As in everything, nature is the best instructor, even as regards selection. One couldn't imagine a better activity on nature's part than that which consists in deciding the supremacy of one creature over another by means of a constant struggle."[28] Thus, for Hitler, "salvation consists in the effort that each person makes to understand Providence and the laws of nature."[29] The ideal world would be one "in which every man would know that he lives and dies for the preservation of the species."[30]

This entire outlook can be rightly looked upon as Hitler's "nature religion."[31] Yet his public presentation of these doctrines was quite different. Speaking before the 1938 party rally in Nuremberg, Hitler declared: "National Socialism is a cool-headed doctrine of realities; it mirrors clearly scientific knowledge and its expression in thought. Since we have won the heart of our people for this doctrine, we do not wish to fill their minds with a mysticism which lies outside of that doctrine's goal and purpose. National Socialism is not a cult movement — a movement for worship; it is exclusively a *völkisch,* political doctrine based on racial principles."[32] Indeed, Hitler's indictment of Christianity is directly linked to the notion that science and religion are somehow opposed to each other. Christianity, in his view, was doomed to extinction precisely because it had been "worn away before the advances of science." Nazism, he insisted, must adhere to the "spirit of exact science."[33]

Hitler's vision of both himself and his racial doctrines as the product of scientific thought extends back to his conception of his childhood education. To his table-talk listeners Hitler, discussing what he saw as the "perpetual conflict" between religion and science, recalled that "as a child I suffered from this contradiction and ran my head against a wall. Often I complained to one or another of my teachers against what I had been taught an hour before—and I remember that I drove them to despair."[34] On another occasion Hitler engaged in a long reminiscence of his religion teacher in Linz, a Father Schwarz, an account in which Hitler is at great pains to depict himself as being "completely the master of the material" and as having read "a lot of works by free thinkers" and acquired "ill-digested scientific knowledge," all of which he employed, as he tells it, to drive the good Father Schwarz "out of his wits."[35]

Hitler's depiction of himself as a youthful freethinker who refused to be taken in by priestly superstition cannot, of course, be taken at face value. In fact, as Bradley Smith has shown, the accounts of his childhood provided by the adult Hitler usually represent what he wished to believe was true, as opposed to what actually happened.[36] The fact that Hitler was so determined to give the impression that, even in his youth, he had never come to terms with what he called the "Christian lie" suggests that in reality he may have as a child been genuinely attracted to the Christian faith,[37] only to suffer disillusionment when its doctrines appeared to be exposed as fraudulent by the crude racism which he acquired while in Vienna before 1913 and which to his uncritical mind appeared to be based upon

"scientific" principles.[38] This would explain the personal vin-
dictiveness and vehemence that appear in Hitler's private con-
demnations of Christianity and his insistence upon the latter's
inevitable demise.

Paradoxically, therefore, Hitler's conception of the struggle
for existence embodied in the laws of nature could only function for him as a *religion* so long as he thought of it as the
product of *science*. While Hitler imagined his "nature religion"
to be a set of principles derived from scientific knowledge, it
actually was serving as a sacred cosmos, that is to say, "an
absolute world view which cannot allow any other to intrude
upon it."[39] Certainly Hitler resisted any intrusion that would
threaten the sanctity of his racist sacred cosmos. Accordingly, in
his table talk Hitler urged that the conception of God, or the
beyond, ought not to be given any precise definition or representation, lest it go the way of Christianity, whose concrete
images failed to "stand up to examination."[40] Along the same
lines Hitler opposed efforts to introduce cult practices into
Nazism as he ridiculed those zealots who carried the glorifica-
tion of the German past to the point of urging re-establishment
of worship to the Teutonic god Wotan. "A movement like
ours," the Führer insisted, "mustn't let itself be drawn into
metaphysical digressions."[41]

The single-minded and fanatical zeal with which Hitler
pressed his program for "preservation of the species" through
the elimination of those deemed inferior by the laws of nature is
in itself clear evidence that, in the final analysis, he was motivated, not by some "cool-headed doctrine of realities," but
rather by a need to protect a perverted but nonetheless deeply-
rooted sacred cosmos that to him represented the only alternative to chaos.[42] To the end of his life Hitler remained convinced
that his efforts to destroy the Jews was sanctioned by the laws of
nature and by what he once referred to as a "divine Com-
mandment: 'Thou shalt preserve the species.'"[43] In his "Political Testament" Hitler declared that he would "die with a happy
heart" confident even in defeat that six years of death and
destruction were not in vain since they served as a "most
glorious and valiant demonstration of a nation's life

purpose."[44] Thus, Hitler's own suicide became for him a fulfillment of *his* "life purpose"; several years earlier in his table talk he had said that "a man who takes his own life returns finally to nature—body, soul and mind."[45]

While the foregoing analysis of the religious character of Hitler's personal beliefs may be seen as relevant primarily to the workings of the Führer's mind, the concluding segment of this essay will examine how this "nature religion" was reflected in Hitler's public rhetoric and how it might relate to the attraction his movement exerted upon those who gravitated toward National Socialism.

Hitler's speeches were neither the product of reasoned argumentation nor a program offering concrete remedies for specific problems. Hitler relied not upon facts or logic but rather upon what J. P. Stern has called the "self-authenticating" fact of his own inner conviction. According to Stern, Hitler's basic message to his audiences can be paraphrased in these words: "This is the self-validating source of my likes and hates, my scheme of values which is right because it is yours as well as mine, yours by being mine. I am not a man to politick, or haggle with fate. To my every decision my whole existence, and thus yours, is committed. Therefore, follow me, for there is no other way and I cannot go wrong. The forces of History and Nature (or of the Lord, Almighty, or of Fate) are on my side."[46] Hitler, in other words, was speaking in the same way as a fundamentalist preaches the gospel, as a "living witness" who utilizes the strength of his own fervor as a basis for inducing commitment in his listeners. Nazism was presented as a movement in which faith *(Glauben)* preceded understanding *(Erkennen)*.[47]

While it is certainly true that Hitler wished to project the image of a modern political leader, particularly after he came to power, he simultaneously saw himself as a redemptive figure specially destined to bring salvation to Germany. "I feel myself the emissary of fate," he said in a 1931 interview, "the standard bearer as I am sometimes called, and with my movement I shall thump the drum until Germany wakes up."[48] Writing a few years later, Nazi ideologist Ernst Kriech referred explicitly to the religious character of the Führer's role as a leader who directs his "chosen people" to their "destiny." The course of history, Kriech declared, "is suspended between the divine call and the response of man. In the Führer this response is inseparably a religious decision and a political decision, a political leadership rooted in a religious act of will grounded in destiny." He continued, "Religion consists, for every member of the people, in perceiving the destiny, the call, and responding to it . . . The call of destiny is the only divine 'revelation.'"[49] Max Wundt, another Nazi ideologue, echoed the same theme in a lecture given to students at the University of Berlin late in 1932 shortly before Hitler's appointment as chancellor:

> The political purpose of the racial idea is to give the *völkisch* experience of unity the power of a political faith. . . . The realm of the political is now sacred above all else, bringing us grace and liberation . . . . at stake from now on is the primary experience of the German that is sacred to us all, our recognition of the rebirth of Germany, the unshakeable faith in the liberating mission of the Führer. . . . The politically conscious National Socialist will free himself from paralyzing parliamentarianism by his total emotional commitment to the will of the Führer, of blood, of race. . . . Our political faith will bring to completion the secularization process of Revelation.[50]

However turgid their style, such Nazi enthusiasts serve to exemplify a process whereby the realm of politics was endowed with what the Israeli historian Uriel Tal terms a "sacred character": "In this linguistic structure many words acquired new meanings. A word like *fanatisch* was used in a positive sense; *rücksichtslos* ('ruthless') and *brutal* appeared as terms of praise; *unverrückbar* ('immovable'), *restlos* ('to the last drop'), *radikal* ('extremist') indicated ideal qualities to be admired and emulated. Concepts taken from the sphere of theology, such as 'salvation' *(Heil)*, 'kingdom' *(Reich)*, 'confessing,' 'resurrection,' 'faith' and 'mission,' underwent a process of politicization."[51] This "sacralization of politics" reflected in the language of theorists such as Kriech and Wundt is a clear indication that the religious idiom enveloping Hitler's rhetoric, derived from his own "nature religion," was meant to be taken literally by its audiences.

This religious idiom is most evident in two themes running throughout Hitler's speeches, both before and after 1933: the need for a new "faith" and spiritual renewal, and, secondly, the role of sacrifice as salvation. In 1923 Hitler declared that the first priority for Germany was not material armament but "the armament of the spirit";[52] he pledged to create a "new faith" for the masses "which will not fail them in this hour of confusion."[53] In his famous address before the Düsseldorf Industry Club in January 1932, at the same time that Hitler addressed the pragmatic interests of his audience in terms of the benefits National Socialism could bring to the German economy, he did not fail to insist that the ultimate source of Germany's ills lay in her "inner confusion and aberration of mind," which could be remedied only through an inner spiritual renewal.[54] Years later at the height of his power in 1936 Hitler proclaimed that the source of his movement's strength was not "mechanical organization" or "outward lip-service" but "faith."[55]

The theme of sacrifice was even more central since it was intimately connected to Hitler's personal view of life as a divinely ordained struggle for existence. The willingness to accept this struggle and to engage in it brings "salvation" precisely because it represented submission to the laws of nature. Self-sacrifice was once singled out by Hitler as, in his estimation, "the highest virtue."[56] National Socialism, he declared, was "not a doctrine of happiness or good luck, but a doctrine of work and a doctrine of struggle, and thus also a doctrine of sacrifice."[57] In 1922, when the National Socialist movement was still in its infancy, Hitler told prospective supporters: "He who today fights on our side cannot win great laurels, far less can he win great material goods—it is more likely he will end up in jail."[58] Ten years later in his Düsseldorf speech he boasted that his followers "cease to regard material distress as the one and only thing which counts." Consequently, he said, "hundreds of thousands of young men are prepared at the risk of their lives to withstand our opponents."[59] In a similar vein he once attributed the weakness of the Weimar Republic to the unwillingness of its supporters to sacrifice their lives for their cause, in contrast to the Nazis who he asserted were "ready for their ideals to face the last encounter."[60]

Those Nazis killed in the street battles during the pre-1933 *Kampfzeit* were presented as examples for all to emulate. Speaking on the twelfth anniversary of the 1923 putsch, Hitler declared that "from the sacrifice of the first fighters there will ever come anew the strength for sacrifice."[61] The annual ceremonies honoring the "martyrs" of the abortive putsch took on all the character of a religious rite; "the blood which they shed," the Führer proclaimed, "has become for the Reich the water of baptism."[62] These elaborate rituals were designed to convey the notion that such acts of sacrifice represented not death or defeat but redemptive victory. This theme was vividly dramatized in the 1933 film *Hitlerjunge Quex,* an early but notable product of Nazi propaganda that told the story of a young boy, Heni, who, despite his communist parents, is drawn to Nazism only to be killed by a gang of Bolshevik street fighters.[63] Heni's death is the direct result of his faith and commitment to the Hitler movement; nonetheless, he attains "salvation." According to the theologian Gary Lease, who regards this film as "a classic religious presentation": "Salvation takes the form, both in the movie and in National Socialist doctrine, of a triumph over death. Death is not viewed as a tragic final end to human existence, but rather serves a higher purpose and thus is overcome in a transcendental act which establishes a new human nature, namely that of National Socialist allegiance and German nationalism."[64]

Ultimately, the willingness to make such a blood sacrifice became a test of one's faith in National Socialism. By 1943, as the specter of military defeat began to present itself, Nazi propaganda under Goebbels's direction increasingly turned to the theme of "victory in death." Even if the worst came, in accepting a "heroic death an individual might transcend himself and become part of what Adolf Hitler called 'national immortality.'"[65] Thus it was that Hitler himself could die in his bunker "with a happy heart"; *he* had at least kept faith with nature and with his sacred cosmos.

The question remains, however, as to what extent others were influenced by his faith. J. P. Stern has argued that Germans in the years following World War I exhibited a "longing for transcendence" that made them susceptible to the appeal of a "religious" movement like Hitler's—"religious" in the sense of being "total and absolute and an object of faith, rather than of prudential thinking" As Stern puts it: "The more total and 'religious' or (to use one of Hitler's favourite terms) 'fanatical' the demands he makes on them and the more uncompromising his call for the war-like virtues of obedience, hardness and self-sacrifice, the more certain they are that his claim to a god-given authority and to the 'historic' nature of his mission is authentic, that he is the true Messiah."[66] Evidence supporting this view linking Nazism's appeal to its call for spiritual renewal and sacrifice can be found among the autobiographical statements, or "biograms," gathered from nearly six hundred Nazi party members in 1934 by Theodore Abel, a Columbia University sociologist, and subjected to quantitative analysis by Peter Merkl in a study done four decades later under the title *Political Violence under the Swastika*.[67] Merkl observes that many of Abel's respondents cited the "quasi-religious ecstasy" which Hitler and Nazi speakers evoked in them. Despite the often confused manner in which this sort of response is articulated, making it difficult to separate words and meaning, Merkl finds ample confirmation in the Abel biograms that many of Hitler's most dedicated followers were won over not by promises of benefits but rather by the very fact that "the last in effort and sacrifices" was being demanded of them.[68] Nazism, he concludes, was "a virulent faith inspiring large numbers of people to march and fight and proselytize for the greater glory of the cause."[69]

Thus, Hitler's personal beliefs, outlined here as his sacred cosmos and reflected in his public rhetoric, did play a role in attracting others to his movement. Two concluding caveats, however, need to be added. First, any understanding of the popular support received by the Nazis cannot rest on a unicausal explanation. Richard Hamilton's recent impressive study of Nazi electoral successes up to 1933 effectively challenges the "great man theory," which would interpret Nazism as a movement solely created by its leader's unique demagogic talents. The success of National Socialism was as much a product of its organizational skills and the different styles of combat directed against its different rivals as it was a product of the content of its doctrines.[70]

Finally, and of particular relevance to this essay, is the fact that even those who for a time may have been caught up in Hitler's vision of a Germany destined by the laws of nature to reign supreme over the weak and the inferior did not necessarily share faith in Hitler's sacred cosmos. Only those few who, like their Führer, took their lives in the conviction that in doing so they were following the dictates of nature and would thereby find salvation can be regarded as the true believers.[71] Hitler may have died believing that his example in seeking victory in death would be the seed from which a new National Socialism would arise; but in the end the only legacy left by the Führer's faith consisted of ashes—his own and those of over twelve million innocent victims.

Notes

[1] Karl Dietrich Bracher, *The German Dictatorship: The Origins, Structure, and Effects of National Socialism* (New York, 1970), pp. 147–48.

[2] George L. Mosse, *The Nationalization of the Masses: Political Symbolism and Mass Movements in Germany from the Napoleonic Wars through the Third Reich* (New York, 1975), pp. 1–20, 207–16.

[3] Robert G. L. Waite, *The Psychopathic God: Adolf Hitler* (New York, 1977), pp. 27–32.

[4] James M. Rhodes, *The Hitler Movement: A Modern Millenarian Revolution* (Stanford, 1980), pp. 29–84.

[5] Peter L. Berger, *The Sacred Canopy: Elements of a Sociological Theory of Religion* (New York, 1969), p. 25.

[6] Ibid., pp. 26–27.

[7] Gary Lease, "Hitler's National Socialism as a Religious Movement," *Journal of the American Academy of Religion*, 45, no. 3, Supplement (September 1977), D797.

[8] Ernst Christian Helmreich, *The German Churches under Hitler: Background, Struggle, and Epilogue* (Detroit, 1979), p. 123.

[9] J. S. Conway, *The Nazi Persecution of the Churches, 1933–1945* (New York, 1968), p. 2.

[10] Adolf Hitler, *Mein Kampf,* trans. Ralph Manheim (Boston, 1943), pp. 345–46.

[11.] H. R. Trevor-Roper, "The Mind of Adolf Hitler," Introduction to *Hitler's Table Talk, 1941–44; His Private Conversations,* trans. Norman Cameron and R. H. Stevens, 2d ed. (London, 1973), p. xv.

[12] *Table Talk* (15 December 1941), p. 144.

[13] Ibid. (11–12 July 1941), p. 7.

[14] Ibid. (21 October 1941), p. 76; (29–30 November 1944), pp. 721–22. Hitler expressed the same point of view years earlier to Otto Wagener, a Nazi party official (Otto Wagener, *Hitler aus nächster Nähe: Aufzeichungen eines Vertrauten, 1929–1932,* ed. H. A. Turner, Jr. (Frankfurt a.M., 1978), pp. 469–72).

[15] Norman H. Baynes, ed., *The Speeches of Adolf Hitler: April 1922–August 1939* (London, 1942), I, 26 (12 April 1922).

[16] Several examples are cited by Waite, pp. 30–32. Conway, pp. 141–57, also discusses Nazi parodies of Christian ritual.

[17] *Table Talk* (31 March 1942), p. 386.

[18] *Mein Kampf,* p. 351.

[19] William Sheridan Allen, ed. and trans., *The Infancy of Nazism: The Memoirs of Ex-Gauleiter Albert Krebs, 1923–1933* (New York, 1976), p. 166.

[20] *Table Talk* (14 October 1941), p. 60.

[21] Ibid. (14 December 1941), p. 145.

[22] Ibid. (1 August 1942), p. 607.

[23] *Mein Kampf*, pp. 379–80.

[24] *Table Talk* (14 October 1941), p. 61.

[25] Ibid. (24 October 1941), pp. 86–87.

[26] Ibid. (23 September 1941), p. 39. Hitler's racist and Social Darwinistic world outlook is outlined in Eberhard Jäckel, *Hitler's Weltanschauung: A Blueprint for Power* (Middletown, Conn. 1972); on Hitler's view of nature as a "teleological force," see Hans Staudinger, *The Inner Nazi: A Critical Analysis of Mein Kampf*, ed. Peter M. Rutkoff and William B. Scott (Baton Rouge, 1981), pp. 77–83.

[27] Wagener, p. 467.

[28] *Table Talk* (4 April 1942), p. 396.

[29] Ibid. (11 November 1941), p. 124.

[30] Ibid. (15 December 1941), p. 145.

[31] The term *nature religion* is used by Michael D. Ryan, "Hitler's Challenge to the Churches: A Theological Political Analysis of *Mein Kampf*," *The German Church Struggle and the Holocaust*, ed. Franklin H. Littell and Hubert G. Locke (Detroit, 1974), p. 161.

[32] Baynes, I, 394–95 (6 September 1938).

[33] *Table Talk* (14 October 1941), pp. 59, 61.

[34] Ibid. (24 October 1941), p. 84.

[35] Ibid. (8–9 January 1942), pp. 188–91.

[36] Bradley F. Smith, *Adolf Hitler: His Family, Childhood and Youth* (Stanford, 1967), p. 79.

[37] *Table Talk* (27 February 1942), p. 343.

[38] In the opening chapter of *Mein Kampf* (p. 6) Hitler recalled that as a young child he briefly was attracted to a priestly vocation. Although Bradley

Smith dismisses this episode as unimportant in Hitler's development, this is an area where, as the psychohistorians have learned to their dismay, there is a dearth of hard evidence.

[39] Lease, p. D797.

[40] *Table Talk* (15 December 1941), pp. 144–45.

[41] Ibid. (14 October 1941), p. 61.

[42] Perhaps the clearest evidence of the irrational fanaticism that motivated the horrors of the Holocaust lies in the extent to which its implementation was given priority in the allocation of scarce wartime resources even to the detriment of German military performance. On the "cost" of the Holocaust, see Raul Hilberg, *The Destruction of the European Jews* (New York, 1961), pp. 643–46.

[43] *Table Talk* (1–2 December 1941), p. 141.

[44] Office of the United States Chief of Counsel for the Prosecution of Axis Criminality, *Nazi Conspiracy and Aggression* (Washington, D.C., 1946–48), VI, 260–61.

[45] *Table Talk* (1–2 December 1941), p. 141.

[46] J. P. Stern, *Hitler: The Führer and the People* (London, 1975), p. 26–27.

[47] Uriel Tal, "On Structures of Political Theology and Myth in Germany Prior to the Holocaust," *The Holocaust as Historical Experience*, ed. Yehuda Bauer and Nathan Rotenstreich (New York, 1981), p. 51.

[48] Richard Breiting, *Secret Interviews with Hitler*, ed. Edouard Calic (New York, 1971), p. 22.

[49] E. Kriech, *Völkischpolitische Anthropologie* (1935–38), quoted in F. Gregorie, "The Use and Misuse of Philosophy and Philosophers," in International Council for Philosophy and Humanistic Studies, *The Third Reich* (London, 1955), pp. 705–6.

[50] Quoted in Tal, p. 59.

[51] Tal, p. 62.

[52] Baynes, I, 71 (4 May 1923).

[53] Adolf Hitler, *My New Order*, ed. Raoul de Roussy de Sales (New York, 1941), p. 26 (12 April 1923).

[54] Max Domarus, ed., *Hitler: Reden und Proklamationen, 1932–1945* (Munich, 1965), I, 71 (27 January 1932).

[55] Quoted in Manfred Ach and Clemens Pentrop, *Hitlers "Religion": Pseudoreligiöse Elements im nationalsozialistischen Sprachgebrauch* (Augsburg, 1977), p. 54.

[56] Breiting, p. 27.

[57] Domarus, I, 571 (30 January 1936).

[58] *My New Order*, p. 44 (28 July 1922).

[59] Domarus, I, 72 (27 January 1932).

[60] Baynes, I, 74–75 (21 August 1923).

[61] Ibid., I, 139 (8 November 1935).

[62] Ibid., I, 159 (8 November 1934).

[63] David Stewart Hull, *Film in the Third Reich* (Berkeley and Los Angeles, 1969), pp. 32–34; Jay W. Baird, "From Berlin to Neubabelsburg: Nazi Film Propaganda and Hitler Youth Quex," *Journal of Contemporary History*, 18 (1983), 495–515.

[64] Lease, D806–807.

[65] Robert Edwin Herzstein, *The War Hitler Won: The Most Infamous Propaganda Campaign in History* (New York, 1978), p. 257. Herzstein also notes that Goebbels's own rhetoric is replete with religious terminology involving the themes of "faith" and "sacrifice" (pp. 41–44). See also Werner Best, "The National-Socialist Vocabulary," in International Council for Philosophy and Humanistic Studies, *The Third Reich* (London, 1955), pp. 784–96; and Jay W. Baird, "Goebbels, Horst Wessel, and the Myth of Resurrection and Return," *Journal of Contemporary History*, 17 (1982), 633–50.

[66] Stern, p. 96.

[67] Abel's original research can be found in Theodore Abel, *Why Hitler Came to Power* (New York, 1938). Merkl's use of Abel's biograms is explained

in Peter H. Merkl, *Political Violence under the Swastika: 581 Early Nazis* (Princeton, 1975), pp. 5–35.

[68] Merkl, pp. 448–49, 539–40.

[69] Ibid., p. 382.

[70] Richard F. Hamilton, *Who Voted for Hitler?* (Princeton, 1982), pp. 359–60.

[71] Herzstein's study of Nazi propaganda efforts within Germany after 1939 (*The War That Hitler Won*), while a useful contribution to the subject, is in fact mistitled. If, indeed, Hitler's propaganda had been victorious, the German people would have joined Hitler and Goebbels in self-immolation.

IV

The Nazi Press before the Third Reich: *Völkisch Presse, Kampfblätter, Gauzeitungen*

LARRY D. WILCOX

T HE HISTORICAL DEBATE over the development of National Socialism in post–World War I Germany continues
unabated. Some scholars, especially social scientists, still pursue
the elusive mirage of comparative fascism.[1] Others attempt to
measure more accurately, in a quantitative sense, the appeal of
the Nazis.[2] Historians of modern Germany, in particular, have
tried to weigh the relative continuity and discontinuity between
the Nazi experience and previous German national development.[3] More recently, German scholars studying National
Socialism have been debating functions and intentions in the
building of the Third Reich.[4]

The enormous literature on National Socialism reflects the
significance of the problem at hand, but, at the same time, the
sheer quantity of publications makes life very difficult for
students of modern German history. One obvious way to get
better control of this situation is to narrow the research focus
without narrowing the ultimate questions, a necessary resort to
microhistory in an attempt to get a better understanding of the
development of National Socialism. Many historians have followed in the pioneering footsteps of Rudolf Heberele and
William Sheridan Allen with their local studies of the rise of the
Nazis.[5] Reading such regional studies, as well as other mono-
graphic studies of the myriad of Nazi groups and institutions,
leads all too logically back to the interpretation of National
Socialism as a *Sammelbewegung,* an umbrella-shaped political

protest movement that organized more skillfully than traditional parties the massive, though diffuse, discontent in German society following the disaster of World War I.

Since the population seeking shelter under such an umbrella
probably changed substantially during the short life of the
Weimar Republic, the Nazi movement could hardly have represented a coherent and positive ideological assault on this first
German republic. The essence of the Nazi appeal before 1933
remained basically negative, reflecting the shifting revolt of
many discontented groups against the modernization process
in central Europe. Such a view is supported by available statistics that indicate the volatility of Nazi party membership. For
example, according to one calculation, of the 239,000 who
joined the NSDAP before the crucial September 1930 elections, only 44 percent remained on the party rolls by early
1935. In his analysis Hans Mommson argues that the Nazis
penetrated a variety of groups in the later 1920s and early
1930s, but most of their electoral support proved transient
because "it is virtually certain that the NSDAP could not
permanently assimilate its mass following to any significant
extent, apart from the small, predominantly middle class hardcore. Therefore, Mommson concludes "that the mass-
movement aspect of the NSDAP was a transient phenomenon."[6] As such interpretations illustrate, the hardcore support
for National Socialism probably came from the lower middle
classes, especially if one includes the growing appeal of the
Nazis to discontented small farmers in Protestant areas of
Germany, an appeal recognized by some local party leaders
even before the central leadership established a rural department under Walter Darré in 1930.[7]

The success of National Socialism, if one follows this line of
reasoning, reflected the relative skill of the party leadership in
organizing, on all levels, the discontented groups at any one
particular time, for example the inflamed nationalists and de-
mobilized veterans in the early 1920s, the depressed small
farmers of the Protestant north in the later twenties, the ter-
rified middle classes in the early thirties. That they did this in a
sometimes traditional fashion is an argument this essay at-

tempts to illustrate with reference to the development of the Nazi press before 1933.

Nazi publications frequently boasted about their success in organizing propaganda activities in the *Kampfzeit:* "There has probably never been a movement in the whole world which has so systematically and resolutely taken up the exercise and formation of its propaganda, as the NSDAP."[8] Nonetheless, Hitler himself had ridiculed the importance of written propaganda and insisted that "the great upheavals in the world have never been guided by goosequills." Rather, he argued in the same passage of *Mein Kampf,* "the mass meeting is the only truly effective (because directly personal) way of exerting an influence on, and thus possibly winning over, any part of the people."[9]

Historians have generally agreed that the success of National Socialist propaganda owed most to the spoken word. The political rallies, on a larger or smaller scale to fit the circumstances, featuring not only Hitler and his close associates but also innumerable lesser-known graduates of party speaker schools *(Rednerschule)*, were certainly the most spectacular instruments in the Nazi propaganda orchestra before 1933 on all levels. For example, Fritz Reinhardt's speaker school founded in Bavaria in 1928 claimed 2,300 students by 1930 and 6,000 by 1933. The rapidly developing party bureaucracy expended a considerable amount of energy generating materials for offically designated speakers. The records of both the party propaganda office and the main archive contain copious documentation of such oral propaganda activities. Scanning these files makes it easier to understand how the Nazi propaganda apparatus reached every nook and cranny in Germany by the early 1930s.[10] The carefully staged political rallies, whether in a Munich beer hall, a Berlin stadium, or a village gasthof, captured the most public attention at the time, inside and outside Germany, as intended by their producers. They have continued to attract more scholarly attention than other instruments of propaganda. In particular, they have overshadowed the party's adventures into the world of political journalism. In one of the few general studies of Nazi propaganda in English, the role of the party newspaper is barely mentioned, and then only to emphasize that "although it had a certain prestige value for the Nazi leaders, it was not a very suitable vehicle for their propaganda."[11]

Given such emphasis on oral propaganda, one wonders why Hitler and his associates, to quote Zeman again, "believed, possibly quite mistakenly, in the necessity of owning a newspaper?" Why bother with such marginal activities if these party newspapers were "merely an adjunct of mass propaganda?"[12] Why stretch meager party resources to support journalistic activities of admittedly dubious value and even more dubious quality? The financial worries that accompanied the exertions of establishing party newspapers are amply documented in the Hauptarchiv files on their history. Yet, on all levels, party leaders emulated the Führer's example by establishing and developing their own journalistic mouthpieces.[13]

By the Nazi accession to power, more than 150 party-owned or affiliated newspapers had spread all over the Reich.[14] By that time, every gauleiter, and many lesser party leaders, had his own house organ that benefited enormously from the Nazi seizure of power in 1933–34 and the accompanying confiscation of socialist and communist printing plants.[15] Few German towns, however small, lacked their contingent of swastika arm-banded brown shirts hawking the appropriate local Nazi sheet, derisively labeled by some as *Kampf- und Käseblätter,* including Joseph Goebbels in reference to his Berlin party paper, *Der Angriff:* "The paper was bad, the printing inadequate. The *Angriff* gave the impression of a paper useful only for wrapping cheese [*Käseblatt*], appearing somewhere in obscure anonymity and devoid of any ambition of rising in the ranks of the great press organs in the Reich capital."[16]

Superficially at least, few of these Nazi newspapers appeared of little value for anything more than wrapping cheese, or garbage. Party newspapers, however, numbering thirty-one by late 1928 and perhaps sixty-five by September 1930, varied widely in journalistic quality, technical expertise, coverage, target audiences, and financial stability.[17] Few achieved much prominence, or even notoriety, before 1933, with the exceptions of Hitler's *Völkischer Beobachter,* Goebbels's *Der Angriff,* and Streicher's *Der Stürmer.* Contemporary foreign observers of the German press virtually ignored the existence of Nazi newspapers, focusing instead on the more visible SPD, Ullstein, Mosse, and especially the Hugenberg publishing empires.[18]

The NSDAP press, to judge from available and frequently questionable statistics, probably did not reach beyond the hardcore party membership in the years between 1925 and 1933. According to the most optimistic estimates, derived from information supplied to the party archives by the newspapers themselves, party dailies claimed a circulation of about three-quarters of a million (782,121) and the weeklies less than half a million (405,997), both figures for December 1932.[19] In other words, even the claimed circulation for party dailies by late 1932 fell short of the probable party membership at that time of something less than a million.[20] A substantial share of this circulation can be attributed to the central party organ, the *Völkischer Beobachter,* whose dominant position was jealously guarded by Max Amann, who ran the Eher Verlag.[21] Rough comparisons for earlier dates reveal the same statistical similarity between party membership and claimed newspaper circulation. It would appear, therefore, that few of the millions of the new voters attracted to National Socialism in the early 1930s became paid subscribers of the party newspapers, any more than they became dues-paying party members, at least before January 1933. While the NSDAP attracted nearly fourteen million discontented German votes in a national election, a contemporary observer estimated paid subscribers to the Nazi press at a paltry 350,000, in a year when total newspaper circulation in Germany has been estimated at more than twenty-seven million.[22] Reading a Nazi sheet did not necessarily precede, or even follow, millions of individual decisions to cast a vote for the NSDAP. The stranglehold of the "liberal-Jewish press," condemned in point twenty-three of the party program, obviously had not been broken by the skills of National Socialist journalism.[23] Not until 1933 did the party press become "suddenly the central point of German journalism. Now subscriptions came in by the thousands," but not because the quality of Nazi journalism had improved.[24]

An analysis of the pre-1933 development of this Nazi party press system reveals what might be labeled a *Sammelpresse,* a loosely coordinated network that drew upon three major historical types of German newspapers: the fragmented, racist-*völkisch* press of the turn of the century and the early postwar period; the combative but more disciplined political newspapers, like those of the Social Democrats; and the more general coverage and ideologically colorless provincial and local newspapers that appealed to broader audiences with a wide variety of features.[25] The progression from a fragmented, frequently backbiting *völkisch* press in the preputsch period through the "fighting papers not fit for wrapping cheese" of the later 1920s, and finally to the more stable, relatively speaking, provincial party papers of the early 1930s *(Gauzeitungen)* was wildly uneven and probably no more logical than the development of the movement as a whole. Indeed, this progression in the development of the party's press paralleled the changing composition of that *Sammelbewegung* we know as the National Socialist German Workers Party before January 1933.

In the early 1920s numerous *völkisch* organizations emerged in Germany in addition to the NSDAP. Many of these groups formed their own publishing firms that printed or supported the publication of books, pamphlets, and newspapers, flooding Germany "with the most violent and scurrilous anti-Semitic propaganda" even before Hitler became the Führer of the NSDAP.[26] For example, the *Deutschvölkischer Schutz- und Trutzbund* sponsored the weekly *Deutschvölkische Blätter* which, according to one source, sported the swastika on its masthead as early as January 1917.[27]

The first specifically "Nazi" newspapers were likely no more than existing radical nationalist sheets whose editors found the screaming propaganda of early Nazi rallies in Munich consistent with their own equally strident propaganda against the new system in Germany. Such newspapers generally reflected the *völkisch* ideology that had spread around the turn of the century, now inflamed, like so much else in Germany, by the searing experiences of military defeat, political collapse, and humiliating peace. They probably had few strong party affiliations within the maze of *völkisch* politics of the early 1920s, and a disproportionate number seem to have found refuge in the reactionary climate of Bavaria. Many seemed to reflect the personal views and eccentricities of someone like Dietrich Eckart, a minor literary figure who influenced Hitler in the early postwar years. Eckart founded, in December 1920, what the party writers later touted as the first truly Nazi newspaper, the weekly *Auf gut deutsch!*[28]

The early Nazi press constituted just one part of the extreme right-wing press that flourished in the climate of Bavaria in the 1920s. Ideologically, stylistically, even organizationally, it is as difficult to separate the early Nazi press from this *völkisch* milieu as it is the party in general before 1925. A very rough calculation from official party documents is that identifiable NSDAP-affiliated newspapers may have included as many as thirty-five different titles in the period 1920–25. Their titles almost always reflected their *völkisch* origins: *Völkische Zeitung* (Saxony, 1921–23), *Völkische Rundschau* (Frankfurt, 1921–23), *Völkische Wacht* (Württemberg, 1923), *Hakenkreuz-Völkische Soziale Monatschrift* (Halle, 1923), *Völkische Kurier* (Munich, 1924), *Das Völkische* (Weimar, 1924). Most were probably short-lived; some merged in order to survive; those that did survive were likely banned after the abortive November 1923 putsch.

In reality, of course, the *Völkischer Beobachter (VB)* became the first and remained to the end the most important Nazi party newspaper, a mouthpiece acquired for Hitler in December 1920, with funds the source of which has never been clearly identified. The *VB* traced its origins to a four-page weekly, *Münchener Beobachter,* founded in 1887 by a printer named Johann Naderer and purchased in 1900 by Franz Xaver Eher, thus the name of the subsequent NSDAP publishing house run by Max Amann. Eher barely managed to keep the weekly above water financially until his death in 1918, shortly before the end of the war, when the sickly little weekly passed to the Thule Society with the new subtitle "independent newspaper for national and racial politics."[29] When control of the weekly, now renamed *Völkischer Beobachter*, passed to the NSDAP, the Führer's closest associates quickly assumed control of the new party mouthpiece; Dietrich Eckart took over as editor, discontinuing his own paper, until shunted aside by the Baltic German racial ideologue Alfred Rosenberg, who remained editor until 1938. The newspaper became a daily in February 1923 and switched shortly thereafter to the larger format, rare in Germany at that time. The paper also rapidly lost its general *völkisch* character "and became a typical party organ, an exclusive megaphone for the leadership of the NSDAP."[30] Its circulation may have risen as high as 30,000 in 1923.[31]

Other early Nazi ventures into the world of German political journalism remained scattered, isolated, and heavily dependent on the support of private individuals since the NSDAP had enough trouble just keeping the central party organ financially afloat. A 1923 *VB* article proudly noted the existence of six other party papers in Bavaria: *Amsberger Tageblatt, Regensberger Tageblatt, Weisse Fahne, Sturmglocke, Der Schanzer, St. Georg*. Most of these must have been short-lived publishing ventures, for they left few traces in the party archives, except for *Weisse Fahne*, which Julius Streicher claimed as a forerunner of his *Der Stürmer* in Nuremberg.[32] A few early attempts to work together with other *völkisch* groups or individuals in newspaper publishing ventures usually came to naught. For example, the NSDAP apparently cooperated for a time in the publication of the *Pommersche Landbund* in northern Germany, presumably because the local Nazis lacked the funds and support to establish their own paper. In any case, the cooperation soon ended, according to the party's local leader, because "National Socialist observations frequently fell victim to the pen of the German nationalist editor."[33] Cooperation for the Nazis always meant subordination of others to National Socialists, not vice versa.

Perhaps the only other personal mouthpiece, other than Hitler's, to survive this *völkisch* period of the party press's development was Julius Streicher's virulently anti-Semitic weekly *Der Stürmer*, founded in 1923 after the failure of several previous ventures in Franconia. Streicher's paper remained his personal organ to the end of the Third Reich, that is, it never became a party-owned newspaper. Yet, because of his special position with the Führer, his weekly survived the *Kampfzeit* to become a prosperous national paper during the Third Reich, representing the extreme racist fringe of the party better than any other newspaper. A February 1945 article in the official journalists' trade paper, *Deutsche Presse,* characterized *Der Stürmer* as the oldest anti-Semitic newspaper which "developed in its first years a stylistic make-up that was calculated to have the maximum effect."[34]

The failure of Hitler's attempt to seize power by force in the context of the 1923 crisis in Germany led to the prohibition of the publication of *VB,* as well as any other papers closely associated with the NSDAP. This ban did not apply to other racist newspapers in Bavaria, which spewed forth a stream of invective against the republic that most contemporaries found indistinguishable from the Nazi sheets. Konrad Heiden later noted that "the school of this National Socialist journalism was the *Miesbacher Anzeiger,* a local sheet that became world famous for a few years because of its characteristic hostility to the Republic."[35] The degree of support for the Nazis from such conservative papers continued to grow throughout the 1920s. Some conservative newspapers later announced their support for National Socialism, for example, Graf Reventlow's *Reichswart.* The *Miesbacher Anzeiger* would become part of a Nazi press combine in southern Germany shortly after Hitler came to power.

Meanwhile, with the *VB* silenced, some Nazi leaders attempted to found substitute newspapers. These tended to reflect the differences between the northern and southern wings of the NSDAP, differences Hitler refused to arbitrate while he languished in Landsberg prison but which he would have to deal with soon after he refounded the party. In 1924 the Bavarian wing of the party, with Hermann Esser in the forefront, founded the *Grossdeutsche Zeitung* and, when that collapsed financially, *Der Nationalsozialist.* A Munich based socialist paper labeled the former the "Munich Hitler sheet" and considered its disappearance in May 1924 "a success of the reactionary-*völkisch* tendency over the revolutionary-*völkisch*."[36] Northern Nazis threw their support to the organ of the Freiheitsbewegung, the *Völkische Kurier*.[37] Nonetheless, it is obvious that neither Hitler nor Max Amann, head of the party publishing house, wanted such substitute newspapers to survive, thus providing potential competition for the *VB* later on.

Surveying the landscape of the party from the perspective of the wreckage of the abortive 1923 putsch, one sees few publishing successes for the Nazi party. Most attempts to found party newspapers within the general *völkisch* framework proved, short-lived, useful only as historical antecedents for later, longer-lived party newspapers. Probably the only significant party publishing ventures to survive 1923 basically intact were the *VB*, the assets of which Amann carefully guarded during the period it was banned, and Streicher's *Der Stürmer*. These two newspapers, respectively the most prominent daily and weekly of the Third Reich, carried the amorphous tradition of *völkisch* publishing into the more organized and more geographically dispersed *Kampfblätter* of the later 1920s. The refounding of the NSDAP after Hitler left prison would also involve the refounding of the party's press. The new "fighting newspapers fit only for wrapping cheese" would draw more on another tradition of the German press.

Hitler had understood from the outset of his political career the need for a central party organ as a vehicle for the transmission of orders and guidelines to the faithful from Munich headquarters of the movement. This became an even more important consideration with his new legal approach to achieving power. Even before Hitler's initial public speech after leaving Landsberg prison, Max Amann had been directed to resume publication of the *VB*. The first issue, printed the day before the official refounding of the NSDAP, carried a major pronouncement by the Führer entitled "Summons to Build a Press Foundation:"

> On 9 November 1923 the nationalist movement lost
> not only its organizational form but also its chief organ,
> the Munich *Völkischer Beobachter*.

If one could measure the worth of a newspaper by the hate of its opponents, then it was the most valuable in Germany. On no paper has so much hate been poured by all Jews and Judaized, by all of the Marxist November criminals, and those with similar views, than on the organ of the National Socialist German Workers' Party, the *Völkischer Beobachter,* the most hated newspaper in the land. After more than a year the movement must now set to work creating a daily newspaper again from nothing, otherwise it would lack today its best and most valuable weapon.

No German forgets the lies and treachery about our people which spew forth daily from the more than 15,000 Jewish organs.

But with what can one oppose them?

Till today almost nothing.

The *Völkischer Beobachter* as central organ of the National Socialist movement in greater Germany shall not only assist with this in its external struggle but shall also help to support within the leading circles of the movement every unifying tendency without which the inner unity of the party would be inconceivable.

On this basis I summon the supporters of the movement to participate in the building of a press foundation and to contribute all their strength to its growth.

Everyone should consider how small the sacrifice is that is demanded of him in relation to that which many of the best within our ranks have already given.

Every party member who has gone to prison for only an hour for his convictions has made a greater sacrifice than money could ever bring.

Can one even measure the sacrifice of death?

I expect the adherents of this movement to enable me to publish the *Völkischer Beobachter* daily again within the next few months.

I hope that the movement that has been in the front lines of the battle of our people against financial slavery can be spared the shame of having to borrow money.[38]

Despite the clear implication that National Socialists should concentrate on helping Hitler rebuild the central party paper, local NSDAP papers reappeared or began publication in greater number than ever before. Such party-affiliated newspapers become a more important and more permanent part of the party organization on all levels. Though the development of local party newspapers appears less systematic than some contemporary observers argued, a slow steady growth, unspectacular but perceptible, in the number of NSDAP newspapers did occur in the period between the refounding of the party in February 1925 and the first major electoral success in September 1930.[39] In late, 1925 a *VB* article listed twenty-two party newspapers, of which only four appeared daily and of which only about half appeared within the boundaries of Weimar Germany (the remainder were in Austria and the Sudeten area of Czechoslovakia). By the end of 1928 the number of party organs within Germany had risen to thirty-one. This doubled to about sixty-five by the September 1930 national elections.[40]

The party press during this period moved well beyond its early *völkisch* origins, reflecting the strategy of building a more disciplined political party apparatus that could compete better in election campaigns on all levels. Some contemporary observers even began to speak of a new type of *Kampfzeitung*. Every part of such a "fighting paper" was politically loaded in the battle for public opinion, using techniques such as constant repetition of a few key points expressed in a combative, catchy language that some termed "spoken writing."[41] Political opinions overshadowed standard information reporting, opinions frequently expressed in violent terms.

Party journalists, in their later reminiscences about the development of the party press, almost always emphasized the combative character of their newspapers: "This newspaper was no commercial operation in the usual sense, but it was an organ bearing the spirit of the coming order—fighting in the streets and at meetings with fists and brains and hearts to conquer."[42] Goebbels agreed that "it was not our intention to establish an informational paper;" rather "our goal was not to inform, but to incite, to inflame, to urge on."[43] Local authorities frequently expressed a quite different view of the spread of such Nazi sheets after 1925. For example, the Bavarian political police reported that the strength of a new Nazi paper in Erlangen, *Die Fackel*, "as that of similar National Socialist press ventures, consists solely in the exploitation of local gossip."[44] "The Torch" must not have burned very well, for it was not included on the list of party approved papers at the end of 1928.

Actually, one need look no further than the history of the German Social Democratic press to find a model for such kampfblätter. Goebbels himself admitted that the SPD press served as the teacher *(Lehrmeister)* for Nazi fighting papers such as his own Berlin-based *Der Angriff*.[45] Hitler likewise expressed admiration for the socialist press while commenting on the secrets of its effectiveness: "The Marxist press is written by agitators, and the bourgeois press attempts to carry on agitation by writers. The Social Democratic back-alley editor, who almost always comes to the editorial chair from the meeting hall has an unparalleled knowledge of his customers."[46]

The development and organization of the Nazi press system in the later 1920s paralleled that of the SPD in the later nineteenth century, at least in part because of the more urban-oriented strategy adopted by the NSDAP in the period 1925–28. The Nazi "fighting press" of this period, though characterized by gross linguistic excesses, also fit very well the general definition of the political press provided by a contemporary scholar, who argued that "the party press is that part of the entire press over which a party can legally and morally assert such an influence that this press reflects the uniform opinion imposed upon it in spite of local and personal connections."[47]

Most new NSDAP newspapers developed from the initiative of party leaders on various levels. Not surprisingly, many of these new party organs imitated the *VB* in their titles, though fewer reflected *völkisch* origins. For example, party leaders in the Rhineland founded the *Westdeutsche Beobachter* in Cologne in May 1925 and the *Nassauer Beobachter* in Wiesbaden in April 1927. By that time several party papers had begun publication in the north with the *Norddeutsche Beobachter* (Griefswald, May

1925) and the *Niederdeutschen Beobachter* (Schwerin, June 1925). East Prussian gauleiter Erich Koch finally succeeded in establishing a party organ in his fief in July 1929 when the *Ostdeutschen Beobachter* began publication in Königsberg. Many new ventures assumed titles sometimes indistinguishable from those of left wing sheets of the time. When Goebbels established his Berlin party paper in July 1927, he chose the title *Der Angriff*. Other lesser lights in the party leadership chose similarly stirring titles: *Der Eisenhammer* (Saarpfalz, 1925), *Freiheitsfahne* (Frankfurt a.M., December 1926), *Hessenhammer* (Darmstadt, 1927), *Die Faust* (Worms, 1927), *Kampfruf* (Stuttgart, August 1929), *Erwerblose* (Hamburg, October 1929), *Der Sturm* (Kassel, February 1930), *Freiheitskampf* (Dresden, August 1930). Significantly, though a few new party papers would use *Volk* on their mastheads, like the *Hamburger Volksblatt* (January 1928) or *Volksaufruf* (Herrsching, November 1930), none, except the *VB*, would use the term *völkisch* in their titles. If their titles reflected more militant political tactics than pure *völkisch* ideology, the varied locations of these new party newspapers documents the wider geographical presence of the NSDAP from 1925. Whereas early Nazi papers usually appeared in the south, especially in Bavaria, every major city in Germany gained its Nazi sheet in the later 1920's, as many smaller cities would in the aftermath of the September 1930 elections.

Party influence increasingly dominated the editorial boards of affiliated newspapers, now published primarily for the small circle of party loyalists in a given geographical area. Hitler fired three *VB* editors in 1926 for disobeying his earlier directives against cooperation with non-Nazi *völkisch* papers. This dismissal order, signed by the *VB* chief editor Rosenberg but approved by the Führer, noted that "the party leadership wishes in this way to assure that the *Völkischer Beobachter* be the sole authoritative party organ and furthermore that its editors work for no other newspaper."[48] Party leaders usually served as designated publishers and responsible editors, even though most ventures seem to have been privately financed. The central party organization probably did not have sufficient funds to support adequately the growing number of party newspapers. Besides, Max Amann carefully protected the special position of the *VB* and the Eher Verlag publishing activities of the central party leadership in Munich. He, therefore, took care to limit party liability for other publishing ventures.

The NSDAP archives document copiously the generally shaky financial condition of these new party organs before January 1933. In almost every case, however, local Nazi papers began as small operations and remained so until later on, requiring only modest amounts of capital and large amounts of volunteer labor to write, edit, proof, solicit ads and subscriptions, and deliver the finished product. One of the keys to a "successful" operation seems to have been the ability of local party leaders to find a sympathetic local printer who would extend credit, perhaps against future considerations. For example, the *Ostfriesische Tageszeitung* owed its printer 10,000 RM by early 1933, according to the official account, and the printer refused to extend any further credit. [49] In a detailed printing agreement of 18 February 1929 between the editor of the NSDAP Stuttgart-based *Kampfruf,* Josef Geiger, and Zuffenhausener G.m.b.H., printing costs were set at 100 RM for 1,000 with specific provisions on ads and delivery of copy. Even with such modest costs, Geiger's paper did not survive long, but the Stuttgart Nazis finally got a party paper off the ground in early 1930, after the demise of at least four previous ventures because of financial difficulties.[50] All of this is consistent with the reported experiences of other political press systems, such as the SPD, as noted by a leading scholar of the German press, Otto Groth, who concluded "as long as a party is still numerically and financially weak, the first newspapers will as a rule be founded by leading individuals within the party or groups in basic agreement with the organization."[51]

In spite of the local origins and financing of the kampfblätter, the central party leadership did attempt to bring some order and discipline to the emerging party press system, while still preserving the dominant position of the *VB* and other Eher Verlag publications. Numerous party circulars *(Rundschreiben)* emphasized the supreme importance of support for the *VB,* reinforcing the Führer's original "Summons to Build a Press Foundation" in the first issue of the refounded *VB*. One of these, dated 12 September 1925, opened with the admonition that "the organ of Adolf Hitler, the *Völkischer Beobachter*, is to be received as a compulsory organ at all levels." Another of 6 May 1927 insisted that "it is much more important for the total movement that the central party organ be received by local NSDAP and be built up further than that they order a few dozen of more or less private weekly sheets." The gauleiter of München-Oberbayern, Adolf Wagner, must have been in a particularly difficult position, as he later noted when he expanded his own local party organ: "The new larger *Front* is very readable as a *Kampfblatt*. Obviously it wished to create no competition for the central party organ of the party, the *VB*, and it was never considered as such by the men of the *VB*."[52]

Munich party leaders also forbade any further support of *völkisch* newspapers that did not join the new NSDAP. The same 12 September 1925 communication cited above spelled out this prohibition in rather specific terms: "Among others the *Deutsche Tageblatt* (Berlin), the *Völkische Kurier* (Munich) and the *Völkische Herold* (Lorsch) are especially to be considered organs which are hostile to Adolf Hitler and the NSDAP, organs on which Adolf Hitler can have no influence or which support the organizations which fight our party. Any support whatsoever of these papers by party officials of the NSDAP is forbidden. No announcements, reports, etc. of *Ortsgruppen* of the NSDAP are permitted to appear in these papers." The *Völkische Kurier*, the official organ of the Freiheitsbewegung, which had served as a *VB* substitute in 1924, attracted special attention when a few days later NSDAP members were forbidden even to subscribe to this leading *völkisch* newspaper.[53]

The central party leadership also regularly threatened drastic action against those who did not follow the party line, as in the case of criticism of the Führer's position on the Germans in the Italian Tyrol, which led to the following pronouncement: "Adolf Hitler recently emphasized that the policies expressed in the *Völkischer Beobachter* are to be followed unquestioningly in speeches and in the press of the movement, especially in reference to foreign policy, and particularly the attitude toward Italy. Violations of this by the press will result in the offending paper losing the right to be designated as an official organ of the NSDAP."[54]

Similar pronouncements dealt with another touchy question, that of the party's attitude toward religion, particularly Catholicism, the dominant religion in Bavaria. Party leaders noted that the recognition system had been established because of "the offenses of papers against one of the first basic rules of the NSDAP which states that attacks on religious groups and their institutions are absolutely forbidden; discussions about these will not be tolerated in the ranks of the NSDAP." Of course, this admonition continued, "the Jews will not be fought on religious grounds, but on national and racial-political grounds."[55] In spite of this strong warning, the party leadership had to reprimand several local leaders. On one occasion they withdrew the Saarpfalz party paper's right to use the party insignia for four weeks because this weekly of Gauleiter Josef Bürckel, *Eisenhammer,* had published a blasphemous poem dealing with Jesuits.[56] At about the same time, the East Prussian gauleiter, Erich Koch, received a reprimand for several anti-Catholic articles in his organ, the *Ostdeutschen Beobachter.*[57]

The central party leadership also had to arbitrate frequent, usually nasty, disputes over the distribution territory of party-recognized newspapers, for example that between Gottfried Feder and Julius Streicher in Franconia. In early 1926 Feder set up a weekly sheet in Bamberg entitled *Die Flamme,* obviously imitative of Streicher's *Der Stürmer* in nearby Nuremberg. Streicher proceeded to accuse Feder of accepting Jewish advertising for his new paper.[58] Though Feder did later obtain party recognition for *Die Flamme,* and its string of subeditions, Streicher's supporters openly blocked the sale of these competing papers at party functions in and around Nuremberg. The local police reported that "occasionally at public rallies in Nuremberg, uniformed SA men selling *Flamme* have been thrown out of the hall by SS people."[59] Hitler tried to arbitrate the conflict between two of his "old fighters" and their "fighting papers," but Feder eventually lost out to Streicher when the last flicker of *Die Flamme* was snuffed out in September 1933 "because the conflict of the *Stürmer* against the *Flamme* had assumed unbearable proportions."[60]

Such conflicts had led to discussions, as early as the 1926 Weimar party congress, on the need for "prophylactic measures for the preservation of the unity of the press." This concern led to a resolution that "every newly established National Socialist newspaper requires the approval of the party leadership."[61] Each officially recognized NSDAP paper would be permitted to use the party insignia, the swastika with wreath and eagle, on its masthead. Editors of such papers, in turn, obligated themselves to follow all party directives, print party announcements free of charge, and refuse all Jewish advertising. Papers that violated these regulations would have their recognition revoked and be subjected to boycott by all NSDAP members, severe punishments for newspapers read almost exclusively by party members.

Such recognition did not always come automatically, as Karl Kaufmann, gauleiter of Hamburg, discovered in 1929 when he requested official party recognition for his new specialized weekly, *Erwerblose,* intended as a competitor for the communist *Arbeitslose.*[62] By this time the central party leadership in Munich had probably given up on the urban strategy advocated by the northern Nazis around the Strasser brothers, as well as Kaufmann and colleague Albert Krebs, who had been instrumental in establishing a party paper in Hamburg. Krebs has left his account of what happened to party journalists who practiced their profession indepedent of the party line from Munich—he would be expelled from the party in November 1932 and more malleable journalists would continue the development of the Hamburg Nazi press, including Kaufmann, who shifted with the changing policy and retained his position as Hamburg gauleiter.[63]

The most serious party press conflict in the later 1920s involved some of the best known kampfblätter of the movement outside Bavaria and reflected the struggle between the Strasser brothers and the new gauleiter of Berlin, Joseph

Goebbels.[64] Out of this battle came the most explicit attempts so far to assert central party direction over a party press that sometimes seemed to resemble the fractious *völkisch* press of the early twenties.

In March 1926 the northern Nazis led by Gregor and Otto Strasser, just reined in at a Bamberg party meeting over the issue of a new program, proceeded to establish their own publishing house, the Kampfverlag, to print their own weekly kampfblatt, *Berliner Arbeiterzeitung.* This followed the earlier establishment in Elberfeld, in October 1925, of the fortnightly theoretical journal for party officials, *NS Briefe.* This venture, consciously intended to spark ideological discussion within the movement, originally had the explicit approval of Hitler and had as its editor the young associate of the Strassers, Joseph Goebbels, who continued as editor even after he moved to Berlin until May 1927, by which time relations had taken a bad turn between the Strassers and their young associate.[65]

Meanwhile, the *Berliner Arbeiterzeitung* and its six sub-editions for various parts of the Reich, became, according to one historian, "the most important propaganda organs of the NSDAP in northern Germany."[66] The Kampfverlag weeklies became official party organs and apparently reached a wide party readership in northern Germany, perhaps attaining a circulation of as high as 25,000 by mid-1929, even challenging the central party Eher Verlag, if Otto Strasser's account is taken seriously. But the Kampfverlag soon found itself locked in competition with the new Berlin party leader who announced plans in November 1926 to establish his own kampfblatt, *Der Angriff.* This may have been partially related to the official ban on his public speaking, as Goebbels's supporters argued then and later, but the immediate effect was an assault on the official position of the *Berliner Arbeiterzeitung* of the Strassers.[67]

The ensuing competition quickly turned into a mud-slinging contest, with veiled references to Goebbels's clubfoot, among other juicy gossip, in an article by Erich Koch, "Consequences of Race Mixing," published in all the Kampfverlag newspapers on 23 April 1927.[68] Goebbels retaliated by loosing his henchmen to sabotage the officially recognized Strasser papers in

Berlin. Though there are some indications that Hitler and the Munich wing of the NSDAP wanted to fan the flames in Berlin in order to weaken the northern wing of the party, such a high level feud still required central party intervention lest it get out of hand.[69] The Führer tried to quiet the squabbling on several occasions, his efforts culminating in a long memo of 2 November 1928, addressed "to all Gau and district headquarters, to all National Socialist newspapers," in which he reviewed the system of NSDAP recognition of newspapers. He emphasized that he would "reprimand, or if necessary expel from the party, any editor in whose paper an attack against a comrade is found, concealed or open." He then reviewed the development of the party press and the problem of an older newspaper which "may lose customers if it does not show itself capable of the greater demands in the resulting competition." He compared this competition to what occurs in nature, an application of Social Darwinism to the development of the party's press, and concluded that "the party leadership therefore forbids all party offices from intervening in the struggle for survival of newspapers which are published according to the party decision in 1927 with the approval of the party leadership, whether it be encouraging or discouraging. Above all, it will not do to hinder or restrict the sale or distribution by official instructions of newspapers already published with the approval and knowledge of the party leadership."

This key document listed thirty-one papers "regarded as National Socialist newspapers whose editors belong to the party and are subordinate to its discipline," of which the first nineteen "have been given the right to use the insignia of the movement."[70] The Kampfverlag papers won the battle of position, numbers three through ten on the list, to the Angriff's number twenty-one, but the Kampfverlag papers would disappear two years later after Otto Strasser broke with Hitler and the NSDAP.

Party directives such as this one seemed to mark the end of the kampfblätter phase of the development of the National Socialist press. Even earlier, in the wake of the party's poor showing in the May 1928 Reichstag elections, the Führer stressed a different role for the party press in a directive addressed "to the editors of the National Socialist press:" "Above all it is the duty of the National Socialist press neither to incite the members of the movement to commit illegal acts nor to prepare such themselves, but to reach the broadest possible audience among the German people and to explain the enormous fraud perpetrated on them. That is your best service for the movement and best way in which to prepare the path to power for National Socialism."[71] From 1928 on, the emphasis shifted to greater central direction of the party press, as well as further geographical spread. The NSDAP would later set up a central press office, headed by Otto Dietrich, in July 1931 to act as a clearing house for central party news service *(Nationalsozialistische Partei-Korrespondenz)*, as well as other specialized services designed for the party press in the final struggle for power.[72]

The third period in the NSDAP press's pre-1933 history, that of the provincial newspapers *(Gauzeitungen)*, illustrates the significant shift of party strategy to broader appeals to more different groups in German society, in many ways a shift away from kampfblätter, not back to the earlier *völkisch* style, but to even more traditional general interest and locally based newspapers. The establishment of a chain of NSDAP district dailies in the period from 1928 to 1933, geographically dispersed and with proliferating subeditions, made possible, perhaps for the first time, more systematic distribution and adaptation of Nazi propaganda. A daily Gau organ might even become "an instrument for spreading National Socialist thought to the masses" as "the time had come when the spoken word no longer sufficed to influence the masses in the sense of the new ideas."[73] It should also be noted that the NSDAP received even more favorable coverage in conservative papers after 1930. Richard Hamilton, in his discussion of the Nazi vote in Berlin, reviews conservative newspaper coverage of the Nazis in the early 1930s and concludes that his "limited review of those city newspapers most likely to have been read by citizens living in the 'best' districts strongly suggests that the conservative press did much, unwittingly perhaps, to aid Hitler on the road to power" by giving him so much favorable publicity.[74]

In many respects the central party organ had already been moved in the direction of a paper with more general appeal. The *VB* had already added in the late 1920s a number of different features designed for its growing audience, at least within the party. One historian even argues the "the *VB* in the *Kampfzeit* was a better party newspaper than Hitler was willing to admit when he reminisced during the war years about the twenties and thirties. Rosenberg and his staff provided enough variety to ensure that the party organ would appeal to the different types who made up the party membership."[75] The party leadership even tried to establish a Berlin edition of the *VB* in 1930–31, but this was apparently beyond the paper's resources and failed in April 1931, to the glee of non-Nazi papers. Only in January 1933 would the Eher Verlag successfully establish a Berlin presence for the main party organ.

Numerous other party newspapers attempted to develop along the same lines as the central party organ in Munich, as each gauleiter consolidated his own provincial daily organ on rather shaky foundations of the militant and more narrowly targeted kampfblätter weeklies of the mid-twenties. Many of the old "fighting papers" shifted to multiweekly or daily publication in the aftermath of the party's startling electoral success of September 1930. About ninety new Nazi newspapers began publication between September 1930 and January 1933. In just one six-month period, from August 1931 to January 1932, at least nineteen new party papers saw the light of day and seventeen existing weeklies shifted to multiweekly or daily publication. By the end of 1932 nearly every party Gau had a daily gauzeitung; only four party districts limped along with mere weeklies. Two of these constituted Streicher's Franconian fief, where he continued to protect *Der Stürmer's* monopoly position; only after the party came to power in 1933 would he support the establishment of a daily party paper in Nuremberg.

The new, or reorganized, party newspapers rarely assumed either *völkisch* or "fighting" titles; usually they carried something more neutral on the masthead, such as *Nationalzeitung, Tageblatt, Tageszeitung,* or just plain *Zeitung.* Of the more than 150 titles verified as NSDAP affiliated newspapers by the end of 1932, the largest number, twenty-three, played it safe with *Beobachter* on their mastheads. Seventeen used "daily newspaper," ten each just plain "newspaper" or "national newspaper," and nine "daily paper." Significantly, by this time only one party newspaper still used *Kampf* in its title, the Dresden-based *Freiheitskampf* which Gauleiter Martin Mutschmann established in August 1930 as a replacement for the former official party organ for Saxony published by the Strassers' Kampfverlag. A few of the mid-twenties kampfblätter, such as *Der Angriff*, carried their titles into the 1930s. Though fourteen papers continued to use *Volk* in their titles, most frequently *Volksblatt* or *Volkswacht*, apparently only two party papers used *völkisch* in their titles in the 1930s, the *VB* and a forerunner of the Koblenz *Nationalblatt* in 1931–32, the *Völkische Merkur*. A January 1937 list of NSDAP newspapers, numbering ninety-seven, includes only two with *völkisch* in their titles, the Munich and Berlin editions of the *VB*.[76]

These "reformed" and "retitled" party papers also frequently stressed their local *(heimatliche)* character in order to "reach the broad masses of the people with our press" in "a definite and relatively small distribution area."[77] Some party leaders even called in press experts "to raise the quality of the papers entrusted to them so that the editorial content could compare with that of the great middle class papers."[78] The reorganization of Gau München-Oberbayern's *kampfblatt* as the *Sonntag-Morgenpost* in November 1932 must have aroused a bit of grumbling since the gauleiter felt it necessary to justify at length the changes in a Gau letter:

> Certainly many party comrades will miss the outspokenly combative character of the Gau newspaper. Understand, however, on reflection that it is above all a matter of gaining ground with our press in non-party circles; it is our strategy to spread National Socialist ideas in an easily digestible form. This adaptation of our Gau newspaper corresponds entirely with the guidelines that representatives of the Führer laid down before the last Reichstag election in the Munich Reich press conference of the NSDAP. Specifically our aspiration must be not only to

equal the neutral and enemy press, but to overtake it in the
quality of the content of our newspapers.[79]

A prospectus for a new party paper in Thuringia provides
another example of how these new publications attempted to
broaden their appeal within a given locality. This new daily
planned to include the following sections: a political article
from the *VB*, *Nationalsozialist*, or other leading paper; a lead
article of any type by the publisher or his associate; official
party announcements; local news of the movement in the
district, city, and surrounding vicinity; announcements of the
authorities; combined daily reports with weekly reviews of the
news for the hurried reader; news from the professions; stories;
letters to the editor; classified ads.[80] Obviously, the founders of
this new party venture hoped to reach out beyond the small
circle of the party faithful and draw in some of the many
thousands of non-Nazis beginning to vote NSDAP in
elections.

Though it is extremely difficult to generalize about over 150
party newspapers, especially without reading all of them, the
Essen *Nationalzeitung* might serve as a representative illustration of the new gauzeitungen that became the framework of
the Nazi press system from 1930 into the Third Reich, perhaps
to the very end.[81] Before the establishment of a daily paper,
Essen Nazis had made do with a small weekly kampfblatt, *Die
Neue Front*, founded in June 1928. This venture was apparently
so insignificant that it deserved no more than passing mention
in the archives of the NSDAP. Typically, according to the
official account, the stimulus to found a more respectable party
paper in Essen came from the gauleiter, Josef Terboven, in the
euphoria following the September 1930 Reichstag elections.[82]
Terboven became the publisher of this new Gau daily, *Nationalzeitung (NZ)*, which began appearing on 15 December
1930 with a capitalization of 20,000 RM. This operation, like
so many others, depended on private financial support, in this
case from a Dortmund printer, Fritz Schmidt.[83] Graf Eberhard
von Schwerin, who formerly worked for the conservative-
nationalist paper *Rheinische-Westfälische Zeitung*, became the

NZ chief editor, promising to faithfully represent Nazi ideas while developing a well-balanced paper with broad general appeal for the masses.[84] Typical coverage in the November 1932 election campaign for this ten-page daily included four pages of political news with lead articles titled "Die Papen-Braun-Severing-Komödie" and "Adolf Hitlers Siegeszug." The following four pages were titled, respectively, "Gross-Dortmunder Beobachter," "Aus Westfalen und Rheinland," "Wirtschaftspolitischer und Handelsteil der N.Z.," and "Turn- und Sportteil der N.Z." The final two pages were devoted to German cultural life ("Deutsches Kulturleben").[85] The *NZ* quickly spread its tentacles into other Rhineland cities, eventually publishing as many as thirteen subeditions. Despite the hopes of a wider audience, the new gauzeitung probably did not attract many readers beyond the NSDAP members in the Ruhr area. Circulation figures later provided by the party archives indicate 14,287 by the end of 1931 with growth to 27,285 by a year later. Even though the number of subscribers did not live up to expectations, if these figures are accurate, the *NZ* reached a wider audience than most other gauzeitungen. The impact on the party press of the party's coming to power in 1933 is illustrated graphically by the Essen party paper's circulation increase to 183,050 by the end of 1933 and the subsequent decline to 132,987 by a year later.[86] But before the party achieved power, the *NZ* hung on the brink of financial disaster and by March 1931 "was no longer in a position to meet current obligations," avoiding bankruptcy only by delaying payment to creditors.[87] By January 1933 extreme pessimism pervaded the offices of the paper; there was some question how much longer the paper could continue to publish: "The specter of bankruptcy appeared repeatedly, and there seemed no possibility of being able to prevent this beyond the first day of February. Then came the real and definite salvation of our *Nationalzeitung* in the appointment of the Führer by Field Marshall von Hindenburg, and with one stroke confidence in the economic reliability of the *Nationalzeitung* was restored again."[88] This must have seemed especially so to the creditors of the *NZ*. Even allowing for the considerable hyperbole in this official account from the post-1933 period, it seems clear that only Hitler's accession to the chancellor's chair saved this Essen party publishing venture, as well as many others. The *NZ* quickly took over several expropriated printing plants of former communist and socialist papers, received 350,000 RM from an unidentified source, gained tens of thousands of new subscribers, and shunted printer Fritz Schmidt out of the now profitable operation.[89] Such examples could be multiplied, almost as many times as the number of party Gaue. By the electoral battles of 1932, few German cities and towns lacked their contingent of swastika arm-banded, brown-shirted street vendors, waving the appropriate local Nazi sheet with the "real" truth about the campaigns. This widely disseminated written propaganda must have added significantly to the drumbeat of the incessant party rallies and must, therefore, have contributed to the growing public impression that the Nazi tide had become irresistible.[90]

What tentative conclusions might be drawn from such a summary of the organization of the Nazi party press before 1933? Obviously, the numerical growth of NSDAP papers remained small before the depression hit Germany. Very few specifically Nazi sheets survived the early 1920s. Only thirty-one bore the coveted swastika with wreath and eagle, at least legally, by the end of 1928, of which only two appeared daily, the *VB* and its Ingolstadt neighbor, *Der Donaubote*. Within two years the number of identifiable Nazi newspapers had doubled, and these would more than double again to over 150 by the end of 1932, of which about 90 appeared daily. Official party circulation statistics, though hardly the independent sources preferred by historians, do reflect the same pattern of growth within the NSDAP press. According to an unpublished party history of its press, total circulation for party dailies increased in this fashion:

1926	10,700
1927	17,800
1928	22,812
1929	72,590
1930	253,925

1931	431,444
1932	782,121
1933	3,197,964
1934	3,375,757
1935	3,900,080[91]

Even more striking than the numerical growth was the pre-1933 geographical spread of the NSDAP press. Before 1925 relatively few Nazi papers began publication outside southern Germany. Probably the first specifically Nazi newspaper published in the Reich capital was the Strassers' *Berliner Arbeiterzeitung* from March 1926. Thereafter, new ventures carried the physical presence of the swastika-masthead kampfblätter to every corner of the Reich, and even beyond to Danzig, Austria, and the Sudetenland. By the fall of 1930 nearly every party district had its own party-affiliated newspaper, even if only a weekly of a few pages. No matter how small their circulation, these kampfblätter must have served as important organizational weapons as the NSDAP tried to spread itself over the entire Reich. They must also have served as a more effective way of spreading party news in a local region, rather than just the Munich and Bavarian news emphasized in the *VB*. If one plots the locations of these kampflbätter on a map of Germany in the interwar period, approximately half of those appearing by the fall of 1930 were north of the Main River, indicating significant organizational growth of the party beyond its Munich roots.

By the end of 1932, these developing gauzeitungen, assisted by their many subeditions and other local sheets, blanketed the Reich with more locally adjusted propaganda, as well as "news from the movement" from Königsberg, Stolp, Swinemünde, Schwerin, Itzehoe, Harburg in the north; or in the west from not only Essen and Saarbrücken but also Altenkirchen and Idar and Alzey; not to mention from Freiburg, Balingen, Heidenheim, Biberbach, Rosenheim, Traunstein, and Hof in the south. The Nazi newspaper, flying the party insignia on its screaming masthead, became one important element of the party's presence in *all* parts of Germany. Like the Führer himself, and the marching brownshirts, the party newspaper seemed to be everywhere at once.

As such an analysis suggests, the Nazi press did accurately reflect the collective nature of National Socialism and its appeal. Reading through a list of the party papers in the early 1930s and their locations gives one a sense of not only the geographical dispersion of the NDSAP but also the broader social and propagandistic appeals that the movement attempted in that period. One finds not only the extreme racism of Streicher's *Der Stürmer,* a carryover from the early 1920s, but also the satirical illustrated weekly *Die Brennessel,* though it could hardly equal its model, *Simplicissimus.* Some urban papers directed party propaganda at unemployed workers, such as the Hamburg *Erwerblose* or the Berlin *Arbeitertum.* Of the latter, one historian has written that it "was one of the best edited, best-written, and most attractive publications that came off the party's press," a paper that "featured charcoal, poster-type, 'socialist-realism' illustrations and excellent artistic photography."[92] Fritz Reinhardt not only directed a speaker's school, mentioned at the beginning of this essay; he also began the specialized economics journal, *Wirtschaftlicher Beobachter,* in 1929. Walter Darré's *NS Landpost* began publication in the fall of 1931 as the official NSDAP peasant newspaper. Both these journals provided party propagandists with material on the economic crisis of the early 1930s and instructions on how to exploit it for the benefit of the NSDAP. The party press system even attracted a few former *völkisch* and conservative newspapers, adding yet another element of respectability to a party with a sometimes unsavory public image. In addition to Graf Reventlow's *Der Reichswart,* which began supporting the NSDAP as early as 1926, Ludendorff's old weekly mouthpiece, *Deutsche Wochenshau,* became part of the Nazi band when Feder took it over in 1931. Two important Hessian papers threw in their lot with the Nazis in the early thirties, the German Nationalist organ in Darmstadt, *Hessische Landeszeitung,* and the German People's Party paper in Alzey, *Rheinhessische Volksblätter.* Many other such papers would join the NSDAP after the takeover, voluntarily at first, then without having much choice as the Nazi regime "coordinated" the

German press with the ideals of National Socialism. Thus, the NSDAP press had become something approximating a coalition press *(Sammellpresse)* by 1932, a *völkisch*-nationalist press for the ideologically committed where necessary, a "fighting press" for the street battles of the industrial cities, a local and provincial press for the many other parts of the Reich less involved in *völkisch* nationalism and the industrial battles of the early thirties, but still representing millions of discontented Germans potentially susceptible to Nazi propaganda appeals in the midst of the economic crisis. This network of NSDAP newspapers, however diverse their origins and their intended audience, would be coordinated during the many election campaigns of 1931–32 through Otto Dietrich's party press office. One example illustrates this particularly well: the mobilization of the party's press by Dietrich's office in the 1932 presidential campaigns. During these campaigns the Reich press office of the party disseminated the reports of Hitler's airborne campaigning, the *Deutschlandflüge,* by relying on local party papers to relay reports to the central headquarters which in turn distributed these reports, with appropriate photos, to selected regional papers with the technical means to feed the reports to smaller party papers in that region. By the following day, the Führer's speech, and the official account of his suitably tumultuous welcome, would be splattered all over the Reich. Coincidentally, this also helped many party newspapers work around their financial and technical weaknesses. All they had to do was to print the accounts that came across the wire or telephone. No need for on-the-spot reporters; no need to rely on non-Nazi, therefore biased, wire services. All a paper really needed was a competent typesetter, some newsprint, and some ink. In at least one instance a former conservative newspaper that had shifted to support of the NSDAP, the *Hessische Landeszeitung,* coordinated such efforts because of its superior technical capabilities.[93]

This network of Nazi party papers also constituted the real beginnings of the coordinated and controlled press of the Third Reich, which reflected a quite different press tradition, one summed up well in one of the Führer's expansive wartime after dinner monologues: "It is only by means of the concentration of the whole machinery of press and propaganda in one single organization that a unified direction of the press can be assured. And a unified press is a prerequisite, if the press is to enjoy the confidence of the people and thus also to become effective as an instrument of popular education. For only a unified press is free from those contradictions of news items, of political, cultural and such-like communications, which is laughable in the eyes of the public, rob it of any prestige as purveyor of truth and of any value as an instrument for the education of public opinion."[94] What this meant for the rest of the German press soon became clear. Max Amann, probably the most powerful figure in the German publishing industry during the Third Reich, admitted to his interrogator after World War II "that the basic purpose of the Nazi press program was to eliminate all press in opposition to the party."[95] Of the more than 4,700 newspapers published in Germany in 1932, only about 900 remained by 1944. The Nazi party owned about a third of those with 80 percent of total newspaper circulation.[96]

Notes

The University of Toledo and the German Academic Exchange Service (DAAD) have provided support for research contributing to this essay. All translations are by the author unless otherwise noted.

[1] Examples of the many different perspectives can be found in Walter Laqueur, ed., *Fascism: A Reader's Guide: Analyses, Interpretations, Bibliography* (Berkeley and Los Angeles, 1976); Stein Larsen et al., eds., *Who Were the Fascists: Social Roots of European Fascism* (Bergen, Norway, 1980). By contrast, however, see also the provocative essay of Gilbert Allardyce, "What Fascism Is Not: Thoughts on the Deflation of a Concept," *American Historical Review*, 84 (April 1979), 367–94.

[2] For example, Peter Merkl reevaluates statistically the well-known Abel autobiographies in the Hoover Institution library in his *Political Violence under the Swastika: 581 Early Nazis* (Princeton, 1975). Richard F. Hamilton takes another look at the available electoral evidence in *Who Voted for Hitler?* (Princeton, 1982), in which he questions the usual emphasis on the predominantly lower-middle-class support of the Nazis. The debate sparked by

Hamilton's work is illustrated by an issue of *Central European History*, 17 (March 1984), devoted entirely to "Who Voted for Hitler?" Two other recent scholarly studies apply statistical analysis to the questions of Nazi party membership and voting support: Michael H. Kater, *The Nazi Party: A Social Profile of Members and Leaders, 1919–1945* (Cambridge, Mass., 1983); Thomas Childers, *The Nazi Voter: The Social Foundations of Fascism in Germany, 1919–1933* (Chapel Hill, N.C., 1983).

[3] Reflections of this continuing debate can be found in Leonard Krieger, "Nazism: Highway or Byway?" *Central European History*, 10 (March 1978), 3–22; Thomas Nipperday, "1933 und die Kontinuität der deutschen Geschichte," *Historische Zeitschrift*, 227 (1978), 86–111; Jürgen Kocka, "Der 'deutsche Sonderweg' in der Diskussion," *German Studies Review*, 5 (October 1982), 365–79; Theodore Hamerow, "Guilt, Redemption, and Writing German History," *American Historical Review*, 88 (February 1983), 53–72; and David Blackbourn and Geoff Eley, *The Peculiarities of German History* (Oxford, 1984).

[4] This controversy among German historians is reviewed briefly by Tim Mason in "Intention and Explanation: A Current Controversy about the Interpretation of National Socialism," in Gerhard Hirschfeld and Lothar Kettenacher, eds., *Der Führerstaat: Mythos und Realität: Studien zur Struktur und Politik des Dritten Reiches* (Stuttgart, 1981), pp. 23–42.

[5] Rudolf Heberle's work on Schleswig-Holstein, the manuscript of which he completed in 1934, has appeared in several editions; the most accessible is the English paperback edition titled *From Democracy to Nazism: A Regional Case Study on Political Parties in Germany* (New York, 1970). William Sheridan Allen's even smaller microcosm study was published as *The Nazi Seizure of Power: The Experience of a Single Town, 1930–1935* (Chicago, 1965), now available in a revised edition extending its coverage to 1945 (New York, 1984). Since these two studies, there has been a flood of regional studies of the NSDAP: Jeremy Noakes, *The Nazi Party in Lower Saxony, 1921–1933* (London, 1971); Eberhard Schön, *Die Entstehung des Nationalsozialismus im Hessen* (Meissenheim, 1972); Geoffrey Pridham, *Hitler's Rise to Power: The Nazi Movement in Bavaria, 1923–1933* (New York, 1973); Wilfried Böhnke, *Die NSDAP im Ruhrgebiet, 1920–1933* (Bonn, 1974). Johnpeter H. Grill, *The Nazi Party in Baden, 1920–1945* (Chapel Hill, N.C., 1983), the most recent of such local party studies, is also one of the few to deal with the entire period to the end of the Third Reich.

[6] Hans Mommsen, "National Socialism: Continuity and Change," in Laqueur, *Fascism*, p. 188. Peter Stachura has also explored the changing strategy of the movement in five different periods, by implication reflecting the changing composition of the discontented groups to which the NSDAP

tried to appeal ("The Political Strategy of the Nazi Party, 1919–1933," *German Studies Review*, 3 [May 1980], 261–88).

[7] On this see Johnpeter H. Grill, "The Nazi Party's Rural Propaganda before 1928," *Central European History*, 15 (June 1982), 149–85.

[8] *Thüringer Staatszeitung*, special edition of 25 February 1934, p. 9. This comes from the major archival source for the history of the party press, the NSDAP Hauptarchiv files filmed by the Hoover Institution. There is an excellent and indispensable guide to this important collection by Grete Heinz and Agnes Peterson, *NSDAP Hauptarchiv* (Stanford, 1964). The files on the party newspapers, numbers 963–1179, comprise materials collected in the mid-1930s for a projected official history of the party press. A preliminary draft manuscript of such a study, never published, is available on microfilm at the University of Virginia library: Franz Hartmann, "Die statistische und geschichtliche Entwicklung der NSDAP-Presse, 1926–1935," dated December 1936. Subsequent references to this microfilm collection will refer to reel number/folder number, title and date of document where deemed necessary; for example, for the *Thüringer Staatszeitung*, HA 48/1063; or HA 47/1028, Hauptarchiv to Reich Press Office, 17 March 1937, which discusses the status of Hartmann's draft manuscript. This manuscript will be referred to by the author's name with the appropriate page numbers. The original Hauptarchiv files have been returned to the Federal Republic and are presently housed in the Bundesarchiv. Another important archival source on the Nazi press is the so-called Schumacher Sammlung, which constitutes part of the National Archives collection of microfilmed captured German documents. References to these materials will indicate the National Archives microcopy number with other relevant data; for example, T-580, 45/260, Hitler "Rundschreiben," 2 November 1928, which includes the list of thirty-one officially recognized party papers at that time.

[9] *Mein Kampf*, Stackpole transl. (New York, 1939), p. 111. Goebbel's published remarks are quite similar; see, for example, *Kampf um Berlin* (Munich, 1939), pp. 18–19, 76, 194.

[10] On these rednerschule, see HA 70–71 and 15A/1529. A good example on the local level is provided by the nearly complete files of a gauredner in southern Germany, one Rudolf Weinbeer, an ortsgruppenführer of Ottobruun, for the years 1925–38, HA 9/185–197.

[11] Z. A. B. Zeman, *Nazi Propaganda*, 2d. ed. (London, 1973), pp. 20–21. K. D. Bracher agrees in his classic *Die Auflösung Der Weimarer Republik*, 4th ed. (Villingen, 1955), p. 126.

[12] Zeman, p. 18; Geoffrey Pridham, p. 245.

[13] Each of the Hauptarchiv files on party newspapers includes a sketch history of the respective newspaper and its forerunners, some very brief, others much longer, such as the revealing forty-five-page historical sketch of the Essen *Nationalzeitung,* which became a major paper after 1933, HA 48/1066. With few exceptions, such accounts emphasize the financial difficulties associated with the party publishing ventures, as well as the heroic sacrifices required. For example, the sketch on the Stuttgart *NS Kurier,* HA 48/1084, notes that "the worst months financially were July 1932 to March 1933, a time in which the fate of the newspaper was daily insecure."

[14] By comparison, the SPD had a total of 203 newspapers by 1929, of which 128 appeared daily, with a combined circulation of about 1.3 million. Kurt Koszyk, *Deutsche Presse, 1918–1945* (Berlin, 1972), pp. 311–14, emphasizes that this was the high point of the SPD press just before the economic collapse. By 1932 the number of SPD newspapers had fallen to 135 and had probably lost at least a quarter of their readers.

[15] On this see Oron J. Hale, *The Captive Press in the Third Reich* (Princeton, 1964), pp. 61–75.

[16] Goebbels, *Kampf um Berlin,* p. 216.

[17] The first figure comes from a "Reichsleitung Rundschreiben" of 2 November 1928, that attempted to quiet dissension among party newspapers, especially that involving Goebbels and the Strasser brothers in Berlin. See the Schumacher Sammlung, NA T-580, 45/260. The 1930 figure has been derived from data in the Hauptarchiv files and the Hartmann manuscript discussed in n. 8.

[18] For example, Osward Garrison Villard, "Hugenberg and the German Dailies," *The Nation,* 20 August 1930, pp. 197–98. Wolf von Dewall, "The German Press," *The Spectator,* 25 June 1932, pp. 892–93, only mentions briefly the *VB* and *Der Angriff,* emphasizing the violence of their language.

[19] Hartmann manuscript, p. 10. These figures probably reflect total copies printed *(Druckauflage),* a figure inflated by large election campaign runs, many of which were distributed free for propaganda.

[20] Peter Merkl, *Political Violence under the Swastika,* p. 557, estimates a membership of 900,000 in December 1932, less than the one million estimate utilized by Theodore Abel in the original analysis of the Nazi party member autobiographies he culled *(The Nazi Movement: Why Hitler Came to Power* (1938; reprint New York, 1966), p. 311). Both these authors rely on published official party statistics such as those included in Hans Volz, *Daten der Geschichte der NSDAP,* 8th ed. (Berlin, 1937). Dietrich Orlow, *History of*

the Nazi Party, 2 vols., (Pittsburgh, 1969), I, 287, uses the figures for January 1933 from HA 2A/239, which indicate 719,446 party members. Kater, *The Nazi Party*, fig. 1, p. 263, provides a graph of Nazi party membership from 1919 to 1945.

[21] Roland Layton, "The *Völkischer Beobachter*, 1920–1933: The Nazi Party Newspaper in the Weimar Era," *Central European History*, 3 (December 1970), 362–63, estimates the central party organ's circulation averaged 15 to 20 percent of the party membership.

[22] The first figure is given in "NSDAP Presse," *Zeitungswissenschaft*, 7 (15 May 1932), p. 181. The second is from the 1932 *Handbuch der Deutschen Tagespresse*, p. 20*.

[23] Hitler, in a *Völkischer Beobachter* special edition of September 1925, demanded that National Socialists fight for their own press in order to destroy the Jewish press, which "is the strongest weapon in the hands of our enemies." Hans Hinkel, an associate of Goebbels, was still complaining about the high circulation of "the November-democratic press" in 1932 when he proclaimed that "every National Socialist [in Berlin] must be a reader of *Angriff* [and] throw the Jewish press out of the house [because] whoever reads the Jewish or so-called neutral press is not a true National Socialist!" This *Der Angriff* article, "Our Press Shall Grow," was reprinted in *Zeitungswissenschaft*, 7 (15 May 1932), p. 183.

[24] Hartmann manuscript, p. 129.

[25] Among the best general studies of the German press and its history are Otto Groth, *Die Zeitung: Ein System der Zeitungskunde*, 4 vols. (Berlin, 1928–30); Walter Kaupert, *Die Deutsche Tagespresse als Politicum* (Freudenstadt, 1932); Kurt Koszyk, *Die Deutsche Presse im 19. Jahrhundert* (Berlin, 1966) and the companion volume on the twentieth century cited earlier; and Heinz-Dietrich Fischer, *Handbuch der Politischen Presse in Deutschland, 1480–1980* (Düsseldorf, 1981).

[26] R. G. L. Waite, *Vanguard of Nazism: The Free Corps Movement in Postwar Germany, 1918–1923* (Cambridge, Mass., 1952), pp. 206–7.

[27] Werner Jochmann, ed., *Nationalsozialismus und Revolution: Ursprung und Geschichte der NSDAP im Hamburg, 1922–1933: Dokumente* (Hamburg, 1963), doc. 1, pp. 5–9. Waite, *Vanguard*, cites the claim of Alfred Roth, founder of the *Schutz- und Trutzbund*, that his organization distributed nearly eight million pieces of propaganda in 1920 alone. See also, Gary D. Stark, *Entrepreneurs of Ideology: Neo-Conservative Publishers in Germany, 1890–1933* (Chapel Hill, N.C., 1980).

²⁸ On Eckart's career, see the Nazi hagiography by Albert Reich, *Dietrich Eckart: Ein Deutscher Dichter und der Vorkämpfer der Nationalsozialistischen Bewegung,* 2d ed. (Munich, 1934); and the more reliable scholarly study of Margarete Plewnia, *Auf den Weg zu Hitler: Der "Völkisch" Publizist Dietrich Eckart* (Bremen, 1970).

²⁹ This change of ownership took place on 31 August 1918 according to Rudolf Freiherr von Sebottendorff, *Bevor Hitler Kam: Urkundliches aus der Frühzeit der Nationalsozialistisches Bewegung* (Munich, 1933), esp. pp. 43–44, 191–96. See also Hale, *Captive Press,* pp. 21–33; and the Layton article cited in n. 21, perhaps the best published summary of the central party organ. This is based on his longer study: Roland V. Layton, "The Völkischer Beobachter, 1925–1933: A Study of the Nazi Party Newspaper in the *Kampfzeit,*" Diss., Virginia, 1965. An authorized party history is not very useful except to verify chronology: Adolf Dresler, *Geschichte des Völkischen Beobachter und des Zentralverlag der NSDAP* (Munich, 1937). The *VB* Hauptarchiv file is HA 49/1143.

³⁰ Hale, *Captive Press,* p. 29.

³¹ Charles Sidman has published an interesting circulation chart for the early *VB:* "Die Auflagen Kurve des Völkischen Beobachters und die Entwicklung des Nationalsozialismus Dezember 1920–November 1923" *(Vierteljahrshefte für Zeitgeschichte,* 13 [1965], 112–18).

³² *VB,* 1 September 1923.

³³ HA 48/1100, historical sketch of the NSDAP *Pommersche Zeitung.*

³⁴ Josef Wulf, *Presse und Funk im Dritten Reich* (Gütersloh, 1964), pp. 250–51. *Der Stürmer's* Hauptarchiv file is HA 49/1129. Probably the best scholarly analysis is Dennis E. Showalter, *Little Man, What Now? Der Stürmer in the Weimar Republic* (Hamden, Conn., 1982).

³⁵ Konrad Heiden, *Geschichte des Nationalsozialismus* (Berlin, 1933), p. 42. See also HA 48/1053 and 48/1055 on the *Miesbacher Anzeiger.*

³⁶ *Münchener Post,* 26 May 1924, in HA 64/1468.

³⁷ HA 71/1530; NA T-580, 45/260.

³⁸ *VB,* 26 February 1925.

³⁹ For example, Karl Bömer, *Handbuch der Weltpresse,* 2d ed. (Berlin,

1934), p. 162, argues that "in order to conduct its struggle for victory in even the smallest villages, the party systematically and stubbornly built up its own newspaper system long before it came to power." Franz Hartmann does not even go this far in his draft history of the party press, and this may be one of the reasons the manuscript was never published by the party. See p. 1.

[40] The first figure comes from the *VB*, 29/30 November 1925; the second from NA T-580, Schumacher Sammlung, 45/260, Hitler "Rundschreiben," 2 November 1928; the third figure is my own calculation from the materials in the Hauptarchiv and the Hartmann manuscript, as supplemented by the 1932 edition of the *Handbuch der Deutschen Tagespresse*.

[41] Martin Plieninger, "Die Kampfpresse," *Zeitungswissenschaft*, 8 (15 March 1933), 65–75. Albert Krebs noted the key concept of "spoken writing" when he argues that Goebbels set up *Der Angriff* in Berlin as a vehicle "through which he could speak *(sprechen)* to the masses even though he was not standing before them on the speaking platform" *(Tendenzen und Gestalten der NSDAP* [Stuttgart, 1959], p. 188).

[42] HA 48/1076, special edition of the *Niedersächsische Tageszeitung*, 1/2 February 1936.

[43] Goebbels, *Kampf um Berlin*, p. 190.

[44] HA 71/1530, "Lagebericht" of 27 July 1927.

[45] *Kampf um Berlin*, p. 190. The best general work on the Weimar SPD press is still Kurt Koszyk, *Zwischen Kaiserreich und Diktatur: Sozialdemokratische Presse von 1914 bis 1933* (Heidelberg, 1958).

[46] *Mein Kampf,* p. 458.

[47] Walter Kaupert, *Die Deutsche Tagespresse,* p. 153.

[48] *VB,* 3 November 1926.

[49] HA 48/1098.

[50] HA 48/1038; HA 48/1084.

[51] Otto Groth, *Die Zeitung,* II, 409, in which section he also notes that by 1929 only two of the 129 SPD newspapers remained in private hands. For other comparisons see Koszyk, *Sozialdemokratische Presse,* pp. 13 ff.; and Kaupert, *Die Deutsche Tagespresse,* pp. 105 ff.

52 Respectively, HA 9/185, 9/187, 49/1126.

53 HA 9/185, "Rundschreiben," 12 and 24 September 1925.

54 HA 9/188, "Rundschreiben," 7 May 1928.

55 NA T-580, Schumacher Sammlung, 45/260, "Rundschreiben," 23 February 1927.

56 Ibid., letter of 8 February 1930; HA 26A/1768, letter of 10 May 1930.

57 NA T-580, Schumacher Sammlung, 25/201, letter of 8 May 1930.

58 Ibid., 45/260, letters of 18 and 20 June 1927. This dispute can also be followed in the reports of the Bamberg city commissioner of 10 March and 26 July 1926 in HA 26A/1768, as well as in the "Lagebericht" of Nuremberg police officials, such as those in 71/1530 dated 1 January 1929, 31 January 1929, 6 June 1929, and 11 November 1929.

59 HA 26A/1768, "Lagebericht," Nürnberg-Fürth, 30 March 1930.

60 HA 47/1002, letter of 25 March 1936. See also Peter Huttenberger's account in *Die Gauleiter: Studie zum Wandel des Machtgefüges in der NSDAP* (Stuttgart, 1969), pp. 63–64. He covers other press battles of the Nazi gauleiter in this same section of his monograph.

61 The *VB* editor's, Alfred Rosenberg's, report to the 1926 party congress in Weimar, 4 July 1926, in HA 21/389, pp. 27–29. Otto Groth, *Die Zeitung*, II, p. 466, also reports the decisions of this party congress on the regulation of the press.

62 NA T-580, Schumacher Sammlung, 21/201, letters of 21 September and 12 October 1929; and HA 47/1028.

63 Krebs, *Tendenzen und Gestalten*, pp. 155–57.

64 The key documentary sources on this conflict are appended to the German edition of Goebbel's early diaries: Helmut Heiber, ed., *Das Tagebuch von Joseph Goebbels, 1925–26* (Stuttgart, 1961). Many of the official party documents are from the file for Gau Berlin-Brandenburg, HA 5/133. Some of these are also in Martin Broszat, "Die Anfänge der Berliner NSDAP, 1926/7," *Vierteljahrshefte für Zeitgeschichte*, 8 (January 1960), 85–118. One of the best secondary accounts of this intraparty stuggle also includes key documents in his appendix: Reinhard Kühnl, *Die Nationalsozialistische Linke, 1925–1930* (Meissenheim am Glan, 1966).

[65] There is not much candid information on the Kampfverlag in the Hauptarchiv or in the Hartmann manuscript. There is some legal documentation on the dissolution of the Kampfverlag in 1930 in HA 11A/1176 and B/1176, and there are some other scattered references in the official reports, such as those of the Bavarian political police dated 20 February in HA 26A/1768. HA 50/1175 includes a copy of the first edition of *NS Briefe* of 1 October 1925, as well as a two-page history dated 8 August 1936. Otto Strasser's account is useful but not always reliable: *Hitler and I* (Boston, 1940). Two secondary accounts of Gregor Strasser's career do not add much to what is already known about the Kampfverlag: Udo Kissenkoetter, *Gregor Strasser und die NSDAP* (Stuttgart, 1978); and Peter D. Stachura, *Gregor Strasser and the Rise of Nazism* (London, 1983).

[66] Martin Broszat, *German National Socialism, 1919–1945* (Santa Barbara, Calif., 1966), p. 74. The subeditions were titled *Der Nationalsozialist für Norddeutschland, Der Nationalsozialist für Westdeutschland, Der Nationalsozialist für Rhein und Ruhr, Der Nationalsozialist für die Ostmark, Der Nationalsozialist für Sachsen, Der Nationalsozialist für Württemberg.* See HA 71/1530, "Lagebericht," 28 April 1926; and HA 26A/1768, typescript dated 1 September 1926.

[67] Otto Strasser, *Hitler and I*, pp. 88–91; R. Kühnl, *NS-Linke*, pp. 48–55. The Kampfverlag was reorganized in early 1929, apparently because of financial difficulties, with Otto Strasser taking de facto control of operations. See the registration documents for this reorganization in HA 11A/1176 and B/1176, dated 7 and 8 January 1929, as well as the Bavarian political police report of 20 February 1929 in HA 26A/1768. *Der Angriff's* Hauptarchiv file, HA 47/968, includes a long article of 30 October 1936 by Dagobert Dürr, an early editor of *Der Angriff.*

[68] This is included in Goebbels's *Tagebuch 1925/26,* doc. 6, p. 126.

[69] Donald McKale, in his study of the NSDAP's arbitration system, also emphasizes Hitler's temporizing attitude in this dispute: *The Nazi Party Courts: Hitler's Management of Conflict in His Movement, 1921–1945* (Lawrence, Kan., 1974), pp. 72–74, 84–86.

[70] NA T-580, Schumacher Sammlung, 45/260, "Rundschreiben," 2 November 1928. See also, Larry D. Wilcox, "Hitler Disciplines His Press: 'The Strongest Survive,' " *Gazette: International Journal of Mass Communication,* 19 (1973), 38–45.

[71] NA T-580, Schumacher Sammlung, 45/260, "Rundschreiben," 27 June 1928.

[72] The other central press services included *Kulturpolitischer Dienst, NS Zeitungshilfsdienst, Wirtschaftpolitischer Pressedienst, Agrarpolitischer Dienst,* and *Nationalsozialistische Anzeigerdienst.* The latter, of course, was supposed to help party papers avoid accepting advertising from Jewish businesses. The establishment of such services illustrates yet another way in which the party attempted to broaden its electoral appeal in 1931–32. Dietrich later also established a party journalists' organization, the *Reichsarbeitsgemeinschaft der NS Journalisten,* which was announced in the *VB* of 4 May 1932. See also HA 89/1857; and Hale, *Captive Press,* pp. 77–82.

[73] Hartmann manuscript, p. 75, in reference to the Düsseldorf-based *Volksparole,* on which see HA 49/1149.

[74] See Hamilton's *Who Voted for Hitler?* pp. 91–99, with quotation from p. 98. Hamilton develops the same argument in his "Braunschweig 1932: Further Evidence on the Support for National Socialism, *Central European History,* 17 (March 1984), 3–36.

[75] Layton, *Central European History,* 3 (December 1970), 382. This assertion is well documented in Layton's unpublished dissertation on the *VB,* see especially chapter 5.

[76] HA 49/1167, list apparently compiled for the Hartmann manuscript.

[77] HA 47/793, on the *Coburger Nationalzeitung,* the daily reincarnation of the weekly kampfblatt, *Der Weckruf.* The latter began in June 1926, the daily in October 1930. See also the Hartmann manuscript, pp. 229–37, which is mainly a repeat of the historical sketch in the Hauptarchiv file; and Franz Schwede-Coburg, *Kampf um Coberg* (Munich, 1939), esp. pp. 185–86.

[78] Hartmann manuscript, pp. 453–54, in reference to the gauleiter of München-Oberbayern, Josef Wagner, and his transformation of his kampf-blatt, *Die Front,* into the *Sonntag-Morgenpost* on November 1932.

[79] HA 9/194, Sammlung Weinbeer; see also HA 49/1126 which includes a twenty-six-page typescript history, "Bericht über den Werdegang des Verlages und der Zeitung *Sonntag-Morgenpost,* nationalsozialistische Sonntagszeitung mit Unfall- und Sterbegeldversicherung."

[80] HA 7/160, *Gau* Thuringia file, prospectus dated May 1932.

[81] The Hauptarchiv *Nationalzeitung* file, HA 48/1066 includes, as noted, a forty-five-page typescript history dated 8 February 1938. There is also a content analysis of this paper's positions on reparations and unemployment: Karl-Gerd Kemmann, *Die Politische Haltung der Essener Nationalzeitung bis*

zur Machtergreifung Hitlers (Cologne, 1964). This paper had close ties to Otto Dietrich and Hermann Goering, and perhaps to heavy industrialists in the Ruhr. Edouard Calic, without solid documentation, argues that Dietrich founded the *Nationalzeitung* with support from several industrialists made possible through the connections of Goering and Dietrich's father-in-law, Dr. Theodor Reismann-Grone, owner, since 1903, of the *Rheinische Westfälische Zeitung*, a mouthpiece for Ruhr industrialists. See Calic, ed., *Unmasked: Two Confidential Interviews with Hitler in 1931* (London, 1971), pp. 12–13. This is also discussed by Richard Hamilton in connection with Ruhrlade industrialists and Henry Turner's discovery that Reismann-Grone was actually a secret member of the NSDAP from January 1930 as a member of Ortsgruppe "Braunes Haus," "a fiction that allowed 'fine' people to join the party without having contact with its local members. It could also be used to keep memberships hidden" (*Who Voted for Hitler*, pp. 620–21, n. 132, and pp. 402 ff.; see also Henry Ashby Turner, Jr., *German Big Business and the Rise of Hitler* [New York, 1985], pp. 146–48). A perusal of a standard German newspaper reference work does indicate that many of the local NSDAP newspapers still exist in German archives and libraries. See Gert Hagelweide, ed., *Deutsche Zeitungsbestande im Bibliotheken und Archiven* (Düsseldorf, 1974). This is organized by cities and dates of publication, by newspaper titles, and by holding institution. A particularly rich treasure trove of such newspapers is the Dortmund Institut für Zeitungsforschung, including a nearly complete run of the Essen *Nationalzeitung*.

[82] HA 48/1066, *NZ*, "Entwicklungsgeschichte," pp. 1–2. Otto Wagener, head of the *Reichsleitung* economic office until he fell out of favor in June 1933, gives a rather different account of the founding of this party paper in Essen in his post–World War II memories: Henry Ashby Turner, Jr., ed., *Hitler aus Nächster Nähe: Auszeichnungen eines Vertrauten, 1929–1932* (Frankfurt a.M., 1978), pp. 213–20. Wagener is also more candid about the financial arrangements surrounding the founding of the *NZ* than the story in the Hauptarchiv file.

[83] HA 48/1066, *NZ*, "Entwicklungsgeschichte," pp. 2–3.

[84] Ibid., pp. 5–11.

[85] *NZ*, 1 November 1932.

[86] HA 48/1066, circulation table.

[87] Ibid., pp. 13–14.

[88] Ibid., p. 16.

[89] Ibid., pp. 16–24.

[90] For example, W. S. Allen notes that the "Thalburgers," that is, the residents of Northeim in Lower Saxony, remained convinced of the inevitability of the Nazi victory despite their decline in the November 1932 Reichstag election (*Nazi Seizure of Power,* rev. ed., pp. 136–38).

[91] This is from the compilation in the Hartmann manuscript, p. 10, which he admits is incomplete since some newspapers did not submit statistics to the party archive. One contemporary estimate is that the NSDAP had about 350,000 subscribers by the spring of 1932 ("NSDAP Presse," *Zeitungswissenschaft,* 15 May 1932, p. 181). The 1932 *Handbuch der Deutschen Tagespresse,* p. 20*, gives a total circulation of 27 million for the more than 4,700 newspapers published in Germany at that time.

[92] Max Kele, *Nazis and Workers: National Socialist Appeals to German Workers, 1919–1933* (Chapel Hill, N.C., 1972), p. 171.

[93] See file in HA 47/1031.

[94] *Hitler's Secret Conversations, 1941–1944,* edited by H. R. Trevor-Roper (New York, 1953), entry 237, 8 June 1942, pp. 525–26.

[95] Deposition of 19 November 1945, *Nazi Conspiracy and Aggression* (Washington, D.C., 1946–48), V, 735–736.

[96] On this see Heinrich Walter, ed., *Zeitung als Aufgabe: 60 Jahre Verein Deutscher Zeitungsverleger* (Wiesbaden, 1954) and *Presse im Fesseln: Eine Schilderung der NS Pressetrust* (Berlin, 1947), as well as Oron J. Hale's *Captive Press in the Third Reich.* A valuable case study is provided by Norbert Frei, *Nationalsozialistische Eroberung der Provinzpresse: Gleichschaltung, Selbstanpassung und Resistenz in Bayern* (Stuttgart, 1980).

V

Poet on Ice: Dionisio Ridruejo and Hitler's Russian Adventure

DOUGLAS W. FOARD

"DEATH TO FRANCE!" With these angry words the volunteers of Spain's Blue Division crossed into German-occupied France in the summer of 1941. They were the vanguard of some 47,000 Spanish troops who for more than two years would risk their lives in the Soviet Union to assist the Wehrmacht in its endeavor to expunge Communism from the planet. Nearly half of these volunteers were to add their names to the endless casualty lists from the Eastern Front. Forty-five hundred perished far from home in Russia's mud and snow.[1]

Leading the chorus of curses against the hapless French was Dionisio Ridruejo (1912-1975), an accomplished poet, former Falangist leader, and now an enlisted man in the ranks of the Blue Division. Along with many of his comrades he was convinced that "Spain's misery and meagerness was the result of Anglo-French hegemony" while fascism offered "the model of a rational Europe."[2]

Although their angry shouts were directed against the French, the Soviet Union was the real target of the attack being prepared by the Spaniards. Hostility toward France was an old theme of Spanish cultural nationalism, but the Blue Division's fury against the Russians was far more immediate in origin. A few days after word reached Madrid that Germany had launched its assault on the USSR, Spain's Foreign Minister, Ramón Serrano Suñer, had harangued a Falangist crowd with the following indictment: "Russia is guilty! Guilty of our civil war. Guilty of the murder of José Antonio, our founder. Guilty of the murder of our brothers and of the murder of so many comrades and so many soldiers who fell in that war brought on by the aggression of Russian Communism. The destruction of Communism is a necessary condition for the survival of a free and civilized Europe."[3]

In spite of Serrano's oratory, Dionisio Ridruejo would later confess that he was prompted to enlist as much by a desire to escape from his situation in Spain as any hostility toward the Russians. He left Madrid in mid-July 1941, trained near Berlin for a mere ten days in August, and was assigned with his comrades to the Novgorod sector before the end of the month. There was little time to arrange proper transport in the midst of these hasty preparations. Regardless of all that the Spaniards had heard of Germany's mechanized Blitzkreig, most walked the 1,000 kilometers into their positions in the Soviet vastness.[4]

Ridruejo's arrival on the Eastern Front was somewhat more glamorous, befitting his background as a onetime associate of the founder of the Falange, José Antonio Primo de Rivera. A French automobile, requisitioned by the Germans from a Madame Trudeau, jostled the poet and several of his associates along the roads between eastern Germany and their destination in Russia. On 12 October 1941 the first elements of the Blue Division entered the German lines around Leningrad under heavy Soviet bombardment. Ridruejo would share all of the miseries that followed. Assigned to an antitank company as a private soldier, he apparently sought no special privileges and was accorded none. One veteran of his unit would later recall: "Dionisio did the same as the rest of us—suffer."[5]

While not privileged, Ridruejo does seem to have been distinctive among his comrades for his everpresent notebook in which he sought to capture the impressions he was gleaning from a land both shattered and frozen. Millions of words have been penned in many languages about Russia's "Great Patriotic War," but certainly none are more poignant than those composed by the Spanish poet as he struggled to stay alive in a totally alien and hostile environment. A river crossing in November 1941 is recalled as follows:

Where is the river? Just ahead of us there is something like a short and concrete plain from which two gentle and frosted slopes arise like a huge cradle. Once we reach this flatness, it seems vast, lonely and brilliant. Certainly it has been a river. About 300 meters separate us from the opposite side. Neither upstream nor down is there a hint of an end to this immense and mysterious plain.

We cross in single file having no idea of what waits for us ahead. Presumably that is where the fighting will begin. At the moment, however, the silence is serene and deep. The stars sparkle excitedly above, but there is only one sound: the tiny crackle of ice under our hobnailed boots. There is something almost angelic, miraculous and indescribable in finding oneself at midnight in this silver world, carried over a sleeping current by thin crystal.

Just as my feet bring me to the center of the river an engine can be heard overhead at some height—the unmistakably halting motor of a Russian bomber. It makes two passes at us. On both banks, the steep edges of the valley, and even at a point a hundred meters downstream from our line of crossing the bombs explode with a terrifying but curiously muffled crash. The flashes come as a weird surprise—color—in what had been a splendor of soft and monotone tints. They nullify the threat posed to us because the surprise has been so "aesthetic" that we hardly felt menace at all.[6]

Not even Ridruejo's aesthetic sensitivities, however, could disguise the perilousness of the mission that he and his fellow countrymen had undertaken so far from home. The Spaniards perished by the thousands that winter as they grappled with Soviet armies in the winterland around Leningrad. Ridruejo, who had already witnessed some action in the civil war of 1936–39, managed once again to be counted among the survivors, but just barely. Suffering from exhaustion and severe respiratory illness, the poet returned to Madrid and a hero's welcome in April 1942.

Another survivor, Alberto Crespo, explains that "Dionisio

enlisted in the Division as a Falangist . . . and returned to Spain with his soul brimming with an incendiary, almost austere and intransigent Falangism." Even before his experience in the Russian crucible, it would have been difficult to have found anyone in Spain who could surpass Ridruejo in his "intransigent" devotion to the nation's incipient fascist movement. While still a university student he had enlisted in the Falange and donned its blue shirt. Although not a founder of the organization, Ridruejo could claim that he had been assigned his first leadership role in the movement by no one less than José Antonio Primo de Rivera and had even lent his poetic talents to the composition of the Falange hymn, *Cara al sol*.[7]

"I gave my allegiance to the tiny Falangist movement," he would later claim, "more because of a juvenile passion to devote myself to something than for any rational hope of actually achieving utopia." Perhaps so, but so dedicated was Ridruejo to Spanish fascism that in April 1937 he risked imprisonment or worse by confronting General Franco personally with criticism of the dictator's treatment of the movement José Antonio had founded.

Decades after the civil war Ridruejo confessed that José Antonio had "impressed me as no other man and he seemed a model of that which every boy seeks instinctively to follow and imitate." The problem in 1937 was that the Falangist leader was dead, the victim of a Republican firing squad, and General Franco was intent on selecting a successor. "I was rather crude," Ridruejo claims, as he argued to preserve the autonomy of the movement within the Nationalist camp.[8]

The general, of course, ultimately did find a successor to command the Falange. He appointed himself to the post, but not before he had officially merged the organization with the ultratraditionalist Carlists creating something called the *Falange Española Traditionalista y de las Juntas Ofensiva Nacional Sindicalista*. However "crude" Ridruejo may have been to the general in their April confrontation, the poet was designated to help draft the new statutes of the party two months later and was officially inaugurated as a member of the organization's executive committee (Consejo Nacional) in August as well as its presidium (the twelve-person Junta politica.)[9]

Even while José Antonio was alive there had been considerable ambiguity in the ideology proclaimed by the Falange. "We are admirers more of Mussolini than Hitler," recalled Ridruejo, "although we considered Italian fascism rather weak on social issues; yet we thought the Germans' excesses were grievous." Now as civil war raged across the land and the emerging Franco dictatorship searched furiously for some ideological justification, it was not only the Falange's organizational structure that proved unequal to the leadership crisis but its political dogma as well. Reflecting back on the sessions of Franco's Junta politica in 1937, Ridruejo confesses: "We spent much time and energy and many words on miniscule battles through which the symbols and phraseology of the Falange came to the forefront in an ornamental form and the cult of the Founder of the Falange ascended all gradations of public consecration, but the fundamental issues eluded us." Point by point the conservatives carried the day against the erstwhile fascist revolutionaries. The new state would be confessional; "the vision of the Falange's 'syndicalist order' dissolved in the fine words of the Labor Charter *[Fuero de Trabajo]*. Of agrarian reform we heard nothing more." The Falangist rout, Ridruejo speculates, was virtually inevitable. Not only was the movement's "theoretical capacity quite limited," but "this syncretism of left and right that we Falangists believed in was a chimera even without the war. Blessed innocence!" They were obliged, he concluded, to answer their conservative opponents on the Junta with quotations from José Antonio regarding situations he had never encountered.

Scoring often and effectively against the youthful Falangist in Franco's formative councils was the distinguished Catholic scholar D. Pedro Sainz Rodríguez, who as minister of education fought to preserve the Church's hegemony in this field against the totalitarian designs of Ridruejo and his associates. In one session of the Junta politica, presided over personally by Franco himself, Sainz reacted with particular hostility to a proposal introduced by Ridruejo for the enhancement of the party's role within the Nationalist state. "The project was, naturally, fascist," the poet admitted.

Sainz recognized the implications of the proposal and rose to oppose it before the dictator. Not only did he present a litany of objections to totalitarianism but he sullied the project by accusing it of being German in its inspiration; specifically, resembling the policies of Hitler's minister of economics, Dr. Karl Schmitt. He concluded his condemnation by informing Ridruejo that his design "exudes in every section a lack of confidence in the government." Before the Falangist poet could even utter a word in his own defense, Franco himself startled the gathering by agreeing with Sainz and adding ominously, "Yes, a lack of confidence not only in the government but above all in the *Caudillo.*" Ridruejo sputtered protestations of loyalty and his proposal was quickly forgotten.[10]

It is ironic that at this moment in his career Ridruejo should have been linked so tellingly with Germany's variation on fascism, particularly through the rather tame policies of Dr. Schmitt. It is true that the poet had just returned from his first trip to the Reich, where he had been introduced personally to Hitler. While Ridruejo recalls the journey as a lark, a holiday that he garnered through his social connections with Spain's foreign minister, his German hosts clearly took the occasion seriously as an opportunity to enhance the Reich's prestige abroad.

Obstensibly the poet and three associates had been invited to Germany to study the *Kraft durch Freude* program at first hand. They were flown to Hamburg, where even William Shirer had been impressed by the low-cost cruises organized for workers by the "Strength through Joy" directors. The Spaniards, however, soon found themselves in the nation's capital, then were flown to lovely Heidelberg, next charmed by a Rhine cruise, and finally treated to a splendid farewell from Munich. Ridruejo knew enough German to realize that he had been introduced to Hitler as a great Spanish orator akin in many ways to Goebbels himself.[11] That German perception of the poet in 1937 may well explain the Reich's generosity in funding this tour. For the next few years, moreover, Dionisio Ridruejo was to hold a position in Franco's Spain not totally unlike that of

Hitler's own celebrated propaganda minister.

While the Falangists' hopes for the creation of a fascist state may have been forestalled by the conservatives in General Franco's ruling councils, the party did manage to gain "effective control of press and propaganda" during the Civil War. In March 1938 Ridruejo captured a strategic post for the Falange when he was officially appointed *jefe* of the National Propaganda Service. A bit more than a year later his authority over the organs of opinion was further enhanced when the dictator granted the poet the title "Director General of Propaganda."[12]

There was merit in these appointments. Stanley Payne long ago concluded that "Dionisio was the most eloquent speaker in the party since José Antonio" and observed that after 1941 his talents earned him "well-deserved literary recognition as one of the two or three best neoclassical poets in Spain." Furthermore, Ridruejo knew something about journalism because as an undergraduate he had spent the 1935–36 session in Madrid learning about the press at a school for budding Catholic writers conducted by the staff of *El Debate,* a prestigious sectarian daily.[13] Talent and training were important components in Ridruejo's rapid advancement in the ranks of the Franco regime (he was only twenty-five when he took over the propaganda post), but the central factor was the personal and political alliance he had formed with Ramón Serrano Suñer, General Franco's dapper brother-in-law.

The two met first in the anteroom of Franco's headquarters in Salamanca in April 1937. Ridruejo had accompanied Pilar Primo de Rivera, sister of the Falange's lamented *jefe,* to a meeting with the Caudillo to intercede on behalf of those Falangists who had incurred the dictator's ire by resisting his usurpation of their movement. Serrano permitted Ridruejo into Franco's office only to have the Falangist criticize the dictator to his face. From this rather inauspicious beginning an important political liaison would emerge.

Few figures rival Serrano Suñer in their significance for the history of Spain in this century and, fortunately, even fewer could be more enigmatic. A partisan of Gil Robles and his Catholic party before the Civil War, Serrano seems to have been

radicalized by the experience of being held captive by Republican forces in 1936 while suffering the loss of two brothers at
the hands of firing squads acting on behalf of Spanish democracy. Serrano reached the safety of Salamanca after having
escaped from Madrid with the assistance of Gregorio Marañon,
one of the authors of the Republic itself. Less than a year later
he had become the Nationalist minister of the interior, and in
October 1940 secured the portfolio of minister of foreign
affairs.[14]

The courtly Alexander Weddell, then United States ambassador to Madrid, regarded Serrano as a "sinister" character,
while recently an American historian concluded that Franco's
brother-in-law "was an ardent fascist."[15] Curiously, Hitler once
dismissed Serrano with contempt, calling him "the political
personification of a priest," and Mussolini's foreign minister,
Count Ciano, seems to have shared that estimation of Serrano,
having labeled him "an arch-Jesuit." The minister himself has
devoted considerable time since his dismissal from office in
1942 to portraying his actions in the critical years, from 1937 to
the conclusion of his government service, as those of a Spanish
patriot fighting desperately to save the independence of his
native land. The distinguished Spanish historian Ricardo de la
Cierva offers some praise for Serrano, claiming that he "conferred a Christian-traditional orientation and the beginnings of
a juridical horizon on the personal and volunteerist totalitarianism that might have directed the regime.[16]

Into this welter of contradictory opinion must be added the
testimony of Serrano's devoted henchman during the 1937–42
period, Dionisio Ridruejo. The two collaborated very closely in
shaping Franco's Spain because, according to Serrano, they had
developed "a mutual friendship that overcame all of their
ideological and tactical differences." They aired those differences, recalled Ridruejo, in long private sessions in the minister's office after they had reviewed the day's work together. On
the basis of that association, Ridruejo would later confess that
Serrano had been "a fascist with reservations."[17]

Whatever the meaning of that phrase, it does suggest that

fascism in Spain was far more influential than the unequal skirmishes between Ridruejo and Sainz Rodríguez might suggest. For example, months before Ridruejo confronted the minister of education in the Junta politica, he and Serrano had worked in tandem in May 1937 hammering out the statutes of the new party Franco had created by forcibly combining the Falange with the Carlists. That collaboration between the ardent young fascist and the dictator's brother-in-law, "a fascist with reservations," may well explain the "compromise" that Stanley Payne detected in the first Nationalist government. It featured, Payne noted, "a cabinet packed with conservatives and monarchists" while the Falangists were effectively able "to control government rhetoric." Not surprisingly, when Serrano gained the Ministry of the Interior early in 1938, he promptly appointed Dionisio Ridruejo to direct the Nationalists' propaganda office.[18]

The liaison with Serrano entailed some dangers. There were still a few *camisas viejas,* the "Old Shirts" of the Falange's inception, who retained their devotion to José Antonio's ideals and to violent methods of obtaining them. Gimenez Caballero, the nation's premier fascist, learned that he had been targeted for assassination by "comrades" in the movement for having been too conspicuous in his acceptance of Franco's leadership. Only the timely intervention, he recalled, of Dionisio Ridruejo had diverted the Falangist gunmen from their mission.[19]

The same kind of suspicion and resentment might easily have been directed by ardent fascists against the new propaganda director. Even though he could control what books and films audiences throughout Nationalist Spain might attain, Ridruejo had acquired his office by collaborating publicly with the Caudillo's brother-in-law. As if to allay the fears of the camisas viejas that José Antonio's legacy would be betrayed, Ridruejo's office contrived elaborate measures to immortalize the fallen leader's memory. His was the responsibility, for example, of staging the massive and rather bizarre ceremony by which in 1939 José Antonio's remains were carried in procession town-by-town from Alicante to the Escorial. Ridruejo even risked a confrontation with the Catholic hierarchy in ordering that José Antonio's name be emblazoned on an exterior wall of every church in the nation.

These efforts notwithstanding, veteran Falangists could not be blamed for doubting Serrano's devotion to their cause or even Ridruejo's independence of action. When, for example, Raimundo Fernández Cuesta, a member of José Antonio's 1935 executive council, showed up at Nationalist headquarters in 1937, Ridruejo did not promptly rally to the side of this last "authentic" Falangist chieftain. Instead he continued to co-operate closely with Serrano, explaining later that he found Fernández Cuesta to have been of "an irresolute and suspicious character who could only reluctantly have been accepted as a leader." The challenge the latter might have presented to Serrano's growing authority was permanently dispelled in August 1939 when General Franco sent the old Falangist abroad as an ambassador and appointed his brother-in-law to preside over the party's Junta politica. Only a few months after the conclusion of the Civil War, therefore, Serrano Suñer had gained command of the remnants of Spanish fascism, having much earlier captured the energies and talents of some of its brightest proponents, such as Dionisio Ridruejo and his associates in the propaganda agency.

There would have been little significance to these maneuverings had the Nationalist armies failed in their efforts to overwhelm the Republic. When Ridruejo took over this new office in Burgos early in 1938, the Civil War was still raging and its outcome was far from certain. The poet was permitted to recruit a sizable staff, which included the future academics Pedro Lain Entralgo and Antonio Tovar and claims to have created in Burgos "a rare center in which it was possible to speak without hesitancy or precautions."[20]

The freedom of expression which he is alleged to have permitted his staff contrasts sharply with Ridruejo's designs for the nation at large. He wanted his agency to do much more than market ideas to win the war for the Nationalist cause. Ridruejo, instead, was pursuing a "more totalitarian" vision of capturing the nation's "cultural leadership and organizing the instruments of public communication at all levels." He added: "In a certain way I was guided by the Falangist dream of the universal syndication of the nation which could obviously have been extended to include the cinema, the plastic arts, mass spectacles. . . . It was probably a sinister plan but it was not banal.[21]

Ridruejo yearned for such authority and had he been permitted to secure it, he might well have been remembered as "the Spanish Goebbels." The historian Ricardo de la Cierva noted the "Falangists' efforts toward unification" during these formative years in the regime's development, but observed that even in the press and propaganda agencies "there was a clear tendency toward Franquist dispersion [of authority]." The Caudillo carefully balanced opposing tendencies in administration and was certain, says Cierva, to make himself the final arbiter of the inevitably resulting disputes. "This scheme," he wrote, "would be repeated almost permanently throughout the long history of the regime."[22] Thus, while Ridruejo, the propagandist, imagined the possibilities of a totalitarian information system, he was obliged on a daily basis to contend with the fact that his office did not control the nation's newspapers nor was it able to exercise absolute authority over the preparation of scripts for radio broadcasts.

Ridruejo was much in demand as a speaker and travelled throughout Nationalist territory during the closing months of the Civil War, rallying support for General Franco's armies and urging still more sacrifice from a weary population. Occasionally he was even escorted to combat zones (Belchite and Teruel) where his oratorical gifts were employed on the troops themselves. Ridruejo would later write that, upon his return to Burgos from such tours, "my ambitious propaganda projects seemed farcical to me."

There was one propaganda campaign that he did not regard as trivial. As the Republican forces began to falter late in 1938, Ridruejo focused the resources of his office upon preparations for the Nationalists' triumphal entry into Barcelona. At his command thousands of leaflets were printed up in Catalan to reassure the population of the city in their native tongue that they had nothing to fear from their conquerors. Ridruejo was also eager to encourage the militant workers of Barcelona to enlist quickly in the National Syndicates that his own efforts in drafting the nation's 1938 Labor Charter had helped create. These workers' organizations were intended originally by their Falangist proponents to be the building blocks of a future national syndicalist state. The process by which they achieved legal status in Franco's Spain had also eviscerated the Syndicates, leaving only an empty shell of the original fascist idea. Unreconciled to the demise of still another Falangist design in the Caudillo's councils, Ridruejo hoped that Barcelona's disciplined work force would demonstrate just how effectively the Syndicates could contribute to the nation's recovery and development. As 1939 began, he remained "a believing Falangist" who yearned "to integrate the working class into the national endeavor and to include the most dynamic and cultured regions into the reconstruction of an ambitious State."[23]

In a noteworthy 1979 article Gilbert Allardyce warned that "the concept of fascism should be de-modeled, de-ideologized, de-mystified, and above all, de-escalated." He added emphatically, "Fascism at present is too hot to handle." Herbert R. Southworth, a celebrated authority on the history of Spanish fascism, seems not to have shared Professor Allardyce's reservations about the term. In 1976 Southworth offered the following definition of the fascist phenomenon:

> Fascism is that manifestation of capitalism which made its appearance within the geographical limits of Western and Central Europe and within the temporal limits of that period which began with the Russian Revolution and ended with the decolonization struggles that followed the Second World War, in the form of a modern, highly organized attempt to save the menaced capitalist structure in certain vulnerable countries through the subversion of the revolutionary élan of the workers, channeling this élan away from the class struggle and toward an enterprise of class collaboration, necessarily and inevitably debouching into an adventure of imperialist conquest.[24]

The Falangist poet-turned-propagandist, Dionisio Ridruejo, evidenced a keen ambition to subvert "the revolutionary élan" of the Barcelona labor force in that winter of 1939. As a dedicated fascist he had helped contrive numerous enterprises "of class collaboration," including the National Syndicates, by which he aspired to make of Spain "an ambitious State." Whatever the general merit of Southworth's definition, portions of his formulation would seem to describe Ridruejo's fascism precisely. Reflecting on this phase of his career, the poet would later define fascism in terms remarkably like Southworth's: "The central dogma of fascism must be: the integration of the people into the nation by lending to it [the nation] a transcendent and expansive definition. The people shall collectively become aristocrats by becoming the denizens of the capital of an empire."[25]

Among the many obstacles in the path of the success of Spanish fascism was what Southworth termed "the factor of national unity, indispensable for the imperialist adventure." The problem was: "The Phalanx programme of imperial conquest could not begin to be put into execution until the Spanish fascists had gained control of the State and unified the country, and three years of civil warfare between the classes and pitiless class repression had divided Spain into two camps of mutual hatred."[26] Ridruejo had truckloads of Catalan handbills to begin plastering over the wounds that divided the nation in 1939 and teams of propagandists who would follow Franco's armies into Barcelona to spread the gospel of an ambitious state.

The Catalan message was never delivered. General Alvarez Arenas, district military commander, had difficulty in accepting Ridruejo's view of the residents of Barcelona as fellow nationals on the brink of some grand collective enterprise. He purportedly claimed to command "a sinful city that had abandoned religion." The general's remedy was not the distribution of Catalan publications but a series of expiatory Masses by which the population could be redeemed. Recalling this stunning personal defeat, Ridruejo wrote: "Instead of an invitation, we brought them a Lenten sermon, our repressive talents, a request to cease being, and as a prize the opiate of 'public order restored.' What incoherence!"

Shortly after this episode in Barcelona, Ridruejo was admitted to a sanitorium at Montseny in Catalonia, where he remained for more than three months recuperating from a respiratory illness and, one might suspect, a case of disillusionment with the emerging dimensions of Franco's Spain. He had, after all, seen his most ambitious projects amended beyond recognition or pigeonholed by his rivals on the Junta politica. Now even the operations of his own agency had been circumscribed by Spanish traditionalism. Tucked away in his hospital bed, Ridruejo returned once again to his poetry and during his convalescence produced *El Primer Libro de Amor*, a work that would even earn the praise of the great lyricist Gerardo Diego.[27]

When the poet returned to his post in June 1939, he quickly discovered that the Nationalist triumph that had occurred during his hospitalization had not substantially improved the Falange's prospects. In August, for example, the primate of Spain, Cardinal Gomá, penned a pastoral letter asserting that the Catholic masses had a right to a voice in the new regime. The Falangist-controlled National Press Service (Servicio Nacional de Prensa) acted to halt the distribution of this seemingly democratic pronouncement. The cardinal defied Ridruejo's colleagues and bestirred the nation's bishops to join him in a public protest. Ultimately, General Franco himself stepped in to arbitrate the noisy altercation and, not surprisingly, stood by the Church against what the historian Cierva called "the fascist deviation of the ideologues and politicians of the F.E.T."

It was also in August 1939 that the Caudillo conducted a major reorganization of his government, shuffling ministers about in such a way that "there was no real Falangist left in the national cabinet." Serrano stayed at the Ministry of Interior and even enhanced his authority by accepting his brother-in-law's nomination to preside over the party's Junta politica. If Ridruejo's assessment that Serrano was "a fascist with reservations" is correct, then the new disposition of forces in the cabinet was not necessarily a blow to the Falange. In fact, Ridruejo was simultaneously promoted to director general of propaganda. Ricardo de la Cierva claims, however, that by 1939 the Falange was merely a "paper tiger," and Stanley Payne asserts that Ridruejo's mentor, Serrano Suñer, was nothing more than "Franco's deputy in diluting the revolutionary fascistic impulse generated during the Civil War."[28]

All of these developments were suddenly eclipsed by the enormity of the events that swept over Europe at the conclusion of that memorable August. Before the significance of the Nazi-Soviet pact could really be comprehended, German troops were streaming over the Polish border and the second great war of the century had begun.

William Shirer recalled that Berlin had remained relatively subdued as these pivotal moments transpired. Allison Peers reported the same from Madrid: "Spain preserved an outward appearance of impassive calm." As the months dragged on, however, passions mounted as well as the apparent influence of the nation's fascists. Shlomo Ben-Ami maintains that "the years from 1939 to 1942 . . . were those of the Falange's greatest splendor." Especially after Italy's intervention in the conflict in June 1940, Peers contended that "strong currents beneath the surface became evident."[29]

The flow of those currents does seem to have been somewhat confused. Again according to Peers: "The dominance of the Phalangists in Spain meant a tightening of relations between Spain and Italy. It was on the Fascist, rather than the Nazi model, that they intended their new State to be contructed." The press, however, was in the hands of the Falange and Charles Foltz of the United Press recalled that the Spanish newspapers were so pro-German in their orientation that their bias "sickened even the Germans." The *New York Times* correspondent in Madrid, Thomas Hamilton, seconded Foltz's view, maintaining that "there was always an underlying preference among the Spanish fascists for Germany." In fairness, he added "that the Phalanx doctrine called for a truly catholic disregard for race."[30]

Whatever the Falange's preferences before the war, Germany's bold acts quickly won Ridruejo's unqualified support. In an editorial in the party daily, *Arriba*, he proclaimed in April 1940 that "our generation demands a hard and terrible decision; we ask and insist upon a place in the fighting." Reflecting upon his own bellicosity years later, the poet explained his wartime attitude as follows: "The most revolutionary group of Falangists—among whom I count myself—had a simplistic understanding of Hitler's enterprise. . . . An Axis triumph held out the hope of a unified, independent and powerful Europe in which Spain somehow would come to play an important role. Domestically, an Axis victory would permit and even require the purging of that plutocratic and clerical complex that was weighing down the State and even eliminate the remnants of nineteenth-century militarism."[31]

Southworth's definition of fascism has the movement's disciples making revolutionary transformations of the state in order to embark upon imperialist adventures. Although there can be little doubt of Dionisio Ridruejo's 1940 credentials as a fascist, the Spanish situation had finally driven him to embrace an agenda that was the exact reverse of Southworth's formulation; that is, Spain should join in an imperial adventure in order eventually to have a revolutionary transformation of the state. That vision of a Spanish regime purged of "plutocratic and clerical" domination had first caused him to follow José Antonio, then Serrano Suñer, and ultimately Hitler. In September 1940, when he was invited to join Serrano on a high-level diplomatic mission to Germany, nothing had occurred to alter Ridruejo's conviction that Spain's salvation would come by joining Hitler's Reich in arms against their common enemies.

The mission was a vital one. Hitler's plans for the invasion of Britain were postponed indefinitely on 17 September 1940. Two days later in Berlin formal meetings began between the Spanish delegation and the Reich's highest officials, including Hitler himself. The German objective in these negotiations, which went on until nearly the end of the month, was to enlist the Franco regime's cooperation in striking a blow against Britain at Gibralter. In pursuit of this objective, Hitler would travel all the way across France to the Spanish border in

October, enjoying no more success in face-to-face discussions with the Caudillo than he had in September with Serrano and his Falangist entourage.

Ridruejo was on hand in Berlin while these fateful negotiations were underway. He recalled that his Falangist colleague Antonio Tovar served as Serrano's interpreter and that Miguel Primo de Rivera, José Antonio's brother, enlivened the hotel bars during breaks in the bargaining. Ridruejo's own function seems far less clear. He recalled doing some public relations work with the delegation's German hosts and providing Serrano with a sympathetic ear after a day's negotiations.

In fact, the ardent young Falangist may not have been so sympathetic to Serrano's cautious dealings with Hitler and Ribbentrop. His memoirs note that on several occasions during their stay in Berlin, the Spaniards were obliged to endure RAF attacks on the city. A special tour arranged for the delegation of the Dunkirk area revealed that the Germans were suspending their plans to invade across the Channel and were instead digging in for a long siege with the British. It was precisely this kind of intelligence that inspired General Franco's prudence in his dealings with the Reich. Ridruejo, on the other hand, returned from his second tour of Germany unshaken in his conviction that Spain should march alongside Hitler's Reich into war.

As noted earlier, Ridruejo did in fact join that march less than a year later. When German forces invaded the Soviet Union in the summer of 1941, the poet was among the first Spaniards to volunteer for service on the Eastern Front. He was prompted not only by admiration for "Hitler's enterprise" but also by the opportunity enlistment in the Blue Division afforded him "to flee the daily contradiction and the state of permanent disgust that I felt for Spanish politics."[32]

It requires little imagination to understand the source of the poet's feelings. While he became a combatant in Hitler's war, Spain was a "nonbelligerent." Neither Hitler's blandishments nor Ridruejo's manipulations of the press had convinced the Caudillo to hazard the war which the poet thought might be Spain's historic opening to a fascist revolution. The "plutocrats" and "clerics" remained in their seats of power in Madrid while Ridruejo was eventually obliged to abandon his post for a place in the line on the Eastern Front.[33]

The career of Dionisio Ridruejo is instructive, underscoring once again the hazards of applying the label "fascism" to the Franco regime. It demonstrates, too, that the Falange's apparent affinity for the German cause in the early years of World War II stemmed less from the Spaniards' agreement with the aims set forth in *Mein Kampf* than from their own frustrated ambitions for a "new Spain." Ridruejo's shattered hopes would quickly lead him from his hero's welcome in the spring of 1942 to banishment to Andalusia before the year's end. That occasion simply marked the beginning of a career of opposition so outspoken that by 1965 he had become in the words of one Madrid correspondent, "the regime's most open, most implacable, but not necessarily most effective, foe."[34]

Notes

Research on this essay was completed with the assistance of a James Hill Summer Fellowship at the University of Kentucky.

[1] Benjamin Welles, *Spain: The Gentle Anarchy* (New York, 1965), p. 217; and Gerald R. Kleinfeld and Lewis A. Tambs, "North to Russia: The Spanish Blue Division in World War II," *Military Affairs,* 37 (February 1973), 12.

[2] Dionisio Ridruejo, *Escrito en España* (Madrid, 1976), p. 28. This and all other translations from the original Spanish are the author's.

[3] Kleinfeld and Tambs, p. 9.

[4] Jesus Aguirre, ed., *Dionisio Ridruejo: De la Falange a la Oposicion* (Madrid, 1976), p. 321; Ridruejo, p. 28; Kleinfeld and Tambs.

[5] Aguirre, pp. 71, 74; Kleinfeld and Tambs, p. 10.

[6] Dionisio Ridruejo, *Casi Unas Memorias* (Barcelona, 1976), p. 232.

[7] Aguirre, p. 80; Ridruejo, *Casi,* pp. 60, 64.

[8] Ridruejo, *Escrito*, p. 19; *Casi*, p. 97.

[9] Aguirre, p. 305.

[10] Ridruejo, *Casi*, pp. 83, 126, 195. For Sainz Rodríguez's orientation in this confrontation, see Douglas W. Foard, "The Spanish Fichte," *Journal of Contemporary History*, 14 (1979), 83–97.

[11] Ridruejo, *Casi*, pp. 187–92.

[12] Ricardo de la Cierva, *Historia del Franquismo* (Barcelona, 1975), p. 123; Aguirre, pp. 308, 313.

[13] Stanley G. Payne, *Falange: A History of Spanish Fascism* (Stanford, 1965), p. 182; Aguirre, pp. 295–96.

[14] Ramón Serrano Suñer, *Entre el Silencio y la Propaganda* (Barcelona, 1977), pp. 146–54; 173–74; Aguirre, p. 308.

[15] Charles R. Halstead, "Diligent Diplomat," *Virginia Magazine of History and Biography*, 82 (January 1974), 24; and, "Spanish Foreign Policy, 1936–1978," in James W. Cortada, ed., *Spain in the Twentieth Century World* (Westport, Conn., 1980), 65.

[16] Cierva, pp. 126, 192, 231.

[17] Ridruejo, *Casi*, pp. 145–46; Aguirre, p. 88.

[18] Aguirre, p. 304; Payne, p. 181; Ridruejo, *Casi*, p. 122.

[19] Ernesto Gimenez Caballero, "Revivencias," *Diario 16* (4 October 1981), p. xi.

[20] Ridruejo, *Casi*, pp. 119, 136, 175; Aguirre, p. 57; Payne, pp. 205–6.

[21] Ridruejo, *Casi*, p. 133.

[22] Cierva, p. 131.

[23] Ridruejo, *Casi*, pp. 129, 163, 171.

[24] Herbert R. Southworth, "The Falange: An Analysis of Spain's Fascist Heritage," in Paul Preston, ed., *Spain in Crisis* (New York, 1976), 1; and Gilbert Allardyce, "What Fascism Is Not: Thoughts on the Deflation of a Concept," *American Historical Review*, 84 (April, 1979), 387, 369.

---

25 Ridruejo, *Escrito*, p. 413.

26 Southworth, pp. 14–15.

27 Aguirre, p. 312; Ridruejo, *Casi*, pp. 170–71.

28 Payne, pp. 206, 231; Cierva, pp. 119–20, 126.

29 E. Allison Peers, *Spain in Eclipse, 1937–1943* (London, 1943), pp. 150–51, 155; Shlomo Ben-Ami, *La Revolution desde Arriba: España, 1936–1979* (Barcelona, 1980), 86.

30 Thomas J. Hamilton, *Appeasement's Child: The Franco Regime in Spain* (New York, 1943), 70–73; Charles Foltz, *The Masquerade in Spain* (Boston, 1948), 147; Peers, 155.

31 Ridruejo, *Escrito*, pp. 138–40; Cierva, p. 155.

32 Ridruejo, *Escrito*, pp. 28–29; *Casi*, pp. 215–22.

33 In spite of the poet's efforts to document his disenchantment with the regime, seconded by Serrano, the exact timing of Ridruejo's resignation of his offices and his membership in the party remains unclear. *Casi Unas Memorias* claims vaguely that the resignation came after Ridruejo's return from Berlin because of "a circumstantial crisis concerning my services with the Press office" (p. 223). The Aguirre commemoration places the date precisely at 4 February 1941 (p. 320), although no immediate cause of this action is recounted. Stanley Payne places the resignation much later (May 1941) and relates Ridruejo's separation from the Falange directly to an article he wrote for *Arriba* that attacked Colonel Valentin Galarza (Payne, p. 228). The ambiguity is important since its resolution may speak volumes regarding Ridruejo's credibility as an opponent of the regime.

34 Welles, p. 217.

VI

German Air Superiority in the *Westfeldzug,* 1940

LEE KENNETT

FOR THAT GENERATION of Europeans who lived through World War II, no military operation produced more profound and more immediate repercussions than the brilliantly successful campaign which the Wehrmacht waged in France and the Low Countries in May and June of 1940. In the space of six weeks a great power was brought to her knees, and the whole political and military complexion of Europe changed. The reverberations spread far beyond Europe itself, producing shifts in power relationships in Asia and the New World.

The first anguished postmortems in the Allied camp tended to the conclusion that in the *Westfeldzug* the Germans could do no wrong, while the British and the French could do nothing right. More than four decades after the event, something of that notion still lingers. Thanks to the researches of H. A. Jacobsen, we know a great deal about *Fall Gelb,* the operational plan for the Wehrmacht's May offensive, but the studies that have been made of its execution are tentative in nature, hardly venturing from the traditional paths of interpretation.[1] A definitive study of the *Westfeldzug* must await a thorough exploitation of the archives of the French army, and since these materials are not yet fully available to scholars, it will be some time before researches there bear much fruit. But recently the Armée de l'Air, the French air force, has made its archives for the May-June campaign available to researchers. While its collection is not so extensive as that of the French army, it is admirably organized and accessible. Materials from this source, added to

manuscript and printed materials already available for the Luftwaffe and the Royal Air Force, permit a comprehensive view of
the air aspects of the *Westfeldzug*. The conclusions drawn here
suggest that as more materials become available, historians may
change their assessments of the Wehrmacht's most dazzling
victory.

To be sure, we will see only part of a larger picture. There was
no separate and independent air war. What happened in the
skies was tied very closely to what occurred on the ground, and
this close relationship was one sought by the leaders of the
Wehrmacht and imposed upon its opponents. This was one of
the fundamental advantages which the Germans enjoyed, since
they alone had recent and valuable experience—gained in
Poland—with a campaign involving intimate cooperation between land and air forces. For the British and French there was
no opportunity, and more specifically no time, to launch strategic air offensives for which their air forces had both the
potential, and in the case of the Royal Air Force, the incli-
nation. The speed and the momentum of Blitzkrieg soon put
the Anglo-French land forces in such peril that bombing fleets
which might have struck at the Ruhr were committed in
desperate attempts to stem the German advance.

The offensive posture that characterized Germany's Blitzkrieg warfare generally paid some supplemental dividends to
the Luftwaffe in the *Westfeldzug*, as it had in operations against
Poland. While aircraft had changed very much in their performance since 1918, the French air defense system still relied on
the same antiaircraft guns and on the same air defense warning
systems as in the previous war. The warning network utilized
telephone relays, entailing such delays that the German bomber
of 1940 could cross the frontier, stike Paris, and be on its return
flight before a fighter interception could be arranged. This is
precisely what happened when the Luftwaffe carried out Operation Paula, a vast bombing expedition to the Paris region on 3
June. Then too, the French air defense system was designed for
use behind a static front; when that front collapsed, forward
observation posts were overrun and the warning system disin-

tegrated. After 20 May French fighters rarely received meaningful data from that system.

There was a remedy already at hand in radar, and in the spring of 1940 a chain of stations was operating in Northern France. But the early sets did not work as effectively over land as over bodies of water. Radar stations in France regularly failed to detect German planes passing nearby, only to have them reported by British stations across the Channel. On the very day the *Westfeldzug* began the commander of the British air forces in France complained of "poor results" with electronic detection.[2] In the Battle of Britain radar would make the difference; in the Battle of France it did not.

The Luftwaffe planners did not fully appreciate this edge which offensive air operations brought them; though it had been evident in the Polish campaign, German military analysts, like French and British ones, felt that lessons from Poland would have only limited applicability against the powerful Allied air forces. The planners of *Fall Gelb* were much preoccupied with the immediate establishment of air superiority and the avoidance of a "Verdun of the air." The means they decided upon was a massive surprise attack on Allied air installations in the first hour of the offensive, destroying the enemy air fleet on the ground. The operation was planned with painstaking thoroughness; the Luftwaffe's *Fernnachrichtengeschwader* of high flying Dorniers kept the scores of Allied airfields under relentless observation. When 10 May arrived Hitler was as anxious about the raids on the airfields as he was about the spectacular airborne operations in Belgium and the Netherlands. Courier planes rushed aerial photographs to the Führer's command post at the Felsennest. The photographs and reports from returning airmen indicated the raids had been very successful, with between four and five hundred aircraft destroyed. General Speidel, who reproduced these figures in his history of the air operations on the Western Front, judged the raids to have been "highly successful."[3] On the French side, historians Paul Berben and Bernard Iselin put losses at about thirty percent of the available Allied aircraft.[4]

In reality, the Luftwaffe's first blow in the air was a patent failure. The attacks were most successful against the Belgian and Dutch air forces, which had few aircraft, a large proportion of them hopelessly obsolete. The Dutch air force, the better equipped of the two, was nonetheless rated by French military intelligence as "negligible."[5] Royal Air Force units stationed in France came through virtually unscathed. As for the Armée de l'Air, by far the largest force, it lost no more than a score of aircraft on the ground. During the entire first day of fighting, it lost from all causes a total of eighty-five aircraft—only two more than the number lost by the Luftwaffe.[6] The explanation for the failure of the German attacks probably lies with the weather. On the morning of 10 May heavy ground fog obscured targets and made navigation extremely difficult. In some cases the bombers were mistaken in their objectives; thus some of them attacked Freiburg thinking it was Dijon.[7] In general, during the campaign the Germans had the benefit of fine weather—*Hitlerwetter,* as they called it. It was a critical factor in the campaign, and only twice did it fail the Luftwaffe. The first time was on the morning of 10 May, and the second—and more crucial—was over Dunkirk during the last four days of May.

We must acknowledge, then, that Allied air power came through this first test largely unimpaired and could thus face the Luftwaffe at full strength. How did the opposing forces compare at the beginning of the campaign? Here there seems to be a deeply rooted notion that the Allies were grievously outnumbered. A recent history of French military aviation indicates that the French air force was outnumbered by a ratio of two to five.[8] A much cited work on the Royal Air Force puts the combined strength of the French and British air forces at 850 planes, which had to do battle against "3,824 modern combat craft" of the Luftwaffe.[9] Data from the French archives permit us to present a fairly complete picture of air strengths, and it is at considerable variance with much that has been written earlier.

Put simply in raw quantitative terms, the Luftwaffe enjoyed no great advantage at the inception of the *Westfeldzug.* The German fighter forces on the Western Front stood at 1,264.

The Armée de l'Air had 940, and in addition there were 96 British Hurricane fighters then stationed in France; what is more, beginning on 10 May, the Royal Air Force began to commit other fighter squadrons to the fighting across the Channel, so that in all some seven hundred British fighters saw action there. The Luftwaffe had available 1,120 bombers (exclusive of dive bombers and ground attack craft). The Royal Air Force had in England and France 544, while the Armée de l'Air had only 242 operational, for a total of 786 Allied bombers. Here then, the Allies would appear to be at a disadvantage in the ratio of two to three. But we should note there were an additional two hundred French bombers in the interior, withdrawn from front-line units because they were obsolescent; yet in fact aircraft of these types would be put into combat before the Battle of France was over. In one category the Germans had a very real advantage: in the nearly four hundred Stuka dive bombers and Henschel ground attack planes. Even here the Allies had more strength than is generally acknowledged. The Armée de l'Air had two groups of low level tactical bombers, and the Aéronavale, the French Navy's air arm, sent in its dive bombing units. All of the air forces had adequate numbers of observation and reconnaissance craft, though in performance some types left a great deal to be desired.[10]

Qualitative assessments of the three air forces are not easy to make. German, French, and British airmen all had approximately the same background of training and represented something of an elite. The chief advantage German airmen possessed was more combat experience, thanks to the Polish campaign. But this was less important than one might think, for in the eight months of the Phony War there was considerable air activity over the Western Front, particularly from March on, when weather conditions improved. In the two months before the German offensive, French fighter units made over 1,300 combat sorties, for example. Deep night-reconnaissance flights over Germany helped sharpen the skills of Allied bomber pilots (the RAF sent bombers on leaflet-dropping missions over Poland and Czechoslovakia). While the greater weight of experience in combat flying still lay with the Germans, a number of

Allied air units had already been blooded before 10 May.

If we may place the airmen of all three belligerents on terms of rough equality in their training and preparation for combat, we must make some distinctions when it comes to matters of morale, psychological readiness for combat, and confidence in one's own forces. All German Luftwaffe officers who left memoirs have attested to the eagerness and the confidence with which the German Air Force undertook the *Westfeldzug;* they had faith in their leadership, in their material, and in their combat doctrines. This high state of morale can be confirmed from an unusual source, interrogations of Luftwaffe personnel captured by the Allies before and during the campaign. Asked which of two Allied fighters he feared the most, a captured bomber pilot replied, "Neither the one nor the other."[11] A similarly high morale seems to have been obtained in the Royal Air Force. This was particularly true in the fighter squadrons, and Captain Peter Townsend has written: "It was the Hurricane, really, which gave us such immense confidence."[12] German pilots acknowledged the fighting spirit of British airmen generally, and General Speidel recalled that the "striking power and fighting morale of the British pilots, most of whom attacked repeatedly and stubbornly, were conspicuously different from those of the French."[13]

Quite early in the Phony War French airmen openly voiced the opinion that their material was inferior to that of the enemy, and this deficiency seems to have weighed on their minds during the winter of 1939–40. They knew that new and better planes were on the way, but feared that when the fighting started those planes would still be, in Saint Exupéry's expression, "phantom birds"—and in many cases they were right. Once fighting began in earnest, morale dropped even more. Bomber pilots noted with alarm that each night their targets were French towns farther and farther to the west. Military censors reported "anxiety" in the letters of airmen from regions of France overrun by the German Army. A fighter pilot wrote his mother in rage and despair: "We are terribly outnumbered by the enemy; the sky is black with swastika planes. . . . We do what we can, but in the end they will get us all."[14] Such emotions were bound to influence combat effectiveness, and hardly for the better. They probably go far to explain why the Germans rated French airmen below their British allies.

With qualitative assessments of German and Allied material the researcher is on relatively solid ground, since the performance characteristics of the various aircraft are well known. It is here, rather than in the matter of numbers, that the Luftwaffe held clear advantage. The German Messerschmitt 109 fighter had as its most frequent adversary the French Morane-Saulnier 406. In September 1939 the French considered the Morane approximately equal to its German counterpart. Though marginally slower, the French fighter was more maneuverable and had superior armament in its twenty-millimeter cannon. But late in 1939 this rough parity disappeared, for the Luftwaffe fighter units on the Western front began to receive an improved version of the 109 fighter, equipped with cannon and a more powerful motor which increased its speed. By November, French pilots were complaining that it was a "material impossibility" to keep up with the Messerschmitt, whose pilot could break off any engagement at will, simply by opening its throttle.[15] German fighter pilots came to characterize French fighters as *bespannter Stoff*.[16] British pilots flying Hawker Hurricanes had less occasion to encounter the Messerschmitt, but in tests with a captured German fighter early in May, they found it thirty to forty miles per hour faster than their own in horizontal flight. Yet the Hurricanes had other qualities, and the reports on comparative tests concluded: "If not surprised, Hurricanes can do very well."[17]

The Messerschmitt posed a serious threat to the Allied bombing forces. The RAF's Fairey Battle medium bomber proved easy prey to the German fighter in occasional encounters in the spring of 1940—this was particularly ominous since ten squadrons of Battles based in eastern France constituted Britain's Advanced Air Striking Force. French bomber crews flew aircraft that were even slower and more vulnerable, though they were slated to receive the ultramodern Léo 45 during the course of 1940. In truth the Allies had a more realistic idea of what their bombers might do in combat than did the Germans, for the Luftwaffe's Heinkel 111, its standard bomber, rarely came across the lines before 10 May. The Luftwaffe was still somewhat influenced by the notion that the bomber's armament and speed would permit it to operate with little or no fighter escort. According to Werner Baumbach, German bomber losses in the French campaign drove home the lesson that fighter protection was necessary.[18]

While the Messerschmitt was thus a well-known danger to Allied bombing units, it was essentially a potential danger before 10 May; for French and British airmen who flew reconnaissance flights into Germany by day, the German fighter was a constant and mortal danger from the very first day of the war. Both British and French reconnaissance units suffered heavy losses during the Phony War, and the Armée de l'Air was compelled to withdraw from service one outmoded type after the other. In the late fall of 1939 there was a veritable crisis in Allied air intelligence, which was only alleviated in part by the use of specially modified camera-equipped Spitfire fighters. They alone could penetrate German airspace by day with impunity, but they lacked the range for very deep reconnaissance flights. As a direct consequence the Allies knew far less than they should have about German preparations for the overrunning of Scandinavia in April and the buildup before the May offensive. On the other hand the Dorniers of the Luftwaffe's *Fernnachrichtungeschwader* crossed the lines almost at will and were rarely intercepted. Though the French fighter pilots made gallant efforts at interception, they brought down only two Dorniers in the two months before the offensive (the Morane fighter was only about five miles per hour faster than the Dornier).

The contrast between German and Allied air reconnaissance grew even more marked after the offensive began. General Halder recalled that the Luftwaffe kept him so completely informed about the enemy that he was "able to conduct operations as though they had been part of a previously planned war game."[19] Far different was the situation at French headquarters, where in the second week in June notations in the daily situation reports betray a grave failure in intelligence.

"From the sea to the Oise the situation is not entirely known . . . situation uncertain, no information . . . situation confused."[20] Though the French rushed into service the new and efficient Bloch 174 reconnaissance craft—Saint Exupéry described a flight in a Bloch in his memorable *Pilote de Guerre*—it came too late to make a difference.

The basic advantage of the Luftwaffe in the *Westfeldzug* probably lay not in the numbers or excellence of its aircraft, nor yet in the training and fighting spirit of its airmen. At bottom the German Air Force excelled in bringing its strength to bear at critical points in the land struggle. Its offensive missions were essentially of two types, tactical, or close-support, for the army, and indirect support through attacks in the "operational zone" behind the enemy front. German bombing squadrons undertook virtually no "strategic" missions, the Luftwaffe having learned in Poland that there was no purpose in destroying production facilities that would soon be in German hands. The only major offensive operation that did not bear on the land fighting was Operation Paula, in which several hundred bombers from Luftflotten 2 and 3 attacked aviation facilities and factories in the Paris region. Its function was probably to deliver a psychological blow at the enemy's capital just as the second phase of the campaign was opening. (A similar demonstration had been planned against Warsaw at the outset of the Polish campaign, but bad weather forced its cancellation.)

Direct support missions were most critical in the first four days of the campaign, though they remained a feature of German armored thrusts thereafter. In its most classical form tactical, or close-support, work involved air attacks to neutralize or destroy Allied points of resistance that blocked the advance of the German army. General Georges, French commander in the northeast, asserted that German columns could call in air support within a space of no more than fifteen minutes, though German sources indicate the time required ran from forty-five minutes to an hour and a quarter.[21] At the operational level this required the Luftwaffe to be at the beck and call of the army, and sometimes, as when Fliegerkorps 8 accompanied General Von Kleist's armored force from the

Meuse to the Channel, to virtually sever its contacts with its own high command. Such unorthodox command relationships were, in the words of one Luftwaffe general, "rich in potential friction";[22] but in the summer of 1940 both army and air force were still eager to exploit to the fullest the tactical partnership they had formed in the Polish campaign. Based on their experience there, both services had even made a number of improvements. Since it was difficult for pilots to distinguish German troops and vehicles from those of the enemy, ground troops had been issued signal panels, and German vehicles bore distinctive white and yellow lozenges (these greatly mystified Allied intelligence). As a further safeguard against attacking its own troops along a rapidly moving front, the German air force set a "bombing line" each day. The Polish campaign had also taught Stuka pilots the powerful psychological effect of their attacks, and in France this was enhanced by attaching noisemakers both to the planes and to the projectiles they dropped.

Indirect support became the preponderant offensive operation of the Luftwaffe after 14 May, when German ground forces crossed the Meuse. The fundamental goal of attacks behind the enemy front was to disrupt communications and hamper the movement of troops and material. All Allied sources attest to the effectiveness of this effort, and to the serious harassment of both rail lines and highways. By the end of the Battle of France no fewer than three thousand bridges had been destroyed, a great many of them by the Luftwaffe.

The German army fully expected heavy air attacks on its own roadbound columns, some of them stretching fifty miles and more. For the first few days elements in the columns were kept widely spaced so as to limit the damage from air attacks; but as the threat from Allied bombers failed to materialize, the intervals disappeared. Even when advancing units collided with British and French troops, Allied airplanes rarely intervened in the battles which developed; this too mystified German leaders.

For their part the Allies had fully expected to commit air power on such occasions, and discussions of the details were carried to great length.[23] But when the time for action came, cumbersome staff and communications arrangements usually prevented any meaningful commitment of Allied air strength. Requests for air assistance from the French army would produce Allied aircraft after a delay of four hours and more, if indeed they appeared at all. Reconnaissance reports prepared in the morning would not be exploited until the afternoon, when German columns had long since moved somewhere else. Air Marshal Barratt put the blame squarely on "the French system of organization and control," which seemed "suited to the slow and methodical days of trench warfare, and was quite incapable of competing with the fast moving mechanized warfare of today."[24] But British procedures were scarcely better; Barratt sometimes had to relay his requests for air strikes to Bomber Command headquarters outside London. For both Allies, a rapidly evolving campaign simply overwhelmed communications networks designed for static warfare, compelling Allied leaders to fight blind, or very nearly so. In the case of the air war certainly, many of the blows they directed were delivered in a void.

On the Allied side a certain rigidity and overspecialization further hobbled the air forces and prevented their effective use. For years Bomber Command had been preparing for a war on the enemy's industrial centers. Its hasty conversion to night bombing missions against the German army's lifelines brought little help to the Allied cause. Directed against the rail center of a French town, it sometimes did not even attack the correct town (its average margin of error proved to be about five miles). Overspecialization likewise hampered Fighter Command. Its squadrons were organized, trained, and logistically supported for a sole task: to operate from British airfields, intercepting enemy bombers to which they were guided by radar. At the beginning of the war only four squadrons had a more flexible "mobile" organization, and these were sent to France. Other squadrons were to be converted in this way, but little had been done when the storm broke in May. So while the bulk of the British fighter force might be sent on missions over France, and even refuel there, it was not possible to base units there. When the French began to plead desperately for a transfer of fighter squadrons early in June, the British government could not have complied even if it had wanted to. As it was, the commitment of British squadrons seems in retrospect to have been as wasteful as it was ineffectual. Air Marshall Barratt wrote soon after the Battle of France: "We should take it to heart that to throw a number of aircraft into the field with an inadequate or ill-prepared maintenance organization is certain to result in waste."[25]

The Armée de L'Air was similarly fettered and restricted in its operations. Command and communications problems made it almost impossible to amass several groups of fighters on short notice; as a result the French were often outnumbered in their duels with the German fighter force. A standing order barred most French bomber formations from taking the air by day. This preoccupation with cutting losses kept bomber squadrons away from the battlefields when they might have done some good; and no doubt this official recognition of the vulnerability of French bombing planes had a depressing effect on their crews.

We may conclude, then, that the success of the Luftwaffe in the spring of 1940 was rooted essentially in its superior ability to influence the outcome of the land battles. But we should also add that its success was not universal, nor yet without heavy cost to it as well as to its enemies. From 10 May to 1 July the Luftwaffe lost 1,239 aircraft, and in the same period the Royal Air Force lost 931 and the Armée de l'Air approximately the same number. The Germans lost 4,417 flying personnel, the British 1,526, and the French 1,518.[26] Nor do figures tell the entire story. The Luftwaffe's "command" of the air was from first to last a tenuous thing, never totally assured and indeed here and there lost to the Allies. The case of Dunkirk is well known, but there are many others that could be found. In the fourth week in May Allied air power was able to deliver sufficient attacks on the advancing German forces for their commanders to complain loudly about the lack of air protection. At the Berlaimont crossroads French navy dive bombers wrought terrible destruction on a German armored column, stopping its progress for two days. Here and there, perhaps in one mission out of ten, Allied air power succeeded in halting the juggernaut. Seen from the air, then, the German victory of 1940 was neither a foreordained event, nor indeed the easy victory sometimes portrayed. It is even possible to read in Blitzkrieg's most celebrated victory, the potential short-comings that would spell the bankruptcy of that form of offensive warfare—and nowhere could the lessons be read more clearly than in the skies over France.

Notes

[1.] Hans Adolf Jacobsen covers air aspects of the preparations for the offensive in the West in two works: *Fall Gelb: Der Kampf um den deutschen Operationsplan zur Westoffensive 1940* (Wiesbaden, 1957), and *Dokumente zur Vorgeschichte des Westfeldzuges, 1939–1940* (Göttingen, 1956). On the air war of May and June 1940 there is no adequate monograph. Robert Jackson, *Air War over France, 1939–40* (London, 1974) is superficial and episodic. From the British side the air aspects are best treated in L. F. Ellis, *The War in France and Flanders 1939–40* (London, 1953). The only adequate German study is Wilhelm Speidel's "The German Air Force in France and the Low Countries, 1949–50," a four-part typescript prepared under American military auspices in 1955 and available from the Albert F. Simpson Historical Research Center, Maxwell AFB, Alabama (Microfilm K1026-U). French participation is most adequately covered in Charles Christienne and Pierre Lissarague, *Histoire de l'aviation militaire française* (Paris, 1980).

[2] Air Marshal A. S. Barratt to Undersecretary of State for Air, 10 May 1940, R.D.F. Policy, Air 35/97, Public Record Office.

[3] Speidel, "German Air Force," III, 74, 445.

[4] Paul Berben and Bernard Iselin, *Les panzers passent la Meuse* (Paris, 1969), p. 62.

[5] Notice sur l'armée hollandaise, 1 April 1940, Carton 1D31, Archives of the Armée de l'Air (AAA), Vincennes. Translations from this and all other foreign language originals are by this author.

[6] Speidel, "German Air Force," III, 77; Bulletin de renseignements, Grand Quartier Général de l'Armée de l'Air, 10 May 1940, 1D36, AAA.

[7] Luftwaffe bombing units that could not find the airfields assigned to

them as targets were told to bomb industrial sites, and French records show that sixteen such targets were attacked.

[8] Christienne and Lissarague, *Histoire,* p. 373.

[9] Derek Wood and Derek Dempster, *The Narrow Margin: The Battle of Britain and the Rise of Air Power, 1930–1940* (New York, 1961), p. 187.

[10] German air strength has been calculated by Hans Adolf Jacobsen and Jurgen Rohwer in *Entscheidungsschlachten des Zweiten Weltkrieges* (Frankfurt, a.M., 1960), p. 25. British figures are from Ellis, *War,* p. 311. French air strength is to be found in Situation de l'Armée de l'Air, le 10 mai 1940, annex to Dossier 9, Carton 5N586, Archives of the French Army, Vincennes.

[11] Robert Williame, *L'Escadrille des cigognes, Spa 3, 1939–1940* (Grenoble, 1945), p. 232; Interrogations des prisonniers allemands de l'Armée de l'Air, no date, 1D26, AAA.

[12] Peter Townsend, *Duel of Eagles* (New York, 1970), p. 180.

[13] Speidel, "German Air Force," III, 282.

[14] Commission de contrôle postale, rapports des sondages, 29 May 1940, 1D20, AAA.

[15] Extraits des compte-rendus des combats, 22 November 1939, 1D6, AAA.

[16] Interrogations, 1D26, AAA.

[17] Report of Comparative Tests of Hurricane versus Messerschmitt 109, 7 May 1940, Air 35/21, P.R.O.

[18] Werner Baumbach, *Zu spät? Aufstieg und Untergang der deutschen Luftwaffe* (Munich, 1950), p. 34.

[19] Quoted in Speidel, "German Air Force," III, 278.

[20] Bulletin de renseignements, Grand Quartier Général de l'Armée de l'Air, 7, 8, and 10 June 1940, 1D36, AAA.

[21] Note sur les enseignements à tirer des premiers combats, 27 May 1940, 1D35, AAA; Speidel, "German Air Force," III, 181.

[22] H. J. Rieckhoff, *Trumpf oder Bluff? 12 Jahre deutscher Luftwaffe* (Geneva, 1945), p. 214.

[23] See for example Patrick Fridenson and Jean Lecuir, *La France et la Grande Bretagne face aux problèmes aériens (1935–mai 1940)* (Vincennes, 1976).

[24] Air Marshal Barratt, "Report on Operations of the British Air Forces in France," typescript in the Air Historical Branch, Ministry of Defense, London.

[25] Ibid.

[26] Ellis, *War,* p. 325; Speidel, "German Air Force," III, 490, IV, 356; Christienne and Lissarague, *Histoire,* pp. 388–90.

VII

German Policy in Occupied Greece and Its Economic Impact, 1941–1944

HARRY RITTER

O N 9 MAY 1941, shortly after the Axis conquest of Greece, the German army high command submitted its plan for the occupation of the country to Berlin. This proposal, designed to ensure domestic stability at the lowest possible cost, was based on three principles: (1) Italian authority must be limited to the south and west, with Athens, the capital, under German control; (2) the new Greek client regime of General George Tsolakoglou must be required to deal with *"only one controlling authority"*—the commander-in-chief of German forces in the Balkans, who should exercise supreme command over Italian and Bulgarian units as well. "Any arrangement which is more accommodating toward the Italians," the high command affirmed, "involves the danger that there will be a constant center of unrest in Greece"; (3) to quell potential internal unrest, there must be "assistance as soon as possible in eliminating the difficulties with respect to food."[1] These recommendations, which reflected the wishes of Tsolakoglou and Field Marshal Wilhelm List of the German Twelfth Army, were endorsed two days later by the ranking German diplomatic representative in Greece, the Reich plenipotentiary in Athens, Günther Altenburg. "The Greek Government [Altenburg advised] will be able to stay in power in the existing circumstances only if military occupation, above all Italian military occupation, is restricted to a minimum and if the food problem is solved. This presupposes that the Greek government is supported by us in solving the latter question. If the population has enough to eat, it will remain quiet."[2]

Hitler ignored these recommendations, primarily because he was sensitive to Mussolini's claim to Greece as an Italian sphere of influence, but also because his own interest in Greece was peripheral; his eyes were fixed on "living space" for Germany in Poland and Soviet Russia, and he believed that "it is none of our business whether the Italian occupation troops can cope with the Greek Government or not."[3] Accordingly, on 17 May 1941 he issued the following directive: "The aim of German intervention in the southeast has been achieved. . . . The protection of the Greek area . . . henceforth devolves on the Italians. German authorities are therefore not to intervene in the general questions of the protection and administration of the country."[4]

This order did not, however, result in the establishment of exclusive Italian control in Greece. Hitler's military aims in Greece—as elsewhere in the Balkans—were ill-defined, but certainly he wanted to ensure German control of the most strategic points.[5] Thus, there was a de facto partition of Greece, with Germany retaining direct control of certain areas of special military importance: Demotika, which abutted the Turkish frontier; Thessaloniki and its hinterland; Piraeus and the islands of the Saronic Gulf; several Aegean islands; and the western two-thirds of Crete. The remainder of Greece—including Athens—became an Italian administrative zone, with the exception of parts of Macedonia and Thrace, which were occupied by Bulgaria.[6] This arrangement spawned a tangle of overlapping jurisdictions and an occupation system that was an unwieldy combination of Italian pride, German power, Bulgarian brutality, and Greek opportunism. This essay, based largely on German records, will assess the economic consequences of the occupation, a subject recently cited as one of the "virtually unexplored" areas in the "spotty and uneven" historiography of Greece in World War II.[7]

The occupation immediately created two separate but related problems: famine and inflation. The critical shortage of food (along with medical supplies and fuel) was the most urgently pressing problem of the early occupation, and it continued to haunt Greece to 1945 and after. The outbreak of war and a constellation of factors related to the occupation had destroyed the delicate equilibrium of the underdeveloped Greek economy —"precariously balanced even at the best of times."[8] In 1939 only 15.7 percent of the country's land surface was classified arable; most of this was either farmed inefficiently on small plots or devoted to the large-scale cultivation of cash crops— tobacco, currants, olives, figs—for sale on highly unpredictable foreign markets. Before the war Greece normally imported one-third or more of its food staple, grain, and it had a "traditionally unfavorable" balance of trade. Foreign exchange deficits were reduced by revenues from the shipping trade, in which Greece was a world leader, but on the eve of the war the public debt was reckoned at £148 million, of which 83.5 percent was owed to foreign creditors.[9] The country had already been described by the British ambassador in 1935 as "poor, naked, miserable and ashamed."[10]

The Axis occupation and subsequent establishment of a British naval blockade isolated Greece from the foreign suppliers and markets to which the nation's economy was so closely tied. This isolation was the single most important cause of the food crisis, but other factors contributed as well. War with Italy had interrupted the harvest of 1940 and planting in 1941. Macedonia and Thrace, which accounted for 25 to 30 percent of Greece's prewar agricultural production, were reorganized as separate economic zones by German and Bulgarian authorities and sealed off from the Italian-controlled south and the country's largest urban complex, Athens-Piraeus. Distribution of available foodstuffs was also a major problem: priority in the use of Greece's primitive transportation system was reserved for the movement of troops and military supplies, rather than food. Moreover, military units often satisfied their food requirements by requisitioning local supplies.[11] On this last point, however, the popular notion that German requisitioning was a primary cause of the food problem[12] has been strongly challenged in a recent study by Heinz Richter.[13] Whatever the case, it seems likely that the Germans were perceived as plunderers by many Greeks,

From the beginning, German authorities in Greece were acutely aware of the danger of famine; reports by Altenburg and List in the summer of 1941 repeatedly outlined the seriousness of the situation and urged German intervention. On September 30 Altenburg reported that food reserves were exhausted and that a "definite famine prevails."[14]

The question of German aid to the Greek government was a sensitive topic around which Axis leaders maneuvered in the autumn of 1941. The Italians, preoccupied with prestige after their embarrassing showing in the Greek war, resented any suggestion of German meddling. Mussolini was reportedly "uneasy" about the food problem,[15] but reluctant to admit that Italy—suffering food shortages herself—could not solve it. Higher German leaders, seeking to avoid responsibility for provisioning Greece (aside from sustaining Greek workers employed by the Wehrmacht),[16] callously capitalized on Italian pride, maintaining that Germany was merely an observer in Greece and would never interfere in "Italian *Lebensraum.*"[17] Goering stated the German position to Ciano with characteristic brutality: "On the German side . . . there is nothing to be done . . . we cannot worry unduly about the hunger of the Greeks. It is a misfortune which will strike many other people besides them. . . . Perhaps it is well that it should be so, for certain nations must be decimated. But even if it were not, nothing can be done about it. It is obvious that if humanity is condemned to die of hunger, the last to die will be our two peoples."[18] The upshot was famine in the winter of 1941–42. In Athens-Piraeus alone (which, along with certain of the islands, suffered most severely) it has been estimated that over 30,000 people died between October 1941 and March 1942, primarily of starvation.[19]

Paralleling the famine was the second major problem, currency inflation. Before the outbreak of war the value of the drachma vis-à-vis the gold pound was 375:1.[20] The nation's economic health was a matter of perpetual concern, and the

British minister had warned of a possible financial crisis in early November 1939, a year before the Italian attack on Greece.[21] The value of the drachma began to fall sharply during the Italian war, before German intervention; one of the prime causes was the shortage of commodities—particularly foodstuffs—but also of all other consumer goods as well. By the time Greece was occupied, in late April 1941, currency circulation had already doubled.[22] The situation was greatly worsened by occupation levies imposed on the Greek client regime. Greece was required to pay the cost of occupation, and for this purpose Axis authorities devised a system of advance payment, according to which the Tsolakoglou regime was obligated to meet the immediate financial demands of the occupying forces in drachmas and postpone collection of revenue from the population until the economy recovered after the war. Initial costs, fixed by protocols of 5-6 August 1941, were set at three billion drachmas per month: one and one-half billion each for Italy and Germany. Germany used these funds not only to provision troops but also to finance a costly program of transportation and harbor improvements and to maintain interisland shipping and communication.[23]

The demands of the Wehrmacht and the Organisation Todt escalated rapidly from one month to the next, outstripping those of the Italians and creating the impression among the latter that Germany was reaping the fruits of conquest while leaving her Axis ally saddled with the burdens.[24] Meanwhile, the fiscal stability of the Greek government was rapidly undermined. The client regime had no gold reserves (the royal government removed the reserves of the Bank of Greece and other important banks when it fled to Egypt),[25] and it did not enjoy the popular support necessary to enforce a direct tax on the population. Consequently, it simply printed drachmas as needed to meet occupation demands.[26] By early 1942, at the height of the famine, German demands had risen to five billion drachmas per month. In June total occupation costs soared to 23 billion drachmas (17 billion for Germany and 6 billion for Italy), and, for November, Germany's projected requirements alone were 31 billion drachmas.[27] Currency circulation, which stood at 19.4 billion drachmas in April 1941 reached 155.1 billion in August 1942. Simultaneously, the state deficit rose from 13.5 to 33.7 billion drachmas. By October 1942 the ratio of the drachma to the gold pound was 300,000:1. Prices soared as commodities—above all, food—were hoarded by speculators.[28] Unemployment accompanied inflation stride for stride as businesses and workshops not essential to military concerns closed or radically curtailed their operations.[29]

Initially, occupation and native authorities tried to harness inflation by establishing economic controls, but these regulations were totally ineffective; only a strong, efficient government and a loyal public could have made such a system work.[30] Neither the Tsolakoglou regime nor the Italian occupation agencies fit the first description, and, aside from the fact that the Greek public was unused to the idea of economic regulation, the "grotesque spectacle" of the staged Greek surrender to Italian forces guaranteed that the client regime would never enjoy popular support.[31] Speculation, hoarding, and the black market flourished, and Greece rapidly succumbed to the worst economic and financial disaster since the German inflation of 1922–23.

By early 1942 the situation had assumed such extreme proportions that it could no longer be ignored. That the most urgent problem—famine—was confronted and partially solved was not primarily the result of Axis policy, however, but was rather due to the humanitarian activities of the International Red Cross. In the autumn of 1941 the Red Cross initiated efforts to mount a relief mission. After several months of negotiation, it secured the permission of Germany, Italy, and Britain to import and distribute food and medical supplies in Greece on a regular basis. The Axis powers were, in fact, eager to support such a project because they believed that the availability of food and political stability were directly lined; moreover, the importation of food would indirectly support their efforts to shore up the drachma, as will be seen below. It was primarily British reluctance that prolonged negotiations. Between September 1942 and April 1944 the Red Cross distributed a monthly average of 18,000 tons of food in the larger towns and cities of Greece. A detailed account of Red Cross relief lies beyond the scope of this essay. The mission owed nothing to German or Italian initiative, and Axis officials participated only to the extent of scrupulously upholding their side of the agreement, providing transport facilities and allowing Red Cross personnel to operate under close supervision on Greek soil. The relief mission is obviously important to our story, however, because it prevented the recurrence of the mass starvation of 1941–42.[32]

Concerted efforts by the Axis governments to remedy the problem of inflation date only from the spring and summer of 1942. Early in the year Italy, under the urging of the Greek minister of finance, Soterios Gotzamanes, pressed for a reduction of German occupation demands. On 14 March 1942 a German-Italian agreement theoretically revised the protocols of August 1941, which required the Greek government to bear the entire cost of the occupation. According to the new agreement, the Tsolakoglou regime would be expected to pay only to the extent of its ability.[33] In fact, however, Wehrmacht leaders refused to honor the new agreement. They argued that occupation costs were merely a symptom, not the cause, of Greece's economic difficulties, and continued to present the Greeks with ever-larger demands. Berlin—even army headquarters— seems to have exercised little control over the Wehrmacht quartermasters in Greece in the spring and summer of 1942. Indeed, according to one report, no one in the high command knew how funds received from the Greek regime were being used.[34] Statistics already cited concerning the rise of Wehrmacht demands in the summer of 1942 make it obvious that the agreement of March 1942 was never enforced. In early October, General Warlimont, deputy chief of the Wehrmachtführungsstab, visited Greece and repeated the evasive argument that occupation levies were not the root cause of Greece's problems; rather, it was the general war situation.[35]

The situation did not begin to change until the summer of 1942. Following a visit to Athens in July, Mussolini, in a personal letter to Hitler, reported that Greece was on the brink of economic and political collapse. Identifying Wehrmacht expenditures as the source of the problem, the Duce, in effect, demanded that costs be drastically reduced.[36]

Strategic considerations now conspired to force the Reich into a more active involvement in Greece. In North Africa, Rommel's drive toward Egypt was halted at Al-Alamein in late July, and "Operation Hercules"—the Italian plan to capture Malta—was abandoned. In retrospect, it is clear that these events helped to make the "summer of 1942 . . . the watershed of the war."[37] At the time it was obvious that Greece would now assume a much more important role in Hitler's overall war strategy. The task in Greece was no longer merely one of policing the country but of preparing for a possible allied invasion; Italy could no longer be trusted to bear the major burden of the occupation.

In late 1942 Hitler moved to meet the new situation. On 14 September he ordered the strengthening of Germany's position on Crete. On 28 December the command structure in Southeastern Europe was revised. Löhr, commander of Army Group E, was named oberbefehlshaber südost, and placed directly under Hitler's command. In the event of an allied invasion of the Balkans, Löhr would assume tactical command of all Axis troops.

Moreover, Germany now grew increasingly concerned with the problem of resistance, though partisan warfare did not become a serious matter until the spring of 1943. Guerrilla bands began to organize in the mountains in the summer of 1942. On 1 October British commandos landed near Delphi, established contact with resistance groups—not yet sharply divided into communist and anticommunist wings—and carried out the destruction of the Gorgopotamos bridge.

Greece's economic and financial stability now assumed critical importance for the Reich, and Hitler agreed to the appointment of a joint German-Italian committee to study the situation. The committee held talks in a strained atmosphere in Rome and Berlin between August and mid-October 1942. Ciano, the Italian foreign minister, privately considered German policy on Greece "absurd and idiotic."[38] At these meetings the Greek finance minister and Italian protégé Gotzamanes had the chance to carry his proposals directly to the Germans. Gotzamanes urgently requested the importation of food and other commodities that could be sold on the open market to undermine speculation and the black market, which were thriving in the climate of scarcity that existed in Greece. With Italian backing he also requested that occupation costs be drastically curtailed and frozen at one and one-half billion drachmas per month.[39] Unless these requests were met, he threatened, the Tsolakoglou government would resign, throwing the entire economic and political burden of the occupation on Italy and diverting her attention from the general war effort.[40]

Carl Clodius, the Reich diplomatic representative on the joint committee, sympathized with these proposals;[41] they were opposed by the Wehrmacht, however, which at this time was demanding an increase of occupation levies to 31 billion drachmas for November in order to strengthen its position on Crete and the mainland, in accordance with directives of Hitler.[42] A compromise of sorts was finally reached on 13 October. It was agreed that the total obligations of the Greek government would be fixed at 20.3 billion drachmas per month, an amount considerably below the Wehrmacht's demands but one which far exceeded Greek and Italian estimates of the client regime's resources. The Greek government did not resign, as threatened, but the mood was pessimistic as the talks closed in mid-October.[43]

As events unfolded, the most important outcome of these meetings was not the reduction of occupation costs, but the appointment—following a German proposal of 5 October—of a special Axis economic mission to Greece, to be headed by one Italian and one German. Its charge was to enforce the new agreement and, with the help of emergency powers, to combat a further deterioration of the economic situation.[44] On 15 October Hitler named the Austrian Hermann Neubacher, an economic specialist in the foreign ministry, as the Reich's special economic envoy to Greece. Neubacher had already enjoyed success as a diplomatic trouble shooter and special economic minister to Rumania, where he concluded the oil arms pact of May 1940 as well as various agricultural agreements. He had previously been indirectly involved in Greek matters through his efforts to secure Bulgarian foodstuffs for Greek Wehrmacht laborers.[45] The energetic Neubacher was a tireless administrator and astute practitioner of the old imperial Austrian policy of "divide and rule." Later, just before the Italian capitulation in September 1943, he would be named Reich special plenipotentiary for the Southeast, responsible for the formulation and coordination of political and economic policy for the Balkans as a whole.

Neubacher was authorized to deal directly with the Tsolakoglou government in financial and economic matters; Altenburg, as well as Wehrmacht authorities, were to support his decisions.[46] The goal of his mission was to sustain Axis operations in Greece without destroying the Greek economy as a functioning system; in practical terms, this meant preserving the drachma as a unit of exchange for as long as possible. The special economic mission was, from the beginning, understood as a holding action; its purpose was to control the situation until the military outlook in the Mediterranean theater improved. Following the war, Neubacher stated that he had never believed that the stabilization of the drachma was possible—only the maintenance of the currency's exchange value for as long as possible by slowing down the rate of its collapse.[47]

Immediately, Neubacher traveled to Rome for talks with Italian, Greek, and other German officials. On 19 October, Ciano, with Neubacher's endorsement, nominated an executive of the Banca Commerciale named D'Agostino as the Italian member of the mission.[48] Theoretically, the two men shared equal authority, but in fact Neubacher controlled the mission and formed its policies.[49]

Gotzamanes, the Greek minister of finance, had correctly stressed for several months that the acute shortage of commodities in the marketplace was a key factor in the inflation. The vast discrepancy between the meager availability of goods and the circulation of banknotes robbed the currency of its foundation.[50] Neubacher, too, was convinced that the situation could be substantially altered only by an influx of consumer goods—above all, foodstuffs—into the open market. Under wartime conditions, however, there were limits to what could be achieved in this regard. The basic aims of the mission were psychological; policies were designed for their impact on public opinion, to create the impression that the authorities were acting decisively to bring a sudden rush of goods into the marketplace. New programs were announced suddenly, in rapid succession. This was, to a large extent, an exercise in public relations, a field in which Neubacher had long experience as a prewar anschluss propagandist in Austria and former Nazi mayor of Vienna.

Neubacher's first actions involved food. As previously noted, Red Cross distribution of food had begun in the late summer of 1942. Now, in late October, Neubacher announced that all exports of food from the country had been stopped. Arrangements were being made, he declared, to import large quantities of Rumanian grain from the Banat, as well as legumes, sugar, and potatoes from other areas in the Balkans.[51] The production of edible crops, he promised, would be given priority over crops such as tobacco and cotton, and several thousand tons of seed were imported from Germany and Italy for planting in the new year. To ensure more reliable food distribution, Neubacher created the Transport-Arbeits-Gesellschaft (TAG), an agency which registered all motor trucks and required their owners to make them available on demand. Behind the scenes Neubacher established close relations with Red Cross authorities to facilitate the deliveries of food and medicine that had begun in September.[52]

Plans were also announced to increase the general volume of trade between Greece and Germany. Through an agency called the Deutsch-Griechische Warenausgleichgesellschaft (DEGRIGES), which began to function on 1 December 1942, the Reich exported to Greece limited quantities of industrial and agricultural machinery, electrical supplies, chemical and pharmaceutical products, paper, and textiles. In all, the Reich eventually exported manufactured goods valued at 87 million Reichsmarks through this agency.[53]

The most striking aspect of the new economic policy, however, was the lifting of economic controls, which had been established at the beginning of the occupation. Price controls, which worked relatively well in some other areas of occupied Europe, were ineffective in Greece because of the acute shortage of commodities and the related problem of hoarding. Neubacher's announcement in late October that price controls were being lifted had the effect of shock therapy. Once prices were free to find their own levels, hoarded commodities rushed onto the open market in "explosive fashion," and prices temporarily plunged.[54] Ironically, events in north Africa reinforced the successful effects of the new policy. Axis military reverses in the Sahara aroused hope in the predominantly Anglophile Greek economic community. For Greek speculators, allied victories were perceived as shortening the war and its attendant economic disruptions. Thus, the first momentary successes of the special economic mission to Greece coincided with the initial signs of ultimate Axis defeat.[55]

The effects of lifting price controls were reinforced by other measures designed to reduce military expenditures, discourage speculation, and generally slow down the tempo of the economy. First, payments to suppliers of both occupation armies were temporarily stopped. For the moment Neubacher was able to enforce a reduction in the army's demands on the Greek government, from 20.2 billion drachmas in October 1942, to 4.75 billion in November. They rose to 17.7 billion in December but held steady at 20 billion drachmas in the first three months of 1943.[56] At the same time, to prevent speculators from evading the pressures to sell hoarded commodities by large-scale borrowing, an order of 4 November 1942, established strict limits on the extension of loans by credit institutions. Over the next four months, extensions of credit were reduced by roughly 18 percent. As a consequence of the freeze on military expenditures, the Wehrmacht's outstanding debts to Greek suppliers remained unpaid and, due to the aforementioned financial controls, Wehrmacht creditors had only restricted access to credit. This was an essential part of Neubacher's overall strategy; the unpaid military debt and limitations on credit resulted in a perceived decline in currency circulation, which had a momentary deflationary impact on the entire economy.[57]

The effects of these measures were quickly felt; hoarders and speculators, fearing that imports would drive prices down and confronted by the new restrictions on credit, rushed to sell their stores at the highest possible price. This created a chain reaction that flushed commodities onto the open market. By mid-November, prices had fallen on the average 10 percent, and in some cases as much as 80 percent; the price of food, for example dropped one-fifth of its former level.[58] Wages and prices were roughly balanced for about four months, and inflation, while not arrested, was slowed appreciably; the rate of the drachma to the gold pound, for instance, fell from 300,000 to 112,000.[59]

The new economic "stability" (glorified by German officials as the "miracle of October") prevented the collapse of the client regime in the winter of 1942–43. Although General Tsolakoglou resigned as head of the government, others were found to take his place: Constantine Logothetopoulos, a German-trained physician and former rector of the University of Athens, who served until April 1943, and then John Rallis, an experienced anti-Venizelist politician who served until the German withdrawal.[60]

The brief respite of stability in the winter of 1942–43 was, however, accompanied by an intensification of administrative rivalries within the German camp. *Behördenkrieg* (war of authorities) was a recurrent feature of National Socialism, and Nazi rule in Greece was no exception. Wehrmacht commanders in Greece and Berlin never willingly accepted the agreement of 13 October 1942, arguing that reductions in expenditure were unacceptable—especially after the German surrender at Stalingrad in January 1943. A conflict between Neubacher, the foreign ministry representative, and the army was unavoidable, and, given the growing urgency of the military situation, the army was certain to win.

Throughout the winter of 1942–43, the headquarters of Generaloberst Alexander Löhr, the new oberbefehlshaber südost, complained that Neubacher's policies were preventing

vital operations. On 28 January 1943 Löhr demanded that
Altenburg petition Hitler to recall Neubacher. This produced a
conference of army and foreign ministry officials on 5 February,
at which Neubacher gained a fleeting triumph by successfully
defending the position that occupation costs must be frozen at
20.3 billion drachmas per month. For the time being the army
was forced to agree to inform him of any new plans that might
affect the economy, and it recognized in principle Neubacher's
supreme authority in economic matters. Keitel, chief of the
high command, formally acknowledged the beneficial work of
the special economic mission in Greece.[61]

In view of Germany's declining fortunes in the war, however,
the policies introduced in October–November 1942 were
destined to fail. Fear of an Anglo-American invasion of the
Balkans via Greece or southern Albania increased Berlin's re-
ceptivity to the army's demands—for the construction of roads,
landing strips, coastal batteries, port improvements, and the
like. At the same time, guerrilla operations disrupted Greece's
primitive transportation system (there was only one rail line
between Athens and Salonika), which undermined credibility
regarding Germany's ability to maintain a flow of commodities
from the outside.

In April 1943 the situation began to deteriorate rapidly. The
cost of living in Athens shot upward, doubling between June
and September, then increasing four times before the end of the
year. On 8 September, Rome capitulated, and the Wehrmacht
had to fill the vacuum created by the loss of Italian divisions
previously stationed in the Balkans. Limitations on occupation
levies were forgotten. At the end of May the Greek government's obligations increased to 30 billion drachmas, and by
December they soared to 440 billion. Currency circulation—
460 billion drachmas on 31 May—rose to 3,114 billion at the
end of the year. The gold pound, worth 162,670 drachmas at
the beginning of the same period, climbed to 1,541,667 drachmas.[62]

Meanwhile, following Mussolini's fall in July and an-
ticipating Italy's collapse, German authorities undertook an
administrative reorganization in the Balkans designed to

rationalize the tangle of military, diplomatic, and party jurisdictional lines.[63] In Greece all nonmilitary agencies—with the sole exceptions of the offices of Altenburg and Neubacher—were placed under the new commander-in-chief southeast, Field Marshal Maximilian von Weichs. On 1 November the positions of Reich plenipotentiary in Athens and special minister for economic questions were abolished; Altenburg was recalled and diplomatic authority in Greece devolved upon Neubacher, who had already been promoted to the new position of special plenipotentiary for the southeast (sonderbeauftragter südost) on August 24, with headquarters in Belgrade. In this capacity Neubacher would serve as chief formulator of political, economic, and antipartisan policy in the Balkans until the German withdrawal in late 1944; in Greece he was represented by a deputy, Consul General von Grävenitz, and an economic expert, Paul Hahn. During the last year of the occupation, Neubacher visited Athens periodically to coordinate political and economic matters.[64]

The longed-for improvement in Germany's general military position failed to materialize, and organized native resistance—not significant before early and mid-1943, and in any case mainly a concern of Italy—now became a serious matter. Reich economic policy, previously concerned mainly with the technical problems of sustaining the client regime's capacity to finance army operations, now became an adjunct of antipartisan strategy as well.[65] Since the beginning of the war, the Wehrmacht had advocated a draconic reprisal policy as a safeguard against the growth of guerrilla activity. By mid-1943, however, even some army commanders concluded that reprisals were actually driving many people into the arms of the resistance. For this reason, Neubacher, as sonderbeauftragter südost, was entrusted in November 1943 with the coordination of a new Balkan antipartisan strategy which de-emphasized reprisals and stressed the mobilization of native anticommunist forces. In Greece this involved the establishment of native Security Battalions, generally under royalist commanders who, despite their pro-British sympathies, were nonetheless ready to participate with the Germans in a struggle against the communist-led ELAS. The problem of financially shoring up the puppet regime now became doubly urgent, for German officials feared that an economic collapse might precipitate a general uprising in which the newly created and armed Security Battalions might themselves turn on the Reich.

In consultation with Hahn and Hector Tsironikos (the new Greek finance minister), Neubacher considered several possible ways to brake the inflation. The introduction of an entirely new currency—based either on government lands or olive oil reserves—was discussed, but it was rejected on the grounds that a new unit of exchange stood no chance of winning popular acceptance in view of Germany's military situation. In the last resort, a radical plan was adopted: the drachma would be shored up by the sale of German gold on the Athens stock market. The sale of gold had hitherto been forbidden under the occupation, but circumstances now recommended it. Gold was a commodity that could be brought in in sufficient quantities by air, thereby circumventing the problem of rail and highway disruptions which affected the importation of other goods. Moreover, gold had a powerful mystique in Greece, particularly since the royal government had taken the nation's reserves into exile. Through the controlled sale of gold, Neubacher hoped to exploit the greed of Greek speculators, absorb depreciated drachmas, and rein in the inflation.[66] The possibility of handling the problem by simply providing gold to the Wehrmacht for direct payment to Greek suppliers was, with certain exceptions, avoided, on the grounds that direct payments in gold would render the drachma useless. Moreover, the practice would have aroused discontent among suppliers in nearby countries, such as Rumania and Bulgaria, where payments in gold would also have been demanded.[67]

The scheme was approved by the Reich ministries of finance and economics on 8 November 1943, and Neubacher was allotted the sum of one million gold pounds for the purpose. The first sale of 20,000 gold pounds in mid-November succeeded in lowering the exchange rate of the drachma relative to the gold pound from two million to 900,000 to one—a result that convinced Berlin to prolong the operation. By an order of

Goering dated January 20, 1944, an additional monthly sum of 200,000 gold pounds (RM 4 million) was placed at Neubacher's disposal for six months, to be used for his operations in Albania and Serbia, as well as Greece.[68]

This all amounted to a psychological game in which the element of timing was critical. Since German gold supplies were limited, Neubacher and Hahn waited repeatedly until the last possible minute, when the final collapse of confidence in the drachma appeared imminent, before putting just enough gold up for auction to restore a measure of confidence in the currency. Drachmas obtained in exchange for gold were then used to finance two-thirds to three-fourths of the Wehrmacht's requirements into the summer of 1944.[69] At the same time, the operations proved to be a relatively effective instrument in the antipartisan strategy of the occupation, which was based on deepening the rift between native communist and anticommunist forces in Greece.[70]

But the sale of gold could be nothing more than a relatively effective means to postpone the final collapse of the Greek economy for several months. The last auction was held in August 1944, but this final effort to save the drachma already began to break down in mid-May 1944 when the Peloponneseus, in consequence of the rapid growth of guerrilla operations, was declared a battle zone. At this time Hitler personally ordered the reestablishment of economic controls in the region, forbidding open markets, civilian shipping, and private motor traffic. This resulted in a new food emergency in the Peloponnesian villages, and in Athens and Piraeus as well. The inflation, which had been slowed but never halted by the sale of gold, soared to unprecedented heights in mid-June, when the value of the drachma to the gold pound rose to 200,000,000:1. At this time a newspaper cost 200,000 drachmas, a cigarette 20,000, and a loaf of bread, 2,000,000. But the figures are really meaningless since by this time most Greeks were living by barter.[71] In September all Greece was declared a battle zone and the final evacuation of the country began; well before this, however, the drachma had become worthless.

In retrospect, it can be said that Germany's economic policy in Greece—always based on the desire to finance Wehrmacht operations with local resources—went through three distinct stages: (1) maximum noninvolvement, leaving Italy to deal with economic problems (May 1941 to October 1942); (2) direct intervention in conjunction with Italy to prevent the collapse of the client regime (October 1942 to the summer of 1943); (3) direct control of the economy immediately before the Italian capitulation, when the aims of economic policy were broadened to become part of antipartisan strategy. Late in the occupation political considerations became as important as economic motives: the maintenance of a functioning economy—no matter how crippled—was viewed as a desperate means to combat the growth of mass resistance and foment conflict between communist-led and nationalist forces.[72]

As a noted Greek scholar has recently said, "Foreign intervention has come to be considered the most important factor in the development of recent Greek history."[73] The years 1941 to 1944 are the most severe illustration of the truth of this statement. To be sure, the deliberately exploitative nature of the Axis occupation has often been greatly exaggerated; the persistent idea that economic dislocations in wartime Greece were the result of policies designed to bring about the "systematic destruction of the wealthproducing sources" and "permanent enfeeblement" of the country[74]—a view that once seemed to be confirmed by Italian sources such as the papers of Ciano—can no longer be accepted. But the fact remains that for most Greeks these were times of stark privation and terror inflicted on the population primarily as the result of the actions or the neglect of invading powers—and also, it should be remembered, by the greed of members of the Greek community itself. Moreover, the occupation vastly complicated previously existing tensions within the country, thereby contributing to the origins of civil war and chronic political, economic, and social instability in the postwar era.

Notes

[1] U.S. Department of State, *Documents on German Foreign Policy, 1918–1945,* 13 vols. (Washington, D.C., 1957–64), series D (1937–45) (hereafter *DGFP*), 12:747–48, High Command of the Army to Chief of the High Command of the Wehrmacht, 9 May 1941, doc. 482.

[2] *DGFP,* 12:776, Altenburg to Foreign Ministry, 11 May 1941, doc. 495. See also Klaus Olshausen, *Zwischenspiel auf dem Balkan: Die deutsche Politik gegenüber Jugoslawien und Griechenland von März bis Juli 1941* (Stuttgart, 1973), pp. 142–43, 239–41.

[3] *DGFP,* 12:796, Memorandum by Ritter, 13 May 1941, doc. 510.

[4] *DGFP,* 12:845–47, Führer's Directive, 17 May 1941, doc. 536.

[5] John S. Koliopoulos, *Greece and the British Connection, 1935–1941* (Oxford, 1977), pp. 133, 184–86. Koliopoulos stresses the "bogy" of a new Salonika front which haunted German leaders and maintains that Operation Marita "had very little to do with Italy and very much to do with Britain."

[6] Heinz Richter, *Griechenland zwischen Revolution und Konterrevolution 1936–1946* (Frankfurt a.M., 1973), pp. 131, 133–34; Olshausen, *Zwischenspiel,* pp. 242–45.

[7] John O. Iatrides, Introduction to the author's *Greece in the 1940s: A Nation in Crisis* (Hanover, N.H., 1981), p. 23. This anthology includes an essay by Stavros B. Thomadakis, "Black Markets, Inflation, and Force in the Economy of Occupied Greece," pp. 61–80, which contains some interesting conjectures about the relationship of profiteering to the occupation system and about transfers of wealth that occurred as a consequence of the occupation. It is based on intelligence reports of the OSS. For bibliography on the general history of Greece during the war, see John O. Iatrides, ed., *Greece in the 1940s: A Bibliographic Companion* (Hanover, N.H., 1981). This is an extremely valuable guide to documentary collections and secondary works; Part 1 is an annotated survey of sources on "Greece under the Axis Occupation" by Hagen Fleischer.

[8] Koliopoulos, *Greece and the British Connection,* p. 128. The author cites a British report of 1939 according to which "the standard of living of the bulk of the population is already so low that it can scarcely be further reduced without fear of social disorders" (p. 128, n. 1).

[9] Royal Institute of International Affairs, *Southeastern Europe: A Political*

and Economic Survey (Oxford, 1939), pp. 156–58, 163–64; L. S. Stavrianos, *The Balkans since 1453* (New York, 1958), pp. 678, 680; Paul Hahn, *Griechische Währung und Währungspolitische Massnahmen unter der Besetzung, 1941–1944* (Tübingen, 1957), pp. 2–3. The last title is a slightly altered version of a technical report prepared by Hahn, head of the economic department of the office of Reich plenipotentiary Hermann Neubacher, shortly before the end of the war. For general observations on economic and social conditions in interwar Greece, see Nicholas Svoronos, "Greek History, 1940–1950: The Main Problems," in Iatrides, ed., *Greece*, pp. 4–6; also Thomadakis, "Black Markets," pp. 63–64 in the same volume.

[10] Cited in Koliopoulos, *Greece and the British Connection*, p. 5.

[11] *DGFP*, 13:676–79, Memorandum by Eisenlohr, 24 Oct. 1941, doc. 420; *Report on the International Committee of the Red Cross on Its Activities during the Second World War* (1 September 1939–30 June 1947), 3, *Relief Activities* (Geneva, 1948), pp. 450, 464; U.S. National Archives (hereafter NA), Undated Report [written after 13 February 1945], "Abwicklung Militärbefehlshaber Südost," Microcopy T-501 (German Field Commands), roll 258, frames 557–574 (hereafter T-501/258/557–60, 574).

[12] E.g., Johannes Gaitanides, *Griechenland ohne Säulen* (Munich, 1955), pp. 240–41; Stavrianos, *The Balkans since 1453*, p. 786; John Louis Hondros, "The German Occupation of Greece, 1941–1944," Diss., Vanderbilt, 1969, p. 81; Thomadakis, "Black Markets," p. 65.

[13] Richter, *Griechenland*, pp. 140–41, 147–48. While admitting that quantities of fresh fruits and vegetables were confiscated for use by troops in North Africa, Richter maintains that grain, the staple, was never exported. German grain confiscations were, in fact, part of an unsuccessful program to help the client regime combat the growth of a black market in food by centralizing control of distribution. In light of the Wehrmacht commanders' sensitivity to the food problem, noted above and immediately below, the argument seems convincing.

[14] *DGFP*, 13:676–79, Memorandum by Eisenlohr, 24 October 1941, doc. 420; ibid., pp. 218–19, Memorandum by Wiehl, 25 July 1941, doc. 155; ibid., pp. 512–14, Memorandum by Wiehl, 15 September 1941, doc. 323.

[15] *DGFP*, 13:679–82, Legation in Hungary to Foreign Ministry, 25 October 1941, doc. 421.

[16] The Wehrmacht employed ca. 200,000 native laborers on various projects in 1942–44. Conditions among these workers were relatively good

(U.S. Office of Strategic Services, Research and Analysis Branch, No. 2500.4, *German Military Government over Europe: Greece* [December 1944], pp. 44–45, 48).

[17] Count Galeazzo Ciano, *Ciano's Diplomatic Papers*, ed. Malcolm Muggeridge (London, 1948), pp. 462–63. In conversation with Ciano, Ribbentrop claimed "not to know much about" the Greek situation, although detailed reports had been placed on his desk throughout the summer. For a particularly good account, see Olshausen, *Zwischenspiel*, pp. 246–54.

[18] Cited in Ciano, *Diplomatic Papers*, pp. 464-65.

[19] V. G. Valaoras, "Some Effects of Famine on the Population of Greece," *Milbank Memorial Fund Quarterly*, 24 (1946), 216, 221; also, *Report of the International Committee of the Red Cross*, pp. 450, 464; NA, Ab. Mil. befh. Südost, T-501/258/557–60, 574; William Hardy McNeill, *The Greek Dilemma* (New York, 1951), p. 51; Bickham Sweet-Escott, *Greece: A Political and Economic Survey, 1939–1953* (London, 1954), p. 93. It has been suggested that "as many as four hundred fifty thousand Greeks (of a population of seven million) may have died during the four-year occupation from starvation, malnutrition, and disease" (Iatrides, Introduction, *Greece*, p. 20). Dimitri Kitsikis, "La famine en Grèce (1941–1942): Les Conséquences politiques," *Revue d'histoire de la deuxième guerre mondiale*, 74 (April 1969), 17, cites a Greek government publication of 1946 which estimated the loss of life due to hunger at 360,000.

[20] Hondros, "The German Occupation," p. 86.

[21] Koliopoulos, *Greece and the British Connection*, p. 128.

[22] Hahn, *Griechische Währung*, pp. 11, 15, 3. Even before the war there had been little of the confidence and mystique surrounding the drachma that people normally feel toward their national currency. The national economy was based to such an extent on foreign trade that Greeks were used to thinking in terms of foreign currencies and considered the drachma a second-class medium of exchange.

[23] Hahn, *Griechische Währung*, p. 14; Percy Ernst Schramm, ed., *Kriegstagebuch des Oberkommandos der Wehrmacht (Wehrmachtführungsstab), 1940–1945* (hereafter *KTB/OKW*), 4 vols. (Frankfurt a.M., 1961–65), 4:665. According to the initial agreement, Wehrmacht demands were not to exceed 1.5 billion drachmas. Actually, occupation costs in the last part of 1941 averaged four billion drachmas—one and one-half billion for the Italians and two and one-half for the Germans (NA, Report of Wiehl, July 25, 1942, T-120 [German Foreign Ministry] /1170/2146).

²⁴ For interesting details of German-Italian economic conflicts, in which the Italians actually held their own, see Olshausen, *Zwischenspiel,* pp. 298 ff. Cf. Georg Vogel, *Diplomat unter Hitler und Adenauer* (Düsseldorf, 1969), pp. 78–84, who identifies points of friction but minimizes tensions between German and Italian agencies. Vogel was attached to Altenburg's staff in Athens.

²⁵ Great importance was attached to this by the population (Hahn, *Griechische Währung,* p. 5).

²⁶ NA, Ab. Mil. befh. Südost, T-501/258/470–77; Richter, *Griechenland,* p. 195.

²⁷ NA, Memorandum of Wiehl, 25 July 1942, T-120/1174/468810; Ab. Mil. befh. Südost, T-501/258/537; also, Memorandum of Hudeczek, 16 October 1942, T-120/1174/468768 ff.; Altenburg to Foreign Ministry, 1 October 1942, T-120/1174/468794.

²⁸ German records vary, sometimes widely, regarding statistics. These figures are from NA, Report of Dr. Soterios Gotzamanes (Greek Minister of Finance), 19 September 1942, T-120/1174/468810 ff., and Herman Neubacher, *Sonderauftrag Südost 1940–1945: Bericht eines fliegenden Diplomaten* (Göttingen, 1957), pp. 74–75. Cf. the much higher estimates in Hahn, *Griechische Währung,* p. 41. The price spiral of various commodities is shown in Richter, *Griechenland,* p. 468.

²⁹ NA, Ab. Mil. behf. Südost, T-501/251/566-67.

³⁰ Hahn, *Griechische Währung,* p. 15.

³¹ Richter, *Griechenland,* p. 114. Tsolakoglou as commander of the Third Greek Army capitulated on the understanding that he would surrender only to German forces. Hitler overruled this, and the Greeks were forced to surrender to the Italians as well. "That the Germans have conquered us is no disgrace," the Greeks were heard to say. "But we will never forget that they surrendered us to the Italians" (cited in Ehrengard Schramm von Thadden, *Griechenland und die Grossmächte im zweiten Weltkrieg* [Wiesbaden, 1955], p. 200).

³² For accounts of the Red Cross mission, see *Report of the International Committee of the Red Cross,* 3:472; Karl Brandt et al., *Management of Agriculture and Food in the German-Occupied and Other Areas of Fortress Europe: A Study in Military Government* (Stanford, 1953), pp. 239–48; Conrad Roediger, "Die internationale Hilfsaktion für die Bevölkerung Griechenlands im zweiten Weltkrieg," *Vierteljahrshefte für Zeitgeschichte,* 11 (1963), 49–71.

[33] Hahn, *Griechische Währung,* p. 14.

[34] NA, Report of Hudeczek, 16 October 1942, T-120/1174/468768 ff.

[35] Following the war, Warlimont denied that he had fought a reduction of occupation costs, blaming opposition on the *Kriegsmarine (KTB/OKW,* 2:836–37).

[36] NA, Mussolini to Hitler, 22 July 1942, T-120/1174/468916 ff. Ivone Kirkpatrick, *Mussolini: A Study in Power* (New York, Paperback ed., 1968), p. 494, refers to this as "the last occasion in which [Mussolini] ventured to speak his mind to Hitler." According to Ciano, Mussolini had by this time come to believe that Germany was working against Italy's interests in Greece and that the Reich was trying to bring about the "systematic impoverishment" of the country (Count Galeazzo Ciano, *The Ciano Diaries, 1939–1943,* ed. Hugh Gibson [Garden City, N.Y., 1946], pp. 508, 528).

[37] F. W. Deakin, *The Brutal Friendship: Mussolini, Hitler and the Fall of Italian Fascism* (New York, 1962), p. 24.

[38] Ciano, *Diaries,* pp. 528–29. By this time, according to Deakin, Italian optimism about the war had "evaporated, and a sense of fear and frustration pervaded the Italian scene" (Deakin, *Brutal Friendship,* p. 27).

[39] NA, Report of Gotzamanes, 19 September 1942, T-120/1174/468810 ff.; Memorandum of Clodius, 5 October 1942, T-120/1174/468785 ff.

[40] NA, Report of Altenburg, 1 October 1942, T-120/1174/468795.

[41] Ciano, *Diaries,* p. 527.

[42] NA, Report of Altenburg, 1 October 1942, T-120/1174/468794.

[43] NA, Memorandum of Clodius, 2 October 1942, T-120/1174/468790 ff.; *KTB/OKW,* 3:109; Ciano, *Diaries,* p. 527.

[44] The Italians, suspicious of an extension of German authority into their sphere of influence, originally opposed the idea of a permanent economic mission (NA, Memorandum of Clodius, 5 October 1942, T-120/1174/468785; Ribbentrop to German Embassy in Rome, 17 October 1942, T-120/1174/468774).

[45] NA, Ab. Mil. befh. Südost, T-501, 258/476–79; Neubacher, *Sonderauftrag,* p. 14. Neubacher had been a successful public housing and

financial administrator for the city of Vienna and a leader of the anschluss movement in the interwar period. Following the anschluss, he served as mayor of Vienna from March 1938 to the spring of 1940, when he entered the foreign service. In addition to his war memoir, cited above, see Harry R. Ritter, "Hermann Neubacher and the German Occupation of the Balkans, 1940–1945," Diss., Virginia, 1969, and "Herman Neubacher and the Austrian *Anschluss* Movement, 1918–40," *Central European History,* 8 (1975), 348–69.

[46] NA, Ab. Mil. befh. Südost, T-501/258/476–77; Ribbentrop to Neubacher, 16 October 1942, T-120/1174/468783 ff.; Ribbentrop to Altenburg, 17 October 1942, T-120/1174/468779.

[47] Neubacher, *Sonderauftrag,* pp. 72–73, 90. Also, NA, Ribbentrop to Neubacher, 16 October 1942, T-120/1174/468783; Hahn, *Griechische Währung,* pp. 35, 27.

[48] Ciano, *Diaries,* p. 532; NA, Ribbentrop to Clodius, 17 October 1942, T-120/1174/468781; Neubacher to Foreign Ministry, 21 October 1942, T-120/1174/468751.

[49] Neubacher, *Sonderauftrag,* p. 72, reports that he developed the outlines of Axis policy even before his formal appointment as special minister. I have been unable to determine D'Agostino's given name, which may in itself indicate something about his importance. In the spring of 1943 he was replaced by an industrialist named Vincenzo Faggiuoli. C. M. Woodhouse, *Apple of Discord: A Survey of Recent Greek Politics in Their International Setting* (London, 1948), p. 134, gives a distorted account of the establishment of the economic mission. See also *The Times* (London), 1 December 1942, p. 4.

[50] Hahn, *Griechische Währung,* p. 15.

[51] Rumania, Bulgaria, and Germany eventually supplied about 166,000 tons of food to Greece (NA, Ab. Mil. befh. Südost, T-501/258/558, 566, 582).

[52] Hahn, *Griechische Währung,* p. 21; *Neue Ordnung* (Belgrade), 25 April 1943, p. 6; NA, Ab. Mil. befh. Südost, T-501/258/527–28.

[53] International Military Tribunal, *Trial of the Major War Criminals before the International Military Tribunal* (hereafter *IMT*), 42 vols. (Nuremberg, 1947–49) 11:430–32; NA, Ab. Mil. befh. Südost, T-501/258/558, 566, 581–82; Report of Hudeczek, 16 October 1942, T-120/1174/468768 ff.; Neubacher, *Sonderauftrag,* pp. 80–82; *Deutsche Zeitung in Kroatien* (Zagreb), 17 December 1943, p. 6; Richter, *Griechenland,,* p. 198. Before the

establishment of DEGRIGES, the export trade was ruthlessly exploited by Greek profiteers who purchased German commodities at a fixed rate of 60 drachmas to one RM, then resold them at enormous profits on the inflated Greek market. DEGRIGES prevented such abuses by holding German imports in customs houses until importers paid a special duty corresponding to the difference between the German and Greek value, but leaving the importer a reasonable profit. Three-fifths of the revenue accumulated was used to compensate Greek exporters for losses incurred by shipping goods abroad. The remaining two-fifths was used to help finance the occupation. Italy established a similar agency, the *Società Anonyma Commerciale Italo-Greca* which, according to German sources, functioned poorly; it was liquidated following the Italian capitulation (Hahn, *Griechische Währung*, pp. 24–25).

[54] Neubacher, *Sonderauftrag*, pp. 78–79. Thomadakis, "Black Markets," pp. 74–75, is uninformed on German policy and attributes the dramatic fall in prices solely to the psychological repercussions of Axis reverses in North Africa.

[55] Hahn, *Griechische Währung*, pp. 21–22; Neubacher, *Sonderauftrag*, p. 77.

[56] Hahn, *Griechische Währung*, p. 22.

[57] Ibid., pp. 22–23; Neubacher, *Sonderauftrag*, pp. 78–79.

[58] Hahn, *Griechische Währung*, pp. 22–23; Neubacher, *Sonderauftrag*, pp. 78–79.

[59] Neubacher, *Sonderauftrag*, p. 79; *IMT*, 11:430, 432.

[60] On the motives of these men, see Richter, *Griechenland*, pp. 197–98.

[61] *KTB/OKW*, 3:109; Neubacher, *Sonderauftrag*, p. 93. Cf. Norman Rich, *Hitler's War Aims*, 2 vols. (New York, 1973), 2:307, who presents the Wehrmacht's point of view.

[62] Hahn, *Griechische Währung*, pp. 27–28.

[63] For the broad outlines of the reform and its degree of success, see Rich, *Hitler's War Aims*, 2:286, and Richter, *Griechenland*, pp. 232–33. The suggestion that the reorganization merely complicated administrative matters in Greece (Rich, pp. 308–9) may not be entirely true. See NA, Ab. Mil. befh. Südost, T-501/258/476–79, 511, 527–28, 552, 597–98.

^{64} Walther Hubatsch, ed., *Hitlers Weisungen für die Kriegführung 1939–1945: Dokumente des Oberkommandos der Wehrmacht* (Frankfurt a.M., 1962), no. 48 of 26 July 1943 and no. 48a. of 3 August 1943, pp. 221, 223; NA, Ab. Mil. befh. Südost, T-501/258/476–78; Neubacher, *Sonderauftrag*, pp. 101–2; NA, Directive of Keitel, 7 October 1943, T-501/264/442–44.

^{65} On the growth of Greek resistance see Hondros, "The German Occupation," pp. 173–75, 185–93, as well as the same author's "The Greek Resistance, 1941–1944: A Reevaluation," in Iatrides, ed., *Greece*, pp. 40–41, 43–45. For a brief account of the evolution of German antipartisan strategy in Greece, see Richter, *Griechenland*, pp. 386–91.

^{66} Neubacher, *Sonderauftrag*, p. 77; Hahn, *Griechische Währung*, pp. 29–30, 52.

^{67} NA, Ab. Mil. befh. Südost, T-501/258/539; Hahn, *Griechische Währung*, pp. 29–30, 55–56. In only one instance did Neubacher allow gold to be used for the direct purchase of a Greek commodity. In order to keep the Macedonian silk crop—important for the manufacture of parachutes—out of the hands of profiteers, its direct purchase with gold was approved in 1944.

^{68} Hahn, *Griechische Währung*, pp. 29, 50. For the precise timing and amounts, see the chart on page 51.

^{69} Neubacher, *Sonderauftrag*, p. 88; Hahn, *Griechische Währung*, pp. 32, 53; NA, Ab. Mil. befh. Südost, T-501/258/538–39.

^{70} Richter, *Griechenland*, p. 391.

^{71} *New York Times*, 18 June 1944, p. 11; see also the chart in NA, Ab. Mil. befh. Südost, T-501/258/609, "Entwicklung der Preise der wichtigsten Lebensmittel und Bedarfsartikel in Athen."

^{72} Richter, *Griechenland*, pp. 488–91.

^{73} Svoronos, "Greek History, 1940–1950," p. 1.

^{74} Stephen G. Xydis, *The Economy and Finances of Greece under Occupation* (New York, n.d.), pp. 6, 11; for more recent and better-informed opinions about the general nature of economic policy, see Dietrich Orlow, *The Nazis in the Balkans: A Case Study of Totalitarian Politics* (Pittsburgh, 1968), p. 10; and Vladimir Petrov, *Money and Conquest: Allied Occupation Currencies in World War II* (Baltimore, 1967) pp. 37–38.

VIII

Military Lend-Lease to the Soviet Union and the Defeat of Germany

ROBERT W. COAKLEY

DURING WORLD WAR II the United States carried on an extensive program to supply war materials to her allies under lend-lease arrangements. Though any exact percentage is difficult to calculate, approximately 20 percent of American war production went to satisfy Allied demands during the war years.[1] The largest of these lend-lease programs was for the United Kingdom, for whose benefit lend-lease was invented; the second largest was for the USSR. The method of handling the British and Russian programs differed greatly, reflecting the contrast between the close and cooperative arrangements between British and Americans that, despite all the family quarrels, characterized their relationship during the war, and the degree of mutual suspicion and mistrust that characterized the relationship of the Anglo-American combine with the Soviet Union.

The Soviet Union fought a separate war on its own front, for different purposes, it later proved, from those that motivated Great Britain and the United States. But while the war with Germany was on, there was agreement on the necessity of defeating her in the most expeditious manner possible. Both sides had the same wolf by the ears and neither could afford to let go. To carry the analogy a bit further, during the first two years after Pearl Harbor, the wolf's energies were being absorbed and his strength drained away in an effort to devour the Soviet Union, a situation that permitted the western allies to gather their strength for the kill.

At their first conference in Washington following Pearl
Harbor (ARCADIA) the British and Americans laid down as
the cardinal principle of their strategy that Germany should be
defeated first, before the full force of combined resources
should be turned against Japan.[2] Although in 1942 and 1943
the Americans sometimes honored this principle in the breach,
it was reiterated at every subsequent major conference. Yet for
some two and a half years after ARCADIA, the western allies
did not mount the full scale attack against Germany in Europe
that their strategy clearly called for. For these two and a half
years the Soviet Union bore the brunt of the fighting in
Europe, and its war against Germany was the most important
factor in the realization of the Anglo-American strategy.

It is small wonder then that the effort to furnish supplies to
the Soviet Union received the utmost emphasis and highest
priority. It was not a question of supporting the war aims of the
USSR but a recognition of the hard fact that continuation of
the Soviet Union in the war was indispensable to ultimate
victory over Germany. It was this hard military fact, un-
varnished by any ideological considerations of either love or
hate for communism, that provided the dominant motive for
furnishing supplies to the Russians in generous measure.
Clearly, President Roosevelt, rather than the military leaders,
was the principal architect of Soviet aid policy and frequently
pushed his military advisers beyond the limits to which they
wished to go, but they too shared the feeling of urgency. At the
Casablanca Conference in January 1943, Admiral Ernest J.
King, U.S. chief of naval operations, could state forthrightly:
"Russia is our main reliance in Europe."[3]

There was undoubtedly a good deal of rationalization of the
program in idealistic terms for popular consumption. Certainly, Roosevelt had high hopes that generosity in supply aid
would not only compensate for the delay in opening a second
front but also lead to harmonious relations in the postwar
period. Americans seem unable to undertake any grand project
without some such idealization of its goals or to base their
alliances on totally materialistic aims. There was in America
during the war a growing assumption of Soviet support of

democratic ideals and of Soviet cooperation in shaping a brave new world. This idealization brought eventual disillusionment and led many to question the entire rationale of the Soviet aid program.

Supply to the Soviet Union was regulated by a series of protocols—definite agreements as to exact quantities of material to be furnished by the United States and Great Britain, normally for a twelve-month period.[4] In contrast to arrangements for the supply of Great Britain and other lend-lease recipients, these protocols were rigid diplomatic agreements and any proposal to depart from them could cause serious diplomatic repercussions. True, each contained some sort of escape clause to the effect that they might be adjusted to the changing situation of the war, but the Russians were seldom willing to let anyone take advantage of it. Only at the end of the war in Europe was the escape clause ever specifically invoked, and this, as will appear later, was a part of a drastic change in the whole approach to Soviet aid. Although the western allies did not meet their full commitments under the first two protocols, it was not because of any invocation of the escape clauses.

Requirements of other lend-lease beneficiaries were weighed in terms of their specific relation to approved strategy, deployments of troops, needs of war economies, and other factors. A combined Anglo-American organization, the Munitions Assignments Board, responsible to the Anglo-American Combined Chiefs of Staff (CCS), made final assignments of munitions from month to month. While the board also made the formal assignments of military to the Soviet Union, it neither weighed Soviet needs in the balance not required strategic justification. It simply followed the commitments in the protocols, adjusting the rate of assignment, in some cases, to the ability to move the goods to the USSR. After October 1942 a special body directly responsible to Roosevelt, known as the President's Soviet Protocol Committee and representing all interested departments, took over the formulation and administration of the protocols. Harry Hopkins, Roosevelt's confidential adviser, and to a degree his alter ego, was originally chairman of both the Munitions Assignments Board and the Protocol Committee, thus providing some link between the two organizations.[5]

Aid to the Soviet Union began almost immediately after the German invasion of 22 June 1941. In the early stages of the Russo-German War the president proceeded to develop the program with considerable caution because of the fear of a popular reaction against the support of a communist state. Not until November 1941 did he declare the USSR eligible for lend-lease under the powers granted him under the Lend-Lease Act to designate those nations whose defense was vital to that of the United States. In the meantime commercial arrangements made available limited quantities of supplies, while plans took shape for a program that could only be financed under lend-lease.

Public opinion was not the only bar to extensive aid in 1941, for there were few military supplies available to ship to the Soviet Union. By midyear the United States was heavily committed to an ambitious aid program for Britain, and seriously embarrassed to meet even a small part of British needs without completely compromising the army's own plans for equipping a force of about two million men by the end of June 1942. All available surplus arms had already been sent to England, the major portion of them to reequip the British army after the debacle of Dunkirk. Existing estimates of future production presupposed that anything beyond the minimum needs for American defense would go to Britain, with a small amount to be diverted to China. General George C. Marshall, the army's chief of staff, felt that the War Department had reached the limit of its ability to give away material and still meet its responsibilities, and he did not welcome the prospect of finding additional material for the Soviet Union. Besides, in these early days of the Soviet-German war, the military experts in the War Department were no wiser than those who wrote for the newspapers and concurred in the widespread belief that the USSR could hardly last more than three or four months in the face of the Nazi onslaught.[6]

The president had other ideas. It seems probable that Hopkins's assurances after returning from a mission to Moscow in late July 1941 convinced Roosevelt that the Germans were in for a long war on the Eastern Front. At the conference with Churchill on board the *Prince of Wales* in August 1941, he agreed with the prime minister that a conference should be held in London to determine a combined supply offer to the USSR, following which an Anglo-American mission would proceed to Moscow for further conferences with the Russians. Following his meeting with Churchill, Roosevelt, on 30 August 1941, informed Secretary of War Stimson in no uncertain terms that he deemed it of "paramount importance for the safety and security of America that all reasonable munitions help be provided Russia, not only immediately but as long as she continues to fight the Axis powers effectively."[7] This presidential directive launched the program of military aid to the Soviet Union and made it necessary for the U.S. Army to revise its plans in order to find material to send in the immediate future.

In London the American representatives, headed by W. Averell Harriman, had to fight off a British proposal to control the flow of American supplies to the USSR. Lord Beaverbrook, British minister of supply, wanted the Americans to make an overall allocation to the British, out of which the latter, with American advice, would make sub-allocations to the Soviets. Although this proposal was rejected, the British did manage in the course of the negotiations to preserve most of their own allocations against the threatened encroachment of the new Soviet aid program. In Moscow, on 2 October 1941, the First Soviet Protocol was signed to cover the nine-month period to the end of June 1942. To cite a few examples of the American commitments; they included 2,250 tanks, 1,800 planes, 85,000 cargo trucks, and 562,000 miles of field telephone wire. In order to finance this program, for which the Soviet Union had no resources, the President finally declared the USSR eligible for lend-lease aid on 7 November 1941. The feared adverse public reaction never developed; by then the American public as well as its leaders had been convinced that aid to Russia was a good investment.[8]

Meanwhile, the executive departments, and particularly the army, struggled to fit the protocol pledges into the already

overburdened allocation schedules. While the commitments
were not nearly so great as the Soviets requested, they represented a sizable additional load for the United States in the
existing state of industrial mobilization. The president was
reluctant to sacrifice any of the previous commitments made to
Britain and China in order to make room for the Russian
program. Thus either production had to be rapidly expanded or
the American rearmament program would suffer heavily. The
president did preemptorily order tank production to be
doubled by 30 June 1942 with a 25 percent step-up in existing
delivery dates, but it proved easier to issue orders than to
accelerate production. It was to take some time before tank
production could be increased sufficiently to accommodate all
demands, and so during the last months before Pearl Harbor
the Soviet program forced a cutback in deliveries to U.S. forces.
The situation with regard to aircraft was even more critical.
When aircraft commitments to the Soviet Union were added to
those already pledged to Britain, they amounted to 68 percent
of prospective American plane production over the nine-month
period of the First Protocol. The army seriously considered a
plan, in October and November 1941, to retire some divisions
of the National Guard from active service to make more equipment available for foreign aid.[9]

In fact, these First Protocol commitments turned out to be
more than the Americans could handle. Not only did it prove
impossible in the fall of 1941 to meet the delivery schedules
projected under the protocol, but the Russians found much of
the material in unsatisfactory condition and refused to accept
delivery. The legacy of the pre–Pearl Harbor period was therefore a large deficit, which the Pearl Harbor attack further
increased.

In the immediate wake of the Japanese attack, both materials
and shipping had to be absorbed in the equipping of American
troops and their deployment to the Pacific and England. The
military leaders looked for a readjustment of protocol commitments to meet the new situation, but the president would
have none of it. On 30 December 1941, Roosevelt ordered that
the "Soviet Aid Program as provided in the Protocol Agree-

ment be reestablished beginning January 1," with existing deficits to be made up no later than April.[10] It was a large order, but the military authorities were able to make most of the promised material available, if not by the end of April, at least by the end of the First Protocol period on 30 June 1942. There were some exceptions, notably antiaircraft and antitank guns, where even the president deemed the army's needs so pressing that he approved retention. But otherwise material for the Soviet Protocol got a priority higher than anything except equipment for U.S. troops moving overseas. The Russians were assigned the entire American production of field telephone wire in January 1942, 90 percent of it in February and March. Light tanks had to be taken from troops in training to fill Soviet quotas. The existence of the deficit put the Americans on the defensive in all their dealings, and every Soviet demand had to be met as far as possible. Soviet representatives in Washington were adamant in their insistence that all material be in perfect condition and that special specifications be met. Though those who dealt with these representatives at low levels became thoroughly exasperated, high policy demanded that the Russians be placated.[11] As American production began to mount and Soviet needs could be fitted better into production plans, these problems of the early days of 1942 began to recede. But even as they did, the materials that were being made available at such sacrifice piled up at the docks as ocean shipping and the routes of delivery became the crucial questions.

The initial commitments to the Soviet Union were made without much consideration of the means of delivering them. The British and Americans did promise to "give aid to the transportation of these materials to the Soviet Union," a clause that was to mean, in effect, that they would assume the major responsibility for delivering them.[12] There were three main possible routes of entry to the USSR in 1941: the northern route around the coast of Norway to ports on the Arctic and the White Sea, the southern route around the coast of Africa to the Persian Gulf and across Iran, and the Pacific route to Vladivostok. Each route had its advantages and disadvantages, but all promised to exact a high cost in merchant shipping—at the time the single most important limiting factor on all Allied strategic moves. The northern route was the shortest and the one preferred by the Russians since it would provide supplies closest to the Soviet battlefronts. But it was exposed to German submarine and air attack, and the Soviet northern ports were plagued by ice in winter. The southern route could be kept open year round and would be relatively free of German interference, but it required an excessively long ocean haul and neither the ports nor overland transportation facilities in Iran could carry any appreciable load without extensive development. The Pacific route offered an avenue for transport of civilian supplies in Soviet flag ships, but it was a long haul and after December 1941 not open to British or American ships because it ran close to the Japanese island of Hokkaido. Soviet flag shipping was not plentiful, and there was also the constant danger that the route would be completely closed by a Japanese attack on the Soviet Union.

The Russians at first insisted on the use of the northern route for practically all war supplies, though they used their own limited merchant shipping in the Pacific to carry civilian-type materials, such as foodstuffs, clothing, and petroleum products. The British furnished naval convoys for merchant ships around the coast of Norway, and at first shipments to Archangel over this route proceeded without interruption. With the cooperation of British port experts, the capacity of Archangel was increased, and after the repulse of the German attack in the north, Murmansk was opened as a port of entry. The Russians promised to keep these ports open year around through the use of ice breakers.

American calculations on bringing the protocol shipments up to date after Pearl Harbor were based on shipping almost entirely over the northern route. In the face of an acute shortage of shipping for proposed troop movements anywhere, Roosevelt and Churchill agreed at ARCADIA that shipping for Soviet aid should have a priority second only to that of initial deployment of American troops. When told that ships could not be made available without interfering with the movement of convoys to England and the Pacific, the Allied political leaders simply told Hopkins and Beaverbrook to "find ships" somewhere.[13] But even the indefatigable Hopkins was unable to discover any spare tonnage in the existing stringency. By March 1942 the situation had become so serious that Roosevelt instructed Admiral Emory S. Land, head of the Maritime Commission, that ships must be furnished to bring protocol shipments up to date "regardless of other considerations."[14]

As a result very heavy loadings for the northern route began late in March 1942 and continued through April, when some 63 ships departed American ports for the convoy rendezvous off Ireland. By the end of April over 100 ships carrying American supplies were waiting off Iceland for convoy. The president proposed to place 50 ships monthly on the northern run between March and November, 25 from November through February. The War Shipping Administration calculated that this would require a total commitment of 260 cargo vessels. Hopkins interpreted this to mean that "the Russian protocol must be completed in preference to any other phase of our war program."[15]

The Germans upset these ambitious plans. In April 1942 they moved to concentrate their submarines, aircraft, and surface raiders along the coast of Norway. The British navy found itself engaged in a major naval operation to get each convoy through. And by the end of April losses of both merchant vessels and naval escorts had mounted to such heights that Churchill decided that the convoys must be limited to three every two months, each containing 25 to 35 vessels. Although the planned loadings in the United States had gone forward on the supposition that 107 ships would sail in these convoys in May alone, Roosevelt reluctantly acquiesced in Churchill's decision. Some of the ships off Iceland were moved to England and unloaded; loadings in the United States were cut to a bare minimum; and the diversion of a considerable number to the southern route via the Persian Gulf was proposed. But the southern route was not yet ready to compensate for the northern one. In the end, despite the fact that the Americans had been able to make both materials and shipping available, the commitments under the First Protocol could not be met in full.

American embarrassment vis-à-vis the Soviet Union continued.[16]

Meanwhile The U.S. Joint Chiefs of Staff (JCS) were proceeding on the theory that resources should be concentrated on the invasion of Europe from bases in Britain in the spring of 1943 or in an emergency operation to prevent Russian collapse in the fall of 1942. In London in April 1942 General Marshall and Harry Hopkins got a qualified agreement from the British to proceed with planning for these operations.[17] The JCS reasoned that a second front in Europe would offer far greater relief to the Soviet Union than the forwarding of supplies. As a corollary they calculated that the concentration of resources in England for a cross-Channel blow could hardly be achieved with Russian aid absorbing so much shipping and so many supplies. There was also the drain on British naval resources. While the Chiefs made no serious effort to cut back commitments under the First Protocol, they did propose that future supply aid to the Soviet Union should be adjusted to accommodate the primary Anglo-American effort.[18]

The president in March 1942 had directed the preparation of a second Soviet protocol on the thesis, as he put it, that the army and navy agreed that the continuation of supply to Russia was an essential element in American strategy. As prepared outside the channels of the JCS, a draft second protocol proposed to offer the Russians seven million tons of American supplies and one million tons of British material. From this the Russians would be asked to choose 4.4 million tons to conform to shipping capabilities, estimated at three million tons over the northern route and one million over the southern with a loss factor of 10 percent. The Pacific route did not even enter into consideration because of the supposed imminence of hostilities between Japan and the Soviet Union.[19]

These figures, as military shipping experts protested, were highly unrealistic in the light of the convoy situation and the inadequacy of facilities in the Persian Gulf, even if the need to concentrate on the buildup in the British Isles was not considered. They nevertheless became the basis for discussion between Roosevelt and V. M. Molotov when the Soviet emissary arrived in Washington on 29 May 1942, seeking not only promises of a second front in 1942 but of increased supply aid as well. After a belated appeal by General Marshall and Admiral King, Roosevelt did raise with Molotov the question of curtailing quantities on the Second Protocol, proposing to cut over a million and a half tons of "general supplies" in the interests of getting more shipping for a second front. Molotov's replies were guarded, reflecting both doubts about the Allied commitment to a second front in 1942 and a reluctance to give up industrial supplies. Since Roosevelt's promise of a second front in 1942 had to be equally guarded, and indeed was unwarranted in view of actual Anglo-American capabilities, the question of reducing protocol quantities was quietly dropped. Although the proposed protocol was not formally signed until October 1942, it went into effect with the expiration of the first at the end of June.[20]

At that point the United States and Britain stood virtually committed to delivering more than four million tons of supplies to the Soviet Union over the next twelve months via uncertain supply routes at the same time they were promising to open a second front in Western Europe. The CCS had little doubt from the start that both could never be accomplished simultaneously, and it soon became evident that neither goal could be realized. The British had long favored a diversionary attack in North Africa instead of an immediate cross-Channel invasion as more in keeping with their actual military potential, and Roosevelt was finally won over to this view in late July 1942. The decision to invade North Africa led to a train of events whereby the British and Americans put the major portion of their available resources into the Mediterranean and the Pacific in 1942 and 1943, delaying the cross-Channel attack until 1944.

Even with the invasion of the Continent postponed, the continuation of the northern convoys proved impossible. The British made valiant efforts to get the promised three convoys through in May and June but suffered losses up to 50 percent. Fearing loss of naval control of the Atlantic, Churchill suspended the convoys completely during July and August. They were resumed in September, but the demands of the North African invasion forced their suspension again during October and November 1942.[21] The Americans and British had to face the fact that they could not undertake any amphibious operation in European waters and still maintain convoys to Russia over the northern route. And while shipments of aid to the Soviet Union dwindled, the German advance in the south of Russia moved relentlessly forward and the great battle at Stalingrad began. The embarrassment of both Roosevelt and Churchill vis-à-vis Stalin reached its highest point during this period.

Churchill's fear of Stalin's reaction was so great that he even proposed cancelling the North African operation in favor of a landing to secure the coast of Norway. But Roosevelt held firm, gambling that the Russians could hold out and would not negotiate a separate peace. At the same time he directed on 2 October that every effort be made to utilize other routes of delivery to the maximum extent possible and that equipment be furnished the Soviet Union within protocol schedules in the exact priority they desired.[22]

By October 1942 plans for these other routes were rapidly taking shape. As the Japanese gave no evidence of attacking Siberia, the Pacific was an obvious alternative for civilian-type supplies. In August the War Shipping Administration started a program of transferring merchant shipping in the Pacific to Soviet registry to take advantage of the capacity of this route. During the brief Arctic summer, ships were dispatched from the west coast to Soviet Arctic ports. Meanwhile, an intensive effort began to deliver all planes under their own power. There were two possible air routes and both were used to some extent. The first ran from Alaska to Siberia, and the other via the South Atlantic, across Africa, and thence to the Soviet zone in Iran. The South Atlantic route was very long, could not serve for fighter planes, and required skilled bomber pilots who could better be used elsewhere. Although the southern route was used for some deliveries, the Alaska-Siberia route offered far the better possibilities. But in negotiations over this matter the Russians proved very difficult. They apparently feared having

American bases in Siberia, and finally agreed to the use of the route after several about-faces only on condition that Russian pilots should take delivery of the planes at Fairbanks, Alaska, and fly them the rest of the way. Even after the agreement, the arranging of air bases, development of proper winterization equipment, and the provision of transports to fly the Soviet pilots back and forth took time and delayed use of the route for large numbers of planes until well into 1943.[23]

The most important route of all for shipping was through the Persian Gulf. Since munitions could not be carried over the Pacific route, it was the only alternative to the northern route for military supplies. In September 1941 the British and Russians had moved into Iran, the Russians occupying a zone in the north and the British one in the south. The British had begun to develop Iranian facilities almost immediately, and a small American mission was dispatched to Iran to help them, but progress was very slow. The British did not have the resources to commit to the task, and if the Americans had them they did not wish to use them in the Middle East. But beginning with the curtailment of the northern convoys in May 1942, the need for improvement of facilities in the Persian Gulf became progressively more urgent. More ships were sent to Iranian and Iraqi ports than they could handle, resulting in congestion and waste of shipping.

When the convoys were suspended completely in July 1942, the president proposed, and Churchill accepted, the proposition that the Americans should take over and operate the Trans-Iranian Railway in the British zone. In the end they took over a great deal more. Under the plan put into final form by the CCS in September, the Americans were assigned responsibility for operating the entire supply line to the Soviet zone, including rail, ports, and trucklines. The United States created a special command—the Persian Gulf Command—to carry out the task and eventually deployed about 30,000 service troops to the area. The Americans undertook the task reluctantly, for it promised diversion both of materials and service troops from operations elsewhere. Indeed, it accentuated the scattering of resources that the decision to invade North Africa had engendered. Given the priorities that had to be assigned to Soviet aid, the effort that followed was an intensive one. Yet there were initial shortages of service troops, of shipping, and of heavy construction equipment, and while Persian Gulf capacities increased monthly, it was not until a year later that the southern route was able to compensate fully for the failure of the northern.[24]

Though all the alternatives carried promise, none was, in the fall of 1942, ready to carry the immediate load. Deliveries under the Second Protocol were only half those promised at the end of the year. By January 1943, nonetheless, when the British and American leaders assembled for a grand conference at Casablanca, the situation looked somewhat brighter. After their victory at Stalingrad, the Soviets showed less urgent need for tanks, guns, and other ground munitions, and placed higher priorities on foodstuffs, petroleum, planes, trucks, and signal equipment. Since the petroleum and foodstuffs could be shipped via the Pacific route, the transfer of ships to the Soviet flag was accelerated, promising increased capacity on that route. In December 1942, also, the British were once again able to resume convoys on the northern route. At the same time General Brehon B. Somervell, commander of the American Services of Supply, optimistically predicted that the Persian Gulf would soon reach peak operations.

Since the cross-Channel operation had been, by the time of Casablanca, almost certainly postponed until 1944 and further operations in the Mediterranean accepted as the main Anglo-American effort in the war against Germany in 1943, the urgency of aid to the Soviet Union was now recognized by the military leaders as well as the president and prime minister. As Admiral King put it, it was not a question of placating Stalin but of "implementing the Russians to our own interest." After examining the problem, the CCS agreed that, under a priority second only to the antisubmarine campaign, shipments for Soviet Aid could be brought up to schedule, not by the end of June 1943, but by the end of the year, assuming Third Protocol commitments were to be at the same rate as the second.[25]

For the first six months of 1943, these plans again proved too optimistic. The northern convoys had to be suspended again in April to allow preparations for the invasion of Sicily and were not resumed until October. The development of the Persian Gulf fell behind General Somervell's optimistic predictions and failed to reach peak operation until August 1943. Up to the end of the Second Protocol period, only the shipments in the Pacific (these had not been originally calculated as part of the commitment) exceeded expectations. The deficit at the end of June 1943 was nearly a million long tons, or about 25 percent of scheduled quantities.[26]

Yet it was the steps taken during this period of adversity that laid the groundwork for a swelling flow of supplies to the Soviet Union in the last two years of the war, a flow that produced surpluses on the last two protocols greater than the shortfalls on the first two. By August 1943 the Persian Gulf was in position to handle well over 200,000 tons per month, and the transfer of vessels to the Soviet flag in the Pacific had created a fleet capable of transporting an even greater tonnage to Vladivostok. The Alaska-Siberia ferry by the fall of 1943 was also carrying the major portion of the aircraft. With the northern route also operating intermittently, the Allies were able to exceed a Third Protocol commitment for 5.1 million tons (2.4 million via the Atlantic and 2.7 million via the Pacific) by some 25 percent. Delivery of aircraft was also maintained at protocol rates.[27]

The cost of developing and maintaining these routes of delivery to the war effort of the western allies was substantial—in service troops and shipping as well as in the supplies shipped. The JCS were undoubtedly right in their assessment in 1942 that Soviet aid could not be maintained at the agreed level if the cross-Channel invasion was to be mounted in 1942 or 1943. The operations undertaken in those years in the Mediterranean and the Pacific absorbed fewer marginal resources, such as shipping and certain types of equipment, and the lesser scale of commitment made it possible to divert service troops, who were an essential part of the buildup in the British Isles, to the Persian Gulf Command. Ironically, the failure to mount the second front in 1942 and 1943, of which the Russians complained so bitterly, made possible the swelling flow of supplies to the Soviet Union in the last years of the war.

By mid-1944, however, the economy of scarcity was ended on the side of the western allies by the vast expansion in American production of both material and the ships to transport it, and by the victory over the German submarines that had bec⌐ effected by May 1943. Thus, in the last year of the war, the western allies were able to mount the large-scale offensive in Europe that had waited so long, to keep offensives against the Japanese going at almost the same rate, and simultaneously provide aid to the Soviet Union in unprecedented volume. For the Fourth Protocol (1944–45) the Anglo-American shipping commitment totaled 5.7 million tons with a promise of more if possible, in addition to the aircraft—2,450 pursuit planes and 300 medium bombers—most of which would be flight delivered. The promises were more than fulfilled. By the end of the war in Europe (8 May 1945), nearly two months before the expiration of the protocol period, American aid had already surpassed the shipping commitment.[28] This accomplishment was facilitated by the opening of a new shipping route to Odessa on the Black Sea, once the Russians had regained control of its northern shores in September 1944. This new route offered large economies in shipping as well as in the use of Soviet rail transport, and by May 1945 it had largely supplanted the Persian Gulf as a route of delivery to the USSR.

As of mid-1943 any imminent danger of Soviet collapse had passed and the Red Army had assumed the offensive all along the Eastern Front. Despite this great change in its fortunes, the Soviet Union continued to press the United States for aid on the largest possible scale. American leaders were still compelled to view the continuing contribution of the Red Army in the war against Germany as an indispensable condition to the success of the Anglo-American assault from the west. Moreover, they expected the USSR to enter the war against Japan at a propitious moment after the defeat of Germany and play an important role in the defeat of the Asiatic member of the Axis. Having accepted, very early in the war, these premises as to the essentiality of the Soviet contribution to victory both in Europe and

Asia, there was little tendency to use the USSR's needs for supplies as a bargaining lever. During the first two years after the German attack in 1941, the urgency of Soviet needs had been so great, the threat of Soviet collapse so imminent and foreboding for the Allied cause, that almost any effort or sacrifice seemed justified in order to deliver supplies. This sense of urgency died hard, in spite of changed circumstances. The philosophy was perhaps best expressed in President Roosevelt's directive for the formulation of a fourth protocol on 14 February 1944: "Russia continues to be a major factor in achieving the defeat of Germany. We must therefore continue to support the USSR by providing the maximum amount of supplies that can be delivered to her ports. This is a matter of paramount importance."[29]

Beginning late in 1943, Averell Harriman, who became ambassador to the Soviet Union in October, and Major General John R. Deane, who went to Moscow at approximately the same time to head a military mission, made some efforts to modify the "unconditional aid" policy.[30] Deane, with Harriman's support, recommended that before items in critical supply were allocated to the USSR, his mission should be required to obtain information and make recommendations that would indicate the urgency of the Soviet need. Deane and Harriman wanted not only to give the military mission more leverage in dealing with the Russians but to institute a more critical review of Russian requirements. This sort of critical review was an established part of lend-lease procedure for other countries, and in 1943 and 1944 the Americans considerably tightened the reins on the British in this respect, moving distinctly away from the "common pool" concept that Roosevelt and Churchill had announced right after Pearl Harbor to a reassertion of American national interest in the administration of lend-lease.[31]

The JCS agreed that a more critical approach to Soviet aid was required, but the Protocol Committee rejected the Harriman-Deane proposals, arguing that shipping limitations still kept Soviet shipments within the bounds of necessity and that a more critical policy might be taken by the Soviets as an affront.

Roosevelt acquiesced, and though Deane and Harriman continued to push for some version of their proposal for advance screening by the military mission, they were unsuccessful. In December 1944 Deane expressed his disgust in a letter to General Marshall: "The situation has changed but our policy has not. We still meet their requests to the limit of our ability, and they meet ours to the limit that will keep us sweet."[32]

One of the reasons for this reluctance, as victory in Europe neared, was what was conceived of as a great need for Soviet assistance in the war against Japan. At the Tehran Conference in December 1943 Stalin clearly indicated that the western allies could count on the USSR entering the war against Japan after the defeat of Germany. American military planners, if they did not consider Soviet entry as essential to victory over Japan, did believe it highly desirable. The Americans hoped to use Siberian bases in the strategic bombing of Japan and thought the Soviet Siberian Army could effectively prevent the movement of the Japanese Kwangtung Army from Manchuria to the home islands to oppose an American assault.[33]

One of the purposes of the Deane Mission was to conduct planning, in collaboration with the Russians, for the Siberian air bases and other joint projects that would be necessary to these ends. On none of the major issues of collaboration did Deane make any real progress with the Russians, who seemed mistrustful and suspicious of any American effort to use bases on Soviet territory. Only on the matter of obtaining supplies for a buildup to support their Siberian Army did they show any enthusiasm.[34]

In conferences between British and Soviet officials in Moscow in October 1944, Stalin agreed definitely that the "Soviet Union would take the offensive against Japan three months after Germany's defeat provided the United States would assist in building up necessary reserve supplies and provided the political aspects of Russia's participation had been clarified."[35] The Soviet government presented a list of civilian and semi-military supplies that they wished delivered via the Pacific route before 30 June 1945. The list included transport aircraft, food, trucks, petroleum, and rail equipment, among other things, and amounted to 860,410 short tons of dry cargo and 206,000 tons of liquid petroleum products.[36] This formidable list of requirements arrived in Washington at a time when the American war machine, for all its expansion, was undergoing considerable strain pursuing major offensives in both Europe and the Pacific. With shipping tied up on both fronts for lack of adequate port capacity, another major shipping crisis, reminiscent of the dark days of 1942, had arisen. The president once again insisted the Soviet requirement must be met, and the War Shipping Administration, in a highly critical situation, forced the military services to accept cutbacks to relieve port congestion, and found some thirty-seven ships to transfer to the Soviet flag in the Pacific. Under similar pressure the executive departments managed to find the supplies for the project, designated MILEPOST, perhaps an indication, in the case of the War and Navy departments, of the importance they attached to Soviet entry into the war against Japan. MILEPOST shipments were not far behind schedule when the war in Europe ended. This achievement involved no real sacrifice of regular Fourth Protocol shipments.[37]

On 5 January 1945, President Roosevelt issued the last of his directives on Soviet aid, directing the formulation of a Fifth Protocol covering the period 1 July 1945 to 30 June 1946. He emphasized the importance of aid to the USSR in almost precisely the same terms as a year earlier. Although the reason given continued to be the "defeat of Germany," even the most pessimistic of prophets at the time hardly expected the war in Europe to continue until mid-1946.[38] The inference could clearly be drawn then that Roosevelt intended that aid continue uninterrupted after V-E Day, despite the fact that the USSR would not then be at war with Japan. He died on 12 April 1945, without having clarified his policy further.

Meanwhile, Congress had shown an unmistakable temper to curb the President's flexibility in dealing with lend-lease in its debates over the extension of the Lend-Lease Act in March and early April 1945. In the end it wrote into the extension a positive prohibition against the use of lend-lease for "post-war relief, post-war rehabilitation, and post-war reconstruction."[39]

Plans drawn up within the military departments, responsive to the congressional mood, provided for restricting lend-lease to needs for the war against Japan, once the war in Europe was over. The new president, Harry Truman, participated as a senator in the formulation of this policy and was well aware of the intent of Congress.

The congressional restrictions, together with a growing disillusionment on the part of many Americans toward Soviet behavior, combined to lead to an abrupt change of policy on Soviet aid once the war in Europe was over. Deane and Harriman again took the lead, but this time they found powerful allies in Leo Crowley, head of the Foreign Economic Administration, and Acting Secretary of State Joseph Grew, as well as in military circles. Deane was most concerned because the Russians simply refused to enter into any collaborative planning for the war with Japan. He conducted studies that showed to his satisfaction that Russian cooperation was really not so necessary to the victory over Japan as Americans had thought. At his instigation the JCS agreed to withdraw from participation in all such projects as the Siberian air bases and to await Soviet initiatives to renew it. Harriman supported Deane in this position but his real purpose was to go further and use lend-lease policy as a lever to promote Soviet concessions in Eastern Europe.[40]

In any case, on 11 May 1945, Grew and Crowley persuaded President Truman to agree to a new policy on lend-lease to the Soviet Union, now that the war in Europe was over. So long as it was anticipated that the USSR would enter the war against Japan, deliveries under the MILEPOST program would continue, as well as shipments to complete industrial plants for which some components had already been sent; however, other supplies on hand and on order for the Fourth Protocol were to be delivered only when they were required to support military operations against Japan. "Other lend-lease supplies now programmed for the USSR should be cut off immediately as far as physically practicable, and such goods and the shipping tonnage should be diverted to approved supply programs for western Europe." There would be no Fifth Protocol. Future supply programs for the USSR would be designed to meet new military situations as they arose "on the basis of reasonably adequate information regarding the essentiality of Soviet military supply requirements and in the light of all competing demands for supplies in the changing military situation."[41]

Thus came to an end, quite abruptly, the policy of unconditional aid. The Deane-Harriman proposals for screening were now placed into effect with a vengeance. The policy was at first applied so rigidly that even ships at sea bound for European Russia were ordered turned around. This order was lifted within a few days on protests from the Soviet representatives in Washington, from the War Department which objected to the attendant confusion, and Harriman, who said he had not intended quite so stringent a restriction. When the dust had finally settled the policy was fairly simply defined as permitting all scheduled shipments via the Pacific route to proceed while stopping all further Atlantic sailings.[42]

Under this policy, owing to the large Pacific shipping program in May 1945, shipments for that month totaled 768,400 long tons, the most ever shipped to the Soviet Union in a single month. This situation did not endure long. Shipments in June and July fell to half the May level. By August there remained little cargo under approved programs to ship, for Deane in Moscow found it almost impossible to secure from Soviet officials the detailed justification required by the new policy. At the Potsdam Conference in July, Admiral King indicated his intention to push convoys through to the Amur River ports once the Soviet Union was at war with Japan. Deane from Moscow on 8 August cabled that in proposing convoys the United States seemed to be "taking the initiative in setting up the means to deliver a supply program which under present policy we intend largely to curtail."[43]

The dilemma never had to be resolved. On 8 August 1945 the first atomic bomb fell on Hiroshima, and on 14 August the Japanese government made known its desire to surrender. With what appears to have been unseemly haste, President Truman on 17 August promulgated a new policy cutting off all lend-lease aid to the Soviet Union effective on the formal Japanese surrender (V-J Day). Only ships at sea and those already loaded would be allowed to proceed. Actually the loading of ships had come to an end some days earlier.[44]

The end of the Soviet aid program, announced five days before the general proclamation of the end of lend-lease, came as a climax to the shift in American policy on supplying the USSR that started belatedly with the end of the war in Europe. It was one of the many harbingers of a new period in Soviet-American relations.

The repercussions of this last phase of lend-lease policy toward the Soviet Union go beyond the scope of this essay and have been dealt with by historians of the origins of the Cold War.[45] The focus here is rather with the part that American aid to the Soviet Union played in the Allied war effort against Germany. The total aid furnished amounted to seventeen and one-half million tons of supplies of which one million tons were lost at sea. It was valued at approximately eleven billion dollars. About four million tons moved over the northern route, another four million over the southern route, about eight hundred thousand via the Black Sea, and eight and one-half million tons via the Pacific routes including shipments to the Arctic ports. The materials included five million tons of food-stuffs, over one hundred million yards of cotton cloth, sixty million yards of woolen cloth, two and one-half million tons of steel, 782 thousand tons of nonferrous metals, and nearly three million tons of petroleum. These were all bulk, civilian-type materials, a large portion of which were shipped to Vladivostok and thence over the Trans-Siberian Railway to European Russia. Finished materials included 14,000 planes, 362,000 trucks, 47,000 jeeps, 7,500 antiaircraft guns, 112,000 Thompson submachine guns, a million miles of field telephone wire, much radio equipment including some radar units, and 13,000 units of railway equipment.[46]

It is difficult to evaluate what these supplies meant to the Soviet Union, for in the atmosphere of the Cold War the Russians have consistently minimized their importance. Yet in an unguarded moment at Yalta early in 1945 Stalin charac-terized lend-lease as a "remarkable invention" without which victory would have been long delayed.[47] And Nikita Khrushchev in his memoirs paid particular tribute to the American trucks saying: "Just imagine how we could have advanced from Stalingrad to Berlin without them."[48] Robert H. Jones, writing in 1969, made an extensive analysis of the importance of lend-lease to the Soviet war machine, calculating for various categories how great a proportion of total Soviet supply American lend-lease provided. He concluded that American supplies were particularly vital in feeding and clothing the Red Army and in providing it with the mobility and communications that enabled it to advance so rapidly in its great offensives of 1943–45. In addition, steel, nonferrous metals, chemicals, explosives, and finished industrial equipment played a considerable role in making the achievements of Russian war production, which were admittedly great, possible. Railroad rolling stock contributed about one half of the total number of new locomotives and cars placed on the Soviet rails during the war, while the lend-lease trucks were the mainstay of the Soviet Army, giving credence to Khrushchev's reflection. The American contribution in trucks and communications equipment enabled Soviet industry to concentrate on production of tanks, guns, and planes, for which it was best suited. The Soviet Union did produce for itself by far the lion's share of these armaments, but American equipment sometimes furnished a vital margin of superiority. Thus, although the United States furnished only 10 percent of Soviet aircraft during the war, the American planes contributed much to Soviet air strength. And Jones concludes in the end that United States aid to the Soviet Union generally, by providing supplies in critical areas, "played a much more vital war role than it would appear from the cold statistics."[49]

Clearly, American aid did not provide any vital margin that enabled the Russians to survive the German onslaught in 1941 and 1942. U.S. planes, trucks, tanks, and field wire that had arrived by mid-1942 may have played some part in the victory at Stalingrad.[50] But the major contribution came after Stalingrad in providing the transportation and communications that enabled the Red Army to exploit breakthroughs and move so rapidly in its offensives. Stalin's random observation at Yalta indeed seems to sum up the matter adequately. The Soviet victory over the Germans could not have come so early nor indeed been so complete without American lend-lease aid. It is of some note, too, that Stalin in the 1941 negotiations, making a plea for more American trucks, predicted that the side with the best motor transport would win the war.[51]

It would be unfair to conclude with a note of Soviet in-gratitude for this American contribution without also noting what perhaps was the main reason for it. Anglo-American strategic policy in 1942 and 1943, consciously or uncon-sciously, substituted limited offensives in the Mediterranean and the Pacific combined with supply aid to the Soviet Union on the maximum scale possible for the high risks involved in mounting a cross-Channel assault at the earliest practicable moment. The invasion was only undertaken once the western Allies were reasonably assured of success at a much lesser cost in American and British lives than an earlier attempt, possibly unsuccessful, might have involved. The USSR was left to bear the major human cost of the war against Germany. The Soviets, by their own admission, lost about 20 million dead in the war, about 10 percent of their population in 1941. In contrast the United States and Great Britain suffered only about 400,000 deaths in the military services and merchant marine.[52]

Notes

[1] This percentage is based on the procurement statistics and lend-lease statistics for the War Department compiled after the war but never published. Copies of drafts may be found in the U.S. Army Center of Military History in Washington, D.C.

[2] On the agreements at ARCADIA, see Maurice Matloff and Edwin M. Snell, *Strategic Planning for Coalition Warfare* (Washington, D.C., 1953), pp. 99–102.

[3] Min, 56th Meeting, JCS, 20 January 1943, in Casablanca Conference Book, copy in U.S. Army Center of Military History.

[4] For the official texts of the protocols, see U.S. Department of State, *Wartime International Agreements, Soviet Supply Protocols,* pub. 2759, European Ser. 22 (Washington, D.C., n.d.).

[5] On the arrangements for munitions assignment during World War II, see Richard M. Leighton and Robert W. Coakley, *Global Logistics and Strategy, 1940–43* (Washington, D.C., 1955), pp. 247–53, 560. On the relationship of Roosevelt and Hopkins see Robert S. Sherwood, *Roosevelt and Hopkins: An Intimate History* (New York, 1950).

[6] Leighton and Coakley, *Global Logistics, 1940–43,* pp. 34–36, 84–85, 97–98.

[7] Roosevelt to Stimson, 31 August 1941, U.S. Department of State, *Foreign Relations of the United States: 1941* (Washington, D.C., 1958) I, 826–27.

[8] Minutes of the London Conference are in Defense Aid Division, War Department file under that name, RG 160, Modern Military Records, National Archives (NA); Sherwood, *Roosevelt and Hopkins,* pp. 387–93. For the complete record of the politics of the decision, see Raymond Dawson, *The Decision to Aid Russia, 1941: Foreign Policy and Domestic Politics* (Chapel Hill, N.C., 1959).

[9] Leighton and Coakley, *Global Logistics, 1940–43,* pp. 99–103; Mark S. Watson, *Chief of Staff: Prewar Plans and Preparations* (Washington, D.C., 1950), pp. 360–66.

[10] President to Department and Agency Heads, 28 December 1941, *Foreign Relations,* 1941, I, 865.

[11] Leighton and Coakley, *Global Logistics, 1940–43,* pp. 555–57.

[12] Department of State, *Soviet Supply Protocols,* pp. 1–12.

[13] Sherwood, *Roosevelt and Hopkins,* p. 465.

[14] Roosevelt to Adm. Land, 17 March 1942, War Department, Army Service Forces files, International Division file USSR Mis 319.1, RG 160, NA.

[15] Msg, Hopkins to Harriman and Faymonville, 18 March 1942, MS Index to Hopkins Papers, U.S. Army Center of Military History.

[16] Winston S. Churchill, *The Hinge of Fate* (Boston, 1950), pp. 256–66; Leighton and Coakley, *Global Logistics*, pp. 556–57.

[17] Matloff and Snell, *Strategic Planning*, pp. 175–91.

[18] Memo, Adm King for JCS, 1 May 1942; Mins JCS mtgs of 4, 11, and 18 May 1942, JCS Records, Record Group 218, Modern Military Records, NA.

[19] President to Sec War, 24 March 1942, War Department AG 400.3295 (8-14-41) Sec. 1. RG 407, Modern Military Records, NA; Memo, Gen James A. Burns for JCS, 12 May 1942 in Operations Division of War Department General Staff files ABC 400.3295 Russia (4-19-42) Sec. 1, RG 319, NA.

[20] Sherwood, *Roosevelt and Hopkins*, pp. 570–75; Minutes of Meeting of Joint Planning Staff, 10 June 1942, JCS Records, NA; Department of State, *Soviet Supply Protocols*.

[21] Churchill, *Hinge of Fate*, pp. 267–75.

[22] Ibid., pp. 575–82; Msg, Prime Minister to President, 22 September 1942, in ABC 381 (7-25-42), 4B; Sherwood, *Roosevelt and Hopkins*, pp. 638–41; Roosevelt memo to Department and Agency Heads, 2 October 1942, in Roosevelt Manuscripts, Hyde Park.

[23] Matloff and Snell, *Strategic Planning*, pp. 349–56.

[24] On the Persian Gulf Command, see T. H. Vail Motter, *The Persian Corridor and Aid to Russia* (Washington, D.C., 1952).

[25] CCS 170/2, 23 January 1943, Final Report to President and Prime Minister, Casablanca Conference book; Mins JCS 56th Mtg, 20 January 1943, Casablanca Conference book.

[26] Figures are taken from U.S. Department of State, *Report on War Aid Furnished by the United States to the USSR*, 28 November 1945 (Washington, D.C., 1945).

[27] Ibid.

[28] Ibid; *Soviet Supply Protocols*.

[29] Memo, President for Sec War, 14 February 1944, in International Division, ASF file 031.1, VII, NA.

[30] This is the term used in George C. Herring, Jr.'s excellent study *Aid to Russia 1941–1946: Strategy, Diplomacy, and the Origins of the Cold War* (New York, 1973).

[31] On the common pool concept and its decline, see R. W. Coakley and R. M. Leighton, *Global Logistics and Strategy, 1943–1945* (Washington, D.C., 1968), pp. 627–70. On the Deane-Harriman proposals see John R. Deane, *The Strange Alliance: The Story of Our Efforts at Wartime Cooperation with Russia* (New York, 1947), pp. 96–98. For a full account see Herring, *Aid to Russia*, pp. 121–44.

[32] Dean, *Strange Alliance*, p. 84.

[33] For a detailed treatment of the military views on this subject, see Department of Defense Release, 19 October 1955, *The Entry of the Soviet Union into the War against Japan: Military Plans, 1941–45.*

[34] See Dean, *Strange Alliance*, pp. 226–47.

[35] Ibid., p. 247.

[36] JCS 1138, 26 October 44, Report by Jt Logistics Committee, "Supplies and Equipment Requested by USSR," JCS Records, NA.

[37] Coakley and Leighton, *Global Logistics, 1943–45*, pp. 551–60, 690–93.

[38] U.S. Department of State, *Foreign Relations of the United States: 1945* (Washington, D.C., 1967), V, 944.

[39] For the Congressional background see Herring, *Aid to Russia*, pp. 187–92.

[40] Deane, *Strange Alliance*, pp. 249–66; Herring, *Aid to Russia*, pp. 195–201; JCS 1313, 16 April 1945, "Revision of Policy with Relation to Russia," JCS Records, NA.

[41] Memo, Truman for Grew and Crowley, 11 May 1945, OPD files ABC 400.3295 Russia (19 April 42), Sec 3, NA.

[42] Coakley and Leighton, *Global Logistics, 1943–45*, pp. 695–96; Herring, *Aid to Russia*, pp. 203–7.

[43] Joint Logistics Committee Paper, JLC 304/2/D, 11 August 1945, "Policy on Military Lend-Lease to USSR," JCS Records, NA.

[44] JCS 1325/9, 24 August 1945, "Policy on Military Lend-Lease to USSR," JCS Records, NA.

[45] Herring, *Aid to Russia*, pp. 238–75, is a balanced assessment of the part the change in American policy on lend-lease played in the origins of the Cold War.

[46] Figures taken from State Department, *Report on War Aid*.

[47] *Foreign Relations, Diplomatic Papers, The Conferences at Malta and Yalta* (Washington, D.C., 1945), p. 68.

[48] "Khrushchev Remembers," part 2, *Life*, 4 December 1970, p. 68.

[49] Robert H. Jones, *The Roads to Russia: United States Lend-Lease to the Soviet Union* (Norman, Okla., 1969), pp. 215–39.

[50] Ibid., pp. 232–33.

[51] Sherwood, *Roosevelt and Hopkins*, p. 390.

[52] The Russians did not admit to the 20 million deaths until the 1970s, by which time a whole new generation of young men had grown up to replace these heavy manpower losses. Initial statements of Russian casualties, carried in most standard sources such as the World Almanac, placed Soviet military dead at around seven million. The first indication of a figure as large as 20 million came in studies made in the West on the basis of a comparison of the USSR census data for 1939 and 1959. There still is, however, no detailed statement available from Soviet sources on the casualties of World War II. The American and British figures are based on official compilations. The American ones include both battle and nonbattle casualties.

IX

The Reopening of Heidelberg University, 1945–1946: Major Earl L. Crum and the Ambiguities of American Postwar Policy

JAMES A. MUMPER

WHEN THE MEN of the U.S. Seventh Army crossed the Rhine in the spring of 1945, they found romantic Heidelberg directly in their path, and they took that lovely city, with a minimum of damage, 30 March through 1 April. The military government closed Ruperto-Carola (Ruprecht-Karls-Universität: "Heidelberg University"), and its faculty, staff, and student body faced careful screening, American style—the process known as denazification. Nine months would pass before Heidelberg reopened all her doors, one of the last universities to do so in all of the four zones of occupation. Heidelberg, like her sisters in the American zone, became a test case for the ambiguous and vacillating American policy of "reeducation," a controversial program obstinately pursued long after the British and French had adopted more prudent measures.

No single American agency assumed responsibility for education policy in April 1945. The State Department, the obvious center for such planning, had forged from 1943 until June 1945 a reconstruction policy with the guiding principle that "the reconstruction of the cultural life of Germany must be in large measure the work of the Germans themselves."[1] By

September 1944 the punitive Morgenthau Plan to agrarianize
Germany had President Roosevelt's support. The State Department, therefore, was compelled to put its own more enlightened policy under wraps and keep it there. Beyond this, the
War Department, with problems of its own in 1945, and with
painful memories of civilian interference in North Africa and in
the postbellum American South, obstructed attempts to give
education a high priority within the military. General Lucius D.
Clay, the U.S. military governor, remembered well the car-
petbaggers who had infested the South after the Civil War, and
he had no intention of presiding over a similar bureaucracy in
Germany.[2] Education policy, therefore, fell between two
stools.

For men of good will, whether German or American, the
reopening of Heidelberg became excruciating. Three of the
leaders who successfully endured that complex ordeal were the
renowned philosopher Dr. Karl Jaspers, the distinguished
surgeon Dr. Karl-Heinrich Bauer, and an American classicist,
Major Earl L. Crum. It will be this author's purpose to demonstrate how Major Crum became the American partner—
humane, perceptive, and courageous—for whom Jaspers and
Bauer had waited impatiently.[3] Jaspers is well known in academic circles, Bauer less so, though his story has been partially
told in a festschrift by the Heidelberg historian Fritz Ernst,
honoring Bauer on his seventieth birthday, September 26,
1960.[4]

Among those in Heidelberg who would get to know him
best, Major Crum would leave a lasting impression:

> He led our university with confidence from an autumn of
> despair into a springtime of hope. He could never have
> done that if he had not been a man who pursued humane
> values even in his official capacity and amidst the network
> of official regulations. When he had ascertained that his
> German partners in Heidelberg harbored no devious
> plans, he forged an abiding trust and became our friend,
> one of our own. He did not bestow his friendship lightly,
> but once he had done so, he was the truest of friends. No

suspicion, no political strife could dislodge him. Gruff masculinity and delicate sensitivity were combined in his nature. His eyes often said more than his infrequent words.[5]

Earl Le Verne Crum, born 13 May 1891, in Athens, Pennsylvania, studied at St. John's College, at the University of Maryland, and at Johns Hopkins, where he pursued a major in classical philology. During World War I he served in France as a chaplain. In 1924 he received a Ph.D. from New York University, where he began his teaching career. He then taught at the State University of Iowa, and from 1929 until his retirement in 1956 he was Professor of Greek and Latin at Lehigh University in Bethlehem, Pennsylvania, where he served as chairman of his department. In 1956 Dr. and Mrs. Crum settled in a prerevolutionary house called Villa Avita in Mrs. Crum's hometown of Greenville, Virginia. Until his death on 29 July 1961 Dr. Crum taught at nearby Washington and Lee University. At one point he served as president of the Classical Association of the Atlantic States and later as a vice-president of the Archaeological Institute of America.

Dr. Crum reentered the U.S. Army in July 1943. He was selected for special grooming in the Civil Affairs Training School at the University of Pittsburgh for duty in occupied Germany. In January 1944 the Army sent Crum to England to do historical research for the Supreme Headquarters, Allied Expeditionary Forces (SHAEF). In October 1944 he was attached to the 12th Army Group as an Education and Religious Affairs Officer (E & RA, Detachment E-1) for U.S. Forces European Theater (USFET) at Verdun, Wiesbaden, and then Frankfurt. On 10 October 1945 Major Crum received long-expected orders to become the "Officer in Charge of Heidelberg."[6] Major Crum brought with him to Heidelberg values particularly appropriate for the job at hand. Steeped in the classical tradition, he evinced an abiding devotion to humanitas in both the Socratic and the Ciceronian senses. Indeed, humanitas was the lamp unto his feet. He put it this way at a *dies academicus,* Heidelberg, June 1949: "As a participant in two wars I was determined to come to Heidelberg prepared for common endeavor, in the hope that my actions would be consistent with the best practices of *humanitas*."[7]

Major Crum held humane and ecumenical religious convictions: "Each person is his own philosopher. Whether or not he ever puts his vision down on paper, his actions and his perception of the world around him will be influenced by the all-pervasive nature of his own individuality—his *ingenium*. Perhaps it is like the inner voice which spoke to Socrates."[8] His dedication to academic freedom was uncompromising. As he later promised both faculty and students at Heidelberg in December 1945: "As I see it there is no university in the proper sense of the term without academic freedom, and, so far as I am concerned, you shall have it."[9] He had long been an admirer of German scientific method as exemplified by Ranke and the neohumanism of Wilhelm von Humboldt, "that noble dream," in Charles Beard's words. Fritz Ernst, Crum's longtime friend, wrote in 1960 that "as a classical philologist he completely understood the university of the Humboldt stamp and he came, therefore, with the intention to do everything in his power to reopen Ruperto-Carola."[10] However, the nineteenth-century reforms of Humboldt that had been fashioned for a gifted minority would not sit well with American occupation authorities.

Any consideration of Major Crum's first principles must include his convictions regarding the duties of his own Detachment for Education and Religion (Det. E-1). These he expressed in a speech delivered to fellow officers at Verdun, 27 January 1945, in which he described the special character of the German university before its perversion by National Socialism. He emphasized the unhampered search for scientific truth and the self-government through an elected rector and Senate.[11] He then compared this earlier ideal, so influential in the development of many distinguished American universities, with the Nazi-era university: the arbitrary exclusion of Jews, the purging of libraries, the dismissal of anti-Nazi faculty, the banning of fraternities, and the attempted political indoctrination of students and faculty alike.

Crum's address evoked a natural question: "What exactly *is*

Det. E-1's responsibility in post-war Germany?" Although functioning in a policy vacuum and compelled to act against its own best judgment, a SHAEF meeting in early January 1945 had prepared a revised handbook paying lip service to the Morgenthau views, but opening the door to the more long-range and comprehensive progams envisaged by the State Department. There would be three prerequisites for the re-opening of any German school or university: buildings, screened teachers (black, gray, and white categories—"rejected, conditionally accepted, and unconditionally accepted") and textbooks. Crum pointed out that German universities had never used the textbook method. This illuminated his point that no directive, however well-intentioned, could be sufficient for specific problems in specific places. "It would seem to me," he remarked, "that this level [Det. E-1] is the place where we ought to have control . . . we might make some plans [regarding] what we are going to do *in so far as the directives permit us* . . . [my italics]."[12]

Fifteen years later Fritz Ernst would note that "Crum always represented America's interests, but it was our good fortune that he saw those interests best assured through giving the university entrusted to him the opportunity to demonstrate the value of its former constitution—in both old and new guises."[13] That conservative German educators throughout all three western zones would adamantly resist the imposition of "foreign" systems is a matter Ernst finessed or simply forgot.

Crum had had a love affair with Heidelberg for years. Like many Americans, he had long regarded Heidelberg, with its forty-seven institutes, as "one of the most famous universities in the world. . . . For Americans like me there is, something romantic about Heidelberg. . . . When I arrived in Europe in 1943 I would have found it unthinkable that some day I should be called upon to serve the famous University of Heidelberg."[14]

For Major Crum the problem of identifying his exact role in Heidelberg, "in so far as the directives permit," was not a simple matter. He knew that whatever he did as "Officer in Charge of Heidelberg University" would be subject to JCS 1067, the Joint Chiefs of Staff (JCS) directive for the Office of Military

Government United States (OMGUS), not revealed as official policy until June 1945 and not revised until July 1947, one year after Crum's departure.

General Clay; Robert Murphy, Clay's political advisor; Lewis Douglas, Clay's financial advisor; and William Draper, Clay's economic advisor—had studied JCS 1067 shortly before V-E Day and had concluded that it made little sense.[15] Clay later wrote that he and Douglas were "shocked," but they were in no position to say so openly.[16] The policy reflected in JCS 1067 had been drafted by a civilian State Department under much pressure from devotees of the draconian Morgenthau plan, and the War Department was ordered to implement it.

The first problem created for the latter was that JCS 1067's stated goals seemed incompatible: denazification, demilitarization and trust-busting on the one hand, and democratization on the other. Robert Murphy quoted Douglas as saying that the proposal to turn Germany into a pastoral region had been "assembled by economic idiots" who would "forbid the most skilled workers in Europe from producing as much as they can for a continent which is desperately short of everything."[17] But there were further consequences: the denazification of German governments, the media, and the schools had the highest priority. Yet the definition of a "Nazi" would change three times during Crum's eight-month tenure. How this throttled enlightened efforts to revive the democratic spirit comprises the essence of Major Crum's story.

A second problem for OMGUS proved inevitable in light of the first: conflicting jurisdictions, whereby the right hand neither understood nor wished to understand what the left hand was doing. The upshot was publicly sensational confrontations between one agency of the military government and another, confrontations that embarrassed both parties and raised serious doubts in the minds of perceptive Germans regarding the competence and sophistication of their American masters. The most notorious example would emerge in Bavaria in 1947.[18] Even as late as October 1945, when Major Crum became, ostensibly, "Officer in Charge of Heidelberg University," the most exasperating question in the minds of all concerned was this: Who's running things in Heidelberg? Major Powhida, the military governor for the municipal area? Colonel William Dawson in Mannheim? The Special Branch, generally responsible for denazification? The Counter Intelligence Corps (CIC), rescreening Germans "unconditionally accepted" earlier by both the Special Branch and the CIC? The "Officer in Charge of Heidelberg University? For Major Crum this was an awkward situation indeed, and it would lead very shortly to a crisis of major proportions.

Beyond the problems already mentioned (a policy vacuum, incompatible goals, and conflicting jurisdictions), Major Crum's assessment of his own special task was clouded by the knowledge that the Education and Religious Affairs Detachment had little prestige within the military. As he had told his superior in March 1945, "In the early days of planning, curiously enough, education was not mentioned without a near-laugh, and religion was an unmentionable."[19] The "early days" to which Crum referred were those of the spring of 1944 when an education subdivision was established in the Anglo-American German Country Unit. A modest affair, indeed, the education subdivision never enjoyed the recognition that Legal, Finance, or Economic Affairs received. When the German Country Unit was dissolved in October 1944, most of the American personnel, including Crum, were transferred to a small subordinate subdivision (Det. E-1) of the newly created 12th Army Group, Control Council for Germany. While generals or full colonels usually commanded the various functional subdivisions, Det. E-1 had only captains and majors on its staff. This discrimination persisted. After V-E Day, when hordes of generals and full colonels, finding themselves surplus equipment, sought reassignment in G-5, (Civil Affairs, Military Government) few were attracted to Det. E-1, since its status seemed beneath their dignity.[20] Under circumstances such as these, Major Crum's authority was certain to be limited.

Professor Doctor of Surgery Karl-Heinrich Bauer, chosen by his "accepted" colleagues as rector of Ruperto-Carola in August 1945, was thirty-two years old in 1922–23 when he wrote

Racial Hygiene: Its Biological Foundations. Published in 1925, it received excellent reviews in the democratic press. When the Nazis came to power they banned it, apparently because it delivered less than the title implied: a rationale for Nazi *Rassenwahn*. In spite of its curious title (why not *Eugenics?*) and allegations to this very day that it was racist, Bauer's book was the only work of the Weimar era which attacked such notions as "Aryan supremacy" and "the Master race," calling them "illusionary" and "Utopian." Where intelligence was concerned, Bauer indicated that there was no significant difference between the average German and the average non-German. Beyond that, he concluded that the German people presented "a completely hopeless mixture of races."[21]

Though Bauer may well have capitalized on postwar Social Darwinism as his critics allege, and though some of his conclusions have been revised in the sixty years since the book was written, one thing should be clear: it was not, from the Nazi viewpoint, a handbook for later racial lunacy. The attention it commanded was one factor in Bauer's later appointment to the surgery clinic at Göttingen, where he served until April 1933. Then, before the Nazis consolidated their power, he was named chief surgeon at the University of Breslau. Because of his book and his part-Jewish wife he was subjected for ten years to constant harassment. Much evidence from the Breslau years confirms Karl Jaspers's judgment that Bauer was "an earnest fighter against Nazism"—though too Bismarckian for Jaspers's taste.[22] At Breslau, Bauer stubbornly refused to say, "Heil Hitler!"—using instead "Grüss Gott" or simply "Guten Morgen," which incensed his Nazi colleagues. They ostracized him, intrigued against him, and insulted Mrs. Bauer on every occasion. When the powerful gauleiter there ordered the elevation of an SA man to the rank of assistant, Bauer contrived to expel the candidate from the hospital. Threats from the SA led Bauer to prepare a secret escape route from his home. He twice secured the reappointment of a Jewish orthopedic surgeon whose son was already in a concentration camp, and, when the Jew was at last expelled for all time, Bauer sent him money and words of cheer while the orthopedist was underground.[23]

If Bauer was as audacious in Breslau as testimony alleges, how did he survive in that hostile environment? For one thing, he had powerful backing: two successive oberpräsidenten of Silesia resented the kind of interference exemplified by the gauleiter in what was, after all, a state institution. Both oberpräsidenten eventually found themselves in deep trouble with the party, however. Indeed, one of them, Dr. Lukaschek, was arrested for suspected complicity in the 20 July 1944 plot. Lukaschek later testified that Bauer saved his life.

Furthermore, Bauer had become one of Germany's most distinguished surgeons, and the Nazis needed his expertise. His six-volume series on surgery, in collaboration with Dr. Rudolf Stich, had become the standard work on the subject. He was also a masterful teacher eminently qualified to supply the Third Reich with the surgeons it so badly needed. By 1943 Allied technological superiority was becoming apparent, so Hitler softened his policy toward men of science, allowing them more freedom to pursue their work less hampered by party supervision.[24]

In the Bundesrepublik Bauer would enhance his preeminence; in 1952 he became the president of the German Society for Surgeons, later was elected president of the Society of German Scientists and Physicians, and his six-volume textbook on surgery reached its fifteenth edition. In 1954 Bauer and Stich published the third edition of their *Mistakes and Dangers in Surgical Operations*. Bauer also published *The Cancer Problem,* a very personal subject, since he had undergone surgery for cancer in 1946.

Bauer was by no means a Jacksonian democrat; he was an elitist. He accepted democracy in 1945 for the very pragmatic reason that there *was* no viable alternative; but, like many other German academics, he had serious reservations. German democracy without "the best democrats," as he put it, seemed unthinkable, a view perfectly compatible with the tradition of Wilhelm von Humboldt and his two-track educational system. The "best," now that the nobility were discredited, were Germany's intelligentsia. Bauer was his own best example of such natural leadership, a brilliant man with an iron will and a superb command of realpolitik who could sway his colleagues, already so disposed, toward future rule by "the best democrats." Paradoxical, but true, this attitude was repeated again and again in the American Zone, to the vast consternation of the Military Government.[25] This, then, was the man whom a determined American CIC agent would bedevil throughout the winter and spring of 1945–46, just as he began his demanding work as rector of the newly opened university. This was the man whom a righteously indignant Major Crum would defend before the highest levels in a sensational confrontation.

On 4 April 1945, just six days or so after the arrival of American troops, plans for the reopening of the university began auspiciously. An impeccable ("unconditionally accepted") Committee of Thirteen, initiated by Emil Henk, a trusted resistance fighter, and selected by the highly respected Karl Jaspers, held its first authorized meeting, benevolently attended by two young CIC agents. The committee included at least five professors whom the Nazis had dismissed in 1937: Karl Jaspers himself; Gustav Radbruch, Reich minister of justice in the Weimar Republic; Otto Regenbogen, classicist; Walter Jellinek, legal expert; and Alfred Weber, a sociologist like his famous brother Max. The committee's chairman was the distinguished theologian Martin Dibelius, whose books on early Christianity had greatly enhanced biblical criticism. Eight of its members would later be deans, with two of them to become rectors: Karl-Heinrich Bauer and Fritz Ernst.

Besides its planning, the committee began (after the fashion of the *Federalist Papers*) to prepare a series of essays to enlighten the public regarding the reconstitution of Ruperto-Carola after twelve years of Nazi exploitation. These would be published in the OMGUS organ, the *Süddeutsche Mitteilungen,* until its cessation in September. Thereafter, the *Heidelberger Schriftenreihe* (Springer-Verlag) and the *Rhein-Neckar-Zeitung* provided outlets for university opinion.

Just as auspicious as the prompt recognition given to this blue-ribbon panel was the early arrival in Heidelberg of Dr. Edward Y. Hartshorne, Sidney B. Fay's son-in-law. "Ted"

Hartshorne was a sociologist, an admirer of Max Weber, and an expert on Germany. Since 1933 he had had numerous ties with German academics. He disagreed strongly with the spirit of the Morgenthau Plan and questioned the wisdom of JCS 1067. In September he would become the officer in charge of Marburg University.

Yet on the eve of Major Crum's arrival in mid-October 1945, the academic scene in Heidelberg was a shambles. The Committee of Thirteen, by then transformed into an impotent Senate, was exasperated and frustrated, attacked and humiliated as it was by American and German elements alike. Most ominous was the ill-will generated against the Military Government.[26] What, in heaven's name, had gone wrong?

The seat of the trouble lay in administrative rules. They kept coming down to Major Powhida, Heidelberg's military governor, to the special branch responsible for denazification, and to the CIC as the summer of 1945 unfolded. Both Powhida and his superior, Colonel Dawson, had regarded the early appointment of the Committee of Thirteen as an appropriate and permissible action. When JCS 1067 became official in June, it ostensibly required no more than the closing of all seats of higher learning until further steps were taken by the Control Council in Berlin. There was furthermore an implied promise in the general directive: "The Control Council should devise programs looking towards the reopening of secondary schools, universities and other institutions of higher learning." The CIC's endorsement of the Committee of Thirteen to make plans for the future seemed, therefore, quite in order.[27] Unfortunately, that appointment raised false hopes. Any election of a new rector or Senate, however "white" they may have been, or any adoption of the new constitution (meticulously drafted under Jaspers's supervision), was forbidden until the Control Council should "devise programs."

The programs were not long in coming. Beginning 29 June, after the recent adoption of the generally punitive JCS 1067, directives began to flow. They translated the overall policy directive into precise administrative orders. The first directive stressed denazification, restrictions on political activity, and the necessity for strict military control at all levels. Subsequent directives in October reflected Military Government Law No. 8, which stiffened denazification considerably, broadening rigid categories such as that for "mandatory arrest." "Mandatory arrest" precluded any possibility of an immediate hearing, even for men like the Heidelberg physician Schmidhuber, who had used his party membership again and again to protect, warn, and assist nonparty colleagues. These extenuating circumstances, urgently brought to Major Powhida's attention and to the CIC by the professors whom Schmidhuber had saved, carried no weight whatsoever under prevailing directives. Major Powhida had his orders; so did the CIC.[28]

At this point it cannot be overemphasized that the CIC was an agency completely beyond Powhida's or Dawson's control; originally the sponsor of the Committee of Thirteen, it would, under revised categories of Nazis and changes in personnel, undergo a startling metamorphosis, becoming the Inquisition of the denazification purge. And in Heidelberg one unforgettable CIC agent would become its Torquemada. Among the "unconditionally accepted" professors, especially within the Committee of Thirteen, the new categories of Nazis seemed simplistic and arbitrary. The patent injustice of the Schmidhuber case weighed heavily on their minds. The methods used by certain CIC agents, themselves under strict orders, were repugnant. Some professors would testify later that those methods reminded them of the Gestapo.

In the past few decades many Americans have begun to appreciate how difficult the maintenance of personal integrity can be within a totalitarian system and how necessary it sometimes is to don protective coloration if one is to survive. The heroic figures in the Soviet sphere who scorned to do so have been dealt with ruthlessly. So it was in the Third Reich. There was an active resistance movement, to be sure, small and courageous, but for most Germans there seemed no practical course at the time except "inner emigration," measuring every word, paying lip service to the orthodox political creed, joining the NS-affiliated professional organizations, and serving in the armed forces. *Die Tarnung* they called it, camouflage—

degrading, as many admitted later, but seemingly necessary at the time. Jaspers, whose beloved wife, Gertrud, was Jewish, later wrote: "We watched powerlessly, for twelve years, thoughtfully careful and cautious, heedful of the Gestapo and the Nazi authorities, determined to commit no act and to utter no word which we could not justify. Fortune was with us. I did not tempt it by any imprudence."[29] On the *Fragebogen* (questionnaire) that Fritz Ernst completed on 4 April 1945, he included this advice to the occupation authorities: "Trust the integrity of professors who have shown that they are worthy of this trust. Treat generously former Party members whose primary activities were those of academics."[30]

For the most part Bauer concealed his feeling that the doctrinaire categories set by directives showed little understanding of realities. But not always. He was greatly occupied throughout the summer with finding qualified professors to staff the Medical School when the right time should come, and, in so doing, he boldly brought back into medical practice some "gray" doctors whom he considered innocuous. Dr. Hartshorne and John Muccio, Murphy's assistant, saw trouble brewing here. When American policy stiffened in October, Bauer's "gray" appointees would be categorically removed and Bauer would be accused by the CIC of trying to nazify the university.[31] But he would not budge on the principle at stake. Perhaps there were too many Schmidhubers on his mind. As he put it on 20 February 1946, in a memorandum to Major Crum: "Obviously, someone who is forced to slog through a swamp for twelve long years will get dirt on himself in one way or another."[32]

The worst of the *Entnazifizierungswut* ("denazification madness," as some German observers put it) lay ahead. During the winter and spring of 1945–46 the program would be pursued with a vengeance. Even those "unconditionally accepted" earlier would be screened all over again.[33] Ernst, in the center of the storm, would remember gratefully the conversations which the Committee of Thirteen had in April and May of 1945 with men whom the professors only later discovered were representatives of the Office of Strategic Services.

Here were no humiliating innuendos, no bullying, but simply a desire to understand and to learn. Later interrogations "gave the impression that now, after twelve years of dictatorship in Germany, one was once again butting his head against a wall, this time against a wall of preconceptions, simplistic cliches and, often enough, a wall of less than good-will. . . . Above all, even where completely innocent interrogees were concerned, the interrogations were often harsh and humiliating."[34] Student graffiti in Munich read, "Lord, send us the Fifth Reich! The Fourth is as bad as the Third!"[35]

Not fully aware of the hardening process in the American camp, the Committee of Thirteen had proceeded with its plans. Under Jaspers's conscientious guidance it worked to make the new constitution congruent with American requirements, whatever the conservative professors preferred. It also became obvious that one of the first prerequisites for the reopening of the university would be the return of key buildings requisitioned by the occupation forces: the library, the enormous alte Kaserne on the Neckar, and the buildings of the new university confiscated to serve as headquarters of the Sixth Army Group (the American Seventh Army and the French First Army). Bauer tried persistently to get the military government to move. He had already convinced an American commission that a proposed requisition of the Heidelberg Clinic would have an adverse, even inhumane, effect upon the already crowded patients therein.[36] Though working overtime at the clinic, performing operations and supervising, Bauer played a key role in winning concessions, rather enjoying his adroitness in handling Americans. His trump cards, he slyly told Jaspers, were the words "humanity" and "Christian principles."[37] On 25 June 1945 he wrote a most persuasive letter to Col. Charles Winning, OMGUS, Mannheim, requesting the return of the library and the early reopening of Heidelberg in all of its faculties.[38]

OMGUS met Bauer part way. On 1 August, Major General M. C. Stayer, chief of the Health and Welfare Division, Berlin, informed Det. E-1, Mannheim, that certain premed and refresher medical courses might be resumed at Heidelberg, and on 15 August a purged Medical School was ceremoniously reopened. Though denazification had been haphazard, in John Muccio's opinion, fifty professors or instructors had been evicted.[39] Meanwhile, Bauer prepared articles on the "new spirit" at Heidelberg, and on 26 August he wrote again to Mannheim strongly urging the reopening of all the other schools. He indicated that three-fourths of the accepted personnel were already at work in odd jobs at the clinic, but his major emphasis was upon the wretched physical and spiritual condition of the students waiting in vain for their classes to begin.[40] On 30 September he sought help from Theodor Heuss, who was to become the first President of the Bundesrepublik in 1949.

Before leaving for Heidelberg, Dr. Hartshorne had gotten OMGUS permission for a "white" faculty election to choose a new rector and Senate. Bauer was chosen rector, Ernst prorector and Jaspers first senator. Jaspers had declined to be rector for reasons of health, but he remained in the eyes of the military government the major symbol of Heidelberg's good faith. Other deans chosen were Hölscher, Radbruch, Engelking, Regenbogen, and Freudenberg. Bauer was inaugurated the very day that the Medical School reopened, 15 August 1945. At the Ludolf-Krehl-Klinik both Jaspers and Bauer spoke, the former's remarks receiving the greater attention: "For the first time in twelve years," Jaspers declared, "we have once again freely elected our Rector, our very own Rector."[41] But a prophet is without honor in his own home town. Many students were angered by Jaspers's reminder of the recent crimes committed by men who had once taken the Hippocratic Oath.[42] Bauer's speech was published in the *Süddeutsche Mitteilungen:* "Whose heart will not leap with joy when he hears that Old Heidelberg, once a bastion of German democracy, is commencing anew?"[43] Shortly therafter, the theological faculty began to function, albeit prematurely by OMGUS standards. Lectures were given in church buildings in order to obviate official recognition. No one objected.

In describing Bauer's strenuous days in September— mornings operating and then making his rounds among

patients—Ernst mentions the crowds visiting the Rektorat in
the afternoons. Besides newspaper reporters, students seeking
favors, and university personnel with innumerable problems,
the hordes included members of the occupation who sought,
under the most inexpensive of circumstances, an academic
degree from a university so famous in America.[44] One of those
responsible for a regulation forbidding the receiving of degrees
or honors from universities at our mercy was Major Crum
himself. With that avenue cut off, members of the American
forces sought admission for others. Major Crum told his family
that ranking American officers were forever urging him to
sponsor their lovely German girlfriends. Crum would say,
frigidly, "The Admission Office is *that* way!"[45]

As of August 1945 the reopening of the entire university still
lay five months away. Three of Bauer's petitions had been
rebuffed. In view of the quality of his cadre, he was under-
standably ruffled. Marburg University, also in the American
Zone, would open 28 September, and Major Crum would
address the first dies academicus there. In the British, French,
and Russian zones *six* universities had already fully opened. On
October 1 Bauer puzzled over what lay behind the delay.
Perhaps, he suggested, the Americans feared that Heidelberg
would become a seedbed for leftist extremism.[46] Ernst, on the
other hand, felt that the Americans viewed Heidelberg as a
Brutstätte der Reaktion.[47]

The decisive reasons fell, for the most part, outside Bauer's or
Ernst's field of vision. An already dogmatic policy directive was
about to be articulated in rigorous terms and then translated
into detailed administrative orders that subordinates followed
religiously. If one adds to that factor OMGUS aloofness from
civil affairs, jurisdictional disagreements, a lack of personnel,
the confusion and chaos of rapid demobilization, and American
provinciality and naiveté (Jaspers's judgment) one finds answers for the apparent foot-dragging which are worthy of
thought.[48]

Although the university's announcement that the pos-
sessions of the library had been returned did not come until 17
June 1946, the record should show that the recovery of the

library's scattered property began almost a year earlier. The search, initiated on 6 July 1945, was completed by 14 September. The physical return of discovered items continued bit by bit throughout Crum's tenure.[49] The details of that treasure hunt are revealed in short reports sent by junior officers and ranking noncoms to the Office of the AC of S, G-2, located, ironically, in the requisitioned library itself.[50] Items had been cached as far away as Mainhardt, a distance of 90 kilometers. In the Kochendorf Salt mine were found the equivalent of seven railroad cars of books and magazines. At Tauberbischofsheim, at the Schloss Zwingenberg near Eberbach, at Schloss Neuhaus, at Schloss Bödigheim, at Wiesloch, and in the Heidelberg Schloss itself were found tons of books, laboratory equipment, and priceless works of art. The labor expended in returning these scattered belongings was considerable, but the job was made easier by student volunteers.[51]

One of the most deeply appreciated recoveries was the Manessische Handschrift, Heidelberg's dearest possession. As Dr. Ernst later told Major Crum:

> I shall never forget the moment one afternoon earlier this year (1946) when I entered your office on one of my routine calls. You were standing behind your table and silently pointing at a big book lying on it. I had never seen it before and it took some seconds until I realized that there lay our most precious treasure, the Manesse-Manuscript. We turned over its leaves together, looked at its wonderful miniatures and its poems which are among the finest flowers of medieval lyrical poetry, and I noticed that you were as proud of this treasure and as glad for its safe return . . . as any member of our faculty might ever have been.[52]

On the eve of Major Crum's arrival in Heidelberg the university was deeply troubled. Theodor Heuss could do nothing to expedite Heidelberg's reopening. Two Communists, Bock and Agricola, were conducting a bitter vendetta against the university in the *Rhein-Neckar Zeitung,* stigmatizing it as a tool of the

fascists, demanding representation on departmental committees, and politicizing the leftist students.[53] Simultaneously
the CIC, implementing Military Government Law No. 8,
launched its first attacks against Rector Bauer.[54] The requisition of private homes also increased, especially those owned by
"rejected" persons.[55]

Although Major Crum did not receive his official orders until
10 October, internal evidence suggests that he was aware of his
impending appointment in mid-August, about the time that
Dr. Hartshorne departed. Since 5 August Crum had been the
Chief Education and Religious Officer for USFET at Frankfurt, interviewing priests and ministers and attending church
conferences.[56] Heidelberg, however, is not far from Frankfurt,
and sometime in early August Major Crum must have made a
discreet trip or two to interview Bauer and other senators.
Crum's first act affecting Heidelberg was to request from Bauer
and the Senate a report "on the condition of Heidelberg
University" and whether all of the faculties were prepared to
function. The Senate's response to this request is dated 9
October, one day *before* Crum received his orders.[57] Crum's
initial act bode well: "He called for a report on the faculties'
readiness for action. With that, Bauer found the partner for
whom he had waited so long."[58] The gesture signaled respect
and confidence. As Bauer recalled in 1949: "We shall never
forget the moment during the very first hours of your coming
here, when you accepted our seven memoranda regarding the
situation of the university and immediately made us feel that
you had come to investigate our situation, to understand us,
and to help us."[59]

Upon Major Crum's official arrival he was installed in that
famous landmark *Zum Ritter,* with his office in the Domus
Wilhelmina. Until the later jurisdictional conflict, this building
housed the offices of the CIC as well. This tended to confuse
Germans regarding which authority was which, but, initially,
the two offices seemed part of a common endeavor. Crum's
new colleagues delighted him. As he later stated: "It is nearly
impossible for me to describe the energy and the enthusiasm
with which these professors undertook the reconstruction of

the university. . . . Daily, and often several times daily, we got together to talk over old, new or unforeseen problems. . . . We consulted each other over everything, from electric bulbs to a new Constitution for the university."[60] Major Crum was one of those rare persons who simply *was* what he appeared to be. The evidence supporting his integrity is overwhelming. Bauer and Ernst noted in a protocol: "He never made use of his official position as representative of the victor in dealing with a university of a conquered country. His conscientiousness was always absolute, going far beyond the duties of his office to protect with his own person the often threatened University. He saved us from despair and gave us renewed faith. He was for us a shining example of profound and genuine humanity."[61]

Ruperto-Carola was inundated with applications. For the 331 admissions deemed possible for the Medical School, there had been more than 5,000 applicants. It was therefore essential for the Senate to establish a *numerus clausus;* no more than 3,000 students would be admitted to the university as a whole. Preference would be given to those who had already completed a part of their study.[62]

The Committee of Thirteen was most anxious to recover the alte Kaserne so that at least some students might enjoy the social life and the self-government of a "college." Supported by Major Crum, Bauer received permission in mid-October to establish a collegium in that much-coveted barracks. Not only would the building provide a college for 250; there was also space for the preparatory and refresher courses needed by 650 others.[63] Meanwhile, a mensa had begun to function, but the daily fare was meager indeed. Students often went to bed hungry—this at a time when American GI's dumped half the food in their mess kits into garbage cans.[64]

Under OMGUS regulations fraternities were forbidden, but Major Crum wondered if it might not be possible to create some kind of student organization to represent the students' special concerns, an organization to awaken a feeling of solidarity and to give voice to student opinion.[65] A committee was established to consider the matter. Its reports suggested that, upon the reopening of the entire university, students of each of the five schools should elect three representatives. (For some time to come, a sixth department, political economy, would be absorbed by the School of Philosophy.) From that congress of fifteen should come three students empowered to petition the Senate. This plan, implemented in January 1946, was working smoothly when Dr. Crum returned to Heidelberg in 1949.[66]

On 13 December 1945 Major Crum announced to a delighted Senate that he had just been given permission to reopen the university in all of its faculties. On 7 January 1946, after the Christmas holidays, Ruperto-Carola would be opened fully with pomp and circumstance. It was a day of rejoicing and solemn ceremony in the old Aula. The commander of the Seventh Army, Geoffrey Keyes, was there, attended by an impressive staff, and as the academic procession began, with Bauer and Ernst in the lead, General Keyes rose to his feet accompanied by all of the other officers, including a proud "Officer in Charge of Heidelberg University." Dr. Heuss was there too, as was Dr. Karl Geiler, alumnus and governor of Hesse, along with a host of other German dignitaries.

Rector Bauer began by thanking the military government for liberation from Nazi tyranny and for permission to reopen Ruperto-Carola: "You have given free rein once again to the scientific spirit, for research as well as for the reeducation of German youth." He then thanked Major Crum: "Today we are certain that we know you as a person and we are convinced that it is your pleasure to help us. . . . It is our conviction that your name will enter the history of our university with honor." Crum responded to these compliments in a short speech delivered courteously in German tongue, as he had done at Marburg on 28 September. Bauer then launched into a most eloquent *Festrede* addressed to the young people, "The Philosophy of an Active Life." He portrayed the satisfactions of fruitful living and scientific endeavor, and when he pleaded for tolerance, saying, "without tolerance there is also no democracy and without democracy there is no future for Germany," the students loudly expressed their approval by stamping with one foot in the traditional fashion.[67]

The festivities ended with a short ceremony of matriculation and the newly reopened university got down to business. Within days a free university was functioning once more, but the faculty bore a crushing load. Denazification had reduced their number by half. Of those remaining, two-thirds were in their sixties and seventies. Many had been undernourished for some time and were consequently weakened or sickly. Some bore visible signs of mental suffering after years of insecurity, unlike Ernst, who controlled his anxieties until the very day he took his life.[68] New blood was sorely needed, but to locate and attract first-rate scholars and scientists was difficult indeed, since the middle generation was most decimated by denazification. On 28 January Bauer pleaded again for leniency toward marginal Nazis: "Denazification may be compared with a great operation performed on an organism already weakened considerably . . . precisely German Anti-Nazis . . . plead that the operation should not be more dangerous than the illness for which it is performed . . . [and] ask for grace for those who merely lost their way."[69]

The students at Heidelberg in 1946 were extremely poor, many destitute. Their skepticism sometimes verged on cynicism. For years they had been deceived, and they knew that they had been cheated of their youth. They had witnessed with their own eyes horrors beyond description. Both victor and vanquished had blood on his hands. Any faith in humane ideals, therefore, had been stretched to the breaking point. "What they need," Bauer told Crum, "is quiet and time, much indulgence and much love."[70]

Within a month of the inspiring tableau in the Aula, Crum and his overworked faculty awoke to the fact that disturbing rumors which they had dismissed were all too true. A zealous and determined CIC agent had been preparing since early December a bill of particulars. Agent Daniel F. Penham would set out with a passion to prove that Bauer was a cunning, two-faced Nazi, that the faculty and student body were riddled with Nazis, and that Major Crum was a gullible fool. The fattest folder among the Crum Papers is entitled, in Mrs. Crum's hand, "Earl's biggest headache at Heidelberg."[71] The situation stemmed from Military Government Law No. 8, instituting rigorous denazification in response to articles in the *New York Times* and the *New Republic* attacking OMGUS for tolerating Fritz Schaeffer as Bavaria's minister-president. Schaeffer, an anti-Nazi who had been interned in a concentration camp, had appointed some questionable Bavarians to high public office. Then, in September 1945, when General George Patton had told visiting reporters that "the Nazi thing is just like a Democrat-Republican election fight," he was promptly stripped of his command. General Clay promulgated Military Government Law No. 8 and, after Patton's fall, lesser commanding officers took no chances. An "enormous new wave of denazification" rolled throughout the American zone in October. Daniel Penham was simply an agent of that purge.[72] He leveled forty-four incriminating charges, and, if he could prove them, Ruperto-Carola would close her doors once again and the accused professors, under revised categories of what constituted Nazis, would be ejected from their professions. "Earl's headache" lasted from 12 February 1946 until the end of March, but the very last rumblings of the Penham Affair would not be heard until 4 May, just before a vindicated Major Crum departed for home.

The ordeal began with the appearance of Penham and an associate before a Senate meeting, 12 February, when Penham produced a long list of "monstrous" charges against Bauer and the faculty.[73] It became a crescendo the following month when a righteously enraged Major Crum launched a counterattack. Here was a jurisdictional quarrel, to be sure, highlighting a significant weakness in policy administration, but, with the passage of time, it acquired the flavor of a morality play. Of the forty-four charges which Penham fired at his dismayed suspects, twenty-one were against Rector Bauer, ten against a Dr. Höpke, and the remainder struck Dr. August Seybold, Dr. Willy Andreas, and Professors Becker and Glaeser. Also charged were Dr. Karl Freudenberg, Dr. Ernst Engelking, and a Dr. Spang. After an interrogation of Dr. Höpke of such severity that it led Jewish residents in Höpke's home to protest to the Military Government, the charges were dismissed and the shaken physician was released.[74]

Penham's case against Andreas was convincing. A historian, Andreas had written *The Great Germans from Arminius to Horst Wessel*, a fact he had excluded from his fragebogen. That a "pimp and Nazi 'martyr' like Horst Wessel" should be compared to the great Germans of history outraged Penham, as well it might. But the cases of Becker and Glaeser seemed less conclusive. Becker had taught that the laws of physics are conditioned by blood, race, and soil. Glaeser, a philologist, had interpreted linguistics in a similar light. To what extent were they mouthing Nazi ideology and to what extent were they articulating the now respectable "sociology of knowledge" hypothesis? Both men were rejected.[75] Dr. Seybold, never a party member, had allegedly written to the Nazi Reichskulturminister that anyone who read the English journal *Nature* should be punished to the fullest extent. Seybold was also rejected.[76]

The indictment of Dr. Freudenberg, an unconditionally accepted member of the original Committee of Thirteen and dean of the School of Natural Science, stunned his colleages. Freudenberg, a proven anti-Nazi—as Penham conceded—was accused of covering for Otto Schmidt, a "fanatical National Socialist."[77] Freudenberg was eventually cleared and resumed his duties as dean. Engelking was also unconditionally accepted and Spang was conditionally accepted.

Of the twenty-one charges leveled at Bauer, only six appear in Penham's final report. On the basis of existing documents, twenty-four of the forty-four charges seem inconclusive. The balance may be impossible to prove or disprove at this time, though the highest competent American tribunal in Berlin, with criteria of its own, would brand Penham's charges "trivial and inconsequential."[78] This obscured Penham's valid insights regarding the basically conservative tendencies inherent in the German educational system. It was not, in John Dewey's sense, a system to engender democratic values. Not until American pressures eased did Germans themselves begin to question the premises of their traditional two-track system, which fostered elitism and a certain contempt for those who had not achieved the *Abitur,* the mark of an "educated" German.

But from the viewpoint of the original Committee of Thirteen and of Major Crum, Penham was for weeks a mortal threat, during which he seemed to hold Heidelberg in the palm of his hand as well as the careers and the reputations of his suspects. Even Major Crum was vulnerable. As "Officer in Charge of Heidelberg University" he would be held responsible for every irregularity there.

Daniel F. Penham was born in 1914 in Bad Hersfeld, Germany, as Siegfried Oppenheimer. A German-Jewish refugee, he fled to France in 1933, then came to the United States. He wrote a doctoral dissertation on Budé under Paul Oskar Kristeller, a staunch friend to this very day.[79] Bauer found Penham utterly captivating—for a while. Penham's other suspects conceded that he was highly intelligent and, at first, exceptionally charming—"flamboyant." If Penham lost family and friends to the Holocaust, his unquenchable hatred of Nazis, his extraordinary zeal, and his ungovernable temper are understandable indeed. Beyond this, he had had ample opportunity to observe Nazis first hand in Bad Hersfeld.

Documents regarding Penham's behavior in Heidelberg, however, show that the most frequently cited trait is his repeated rages, screaming at and threatening either a particular suspect or the university at large. This allegation appears twelve times in the documentation. The following are typical. The American UNRRA directors, William Sudduth and Ruth Prager, wrote to Major Crum: "We do not doubt Mr. Penham's complete sincerity but we feel that his health condition has caused him to be overwrought and excitable in his dealings with the students . . . He has shouted at [them], pushed them out of the room without giving them a chance to talk or to make explanations, shoved doors shut in their faces, and generally acted in an abnormal manner."[80] A 22 February Senate report, composed at Major Crum's request, expressed a similar complaint: "Most disturbing of all is Mr. Penham's manner during conversations and interrogations, which is entirely different from that of his predecessors. Time and again he has shouted at professors whom he has interrogated, even those who were previously 'unconditionally accepted.'"[81]

The second most frequently encountered allegation is that Penham exaggerated, or told tall tales, an allegation that appears nine times. For example, Penham is said to have told the Senate as a fact that at the University of Jena students threw a professor out of the window when he mentioned the word *democracy*. Skeptical senators then contacted Jena acquaintances who insisted they knew nothing whatsoever of the alleged incident.[82] Again, while trying to confirm that Bauer had made a compromising remark in one of his classes, Penham stated that he interrogated *fifty* students. Yet, said the Senate, "absolutely nothing regarding such a wholesale interrogation has been brought to our attention. Fifty interrogated students would have doubtless said something about their interrogation concerning the Rector's remarks."[83]

The allegation that Penham made disparaging remarks about Major Crum to Germans or showed his contempt also appears nine times. Crum himself alleges that this was so.[84] As Fritz Ernst discreetly put it to Major Crum: "The Senate is particularly concerned about the fact that Mr. Penham's statements are designed to discredit the decisions of the military government affecting the university."[85] Bauer was more blunt: "Not only that the gentleman in question made derogatory remarks about the 'Officer-in-Charge . . .'—for example, to the Rector. He also gave verbal and written commands which, we felt, were without the knowledge of the 'Officer-in-Charge.'"[86]

There are eight protocols stating that Penham loudly and repeatedly hurled charges against the accepted faculty and students before anyone within earshot: "I am sorry to say that Mr. Penham, even in the secretaries' office, talked about university personnel in a loud voice before complete strangers simply waiting there—indeed, on a number of occasions."[87]

There are six instances, in available sources, where it is suggested in straightforward language that Penham was emotionally distraught. Sudduth and Prager of UNRRA said that he "generally acted in an abnormal manner." Ernst wrote in 1960 that "the fact that he forced a university employee to sing the *Horst-Wessel-Lied* during an interrogation shows the pathological side of his methods."[88] When the interrogee stammered that he knew only the first verse, Penham proceeded to sing the last two verses for him.[89] "In view of his violent temper, his inordinate passion and the great number of interrogees, it cannot be ignored that a general opinion . . . has crystallized that the person in question is indeed a man of high intelligence but is filled with a hatred against the university, and this hatred verges on sickness."[90]

Why Bauer became, in Penham's mind, the incarnation of Nazi duplicity remains unclear. Penham may have intuited that this formidable Bavarian was by no means as committed to American aims as his speeches and writings suggested. Bauer's cavalier acceptance of questionable medical doctors resembled Fritz Schaeffer's appointments in Munich. One also suspects that when Bauer saw Penham's real intentions, he no longer greeted the man with open arms. Initial cordiality undoubtedly chilled.[91] Bauer's schedule was grueling, and he did not feel well, concealing his cancer but becoming, perhaps, abrupt in his manner. Beyond that, Bauer remained a proud, sometimes overbearing man, who had already faced down some very powerful enemies in Breslau. Penham surely perceived this trait, saw it as clearly as a swastika, and became increasingly enraged at Bauer's fencing and guile. Bauer, for his part, had no intention whatsoever of fingering suspects for the CIC. He said so publicly two decades later.[92]

Penham has declined comments to this author, but his old mentor, Paul Oskar Kristeller, never lost faith in his brilliant protégé.[93] Two other witnesses point out that some of Penham's suspicions were surely confirmed by 1968.[94] But it is the intractable nature of the issue here which makes a definitive judgment elusive. "Lack of cooperation in the American aim of denazification"—Penham's major charge against Heidelbergers—becomes confused during discussion with "resistance by conservative German educators to American education theories." James Tent makes this clear in his recent *Mission on the Rhine.*

Penham's major allegations regarding Bauer were as follows: that he had said that he did not intend to let Ruperto-Carola become a Jewish ghetto; that he had made a former SA man the faculty advisor to a student committee screening fragebogen; that he had failed to tell CIC of bribes from hopeful applicants; that he had admonished his colleagues to take it easy with Nazi faculty and students; that he had told one of his classes that history would prove who was responsible for World War II; that in a case under investigation Bauer had leaked Penham's name; that he had aided wounded Wehrmacht personnel to make them fit for combat again; that he had treated a local Nazi and had Mrs. Bauer bring the patient flowers; that he had visited Reichsminister Rust; that he had sent color films of his new surgical techniques to Joseph Goebbels; that he had been a member of the Prussian Board of Health; that he advocated the sterilization of defectives; that he had given a speech commemorating Hitler's seizure of power; that his call to Heidelberg was convincing proof of his high Nazi connections; and, finally, that his book *Racial Hygiene* was filled with racist passages.

Two of these charges are unquestionably true, though honest men might disagree regarding their implications. Bauer *did* take it easy with suspected professors and students. He *did* appoint a former SA man to assist in the screening of students. For each of the other allegations there is a plausible, though not definitive, explanation. It is impossible here to try Bauer's case. Penham's methods, however, deserve scrutiny.

In *Racial Hygiene* Bauer used the dialectical approach still favored in German universities. He would state the position with which he would take issue as clearly as possible, quoting Nietzsche or whomever, and then he would proceed to contest or qualify that position. He attacked simplistic racist notions, warning that "it cannot be emphasized sharply enough that if racial hygiene wishes to be a science, it, like every other science, can only mean a striving toward truth. As such, it can never propagate hate and persecution."[95] "On March 22, 1946, Bauer sent the following memo to Major Crum: Prof. Hoelscher and the instructor, Dr. Bischoff, tell me that Mr. Penham is employing a new method against me. Thus, he put my little book, *Rassenhygiene,* with the title-page hidden, before Dr. Bischoff, told him to read through the last chapter with its underlined passages, and then ordered him to give his written opinion regarding certain points."[96] This author has access to a 1926 copy of *Rassenhygiene* that is undoubtedly the very copy Penham used against Bauer. It bears the stamp and call number of the Universitätsbibliothek Heidelberg. Within it are numerous passages marked in pencil illustrating racist sentiments. These have been photocopied and added to the Crum Papers. But those passages express an ideology with which Bauer was taking issue, not advocating.[97]

On 23 February 1946 Penham sent his report, stamped "confidential," to his superior, 307th CIC Detachment. It portrayed a Heidelberg infested with Nazis. The effect the report produced may be judged by what Penham's superior wrote two days later to *his* superior: "Merely reading this report is sufficient to make the blood of any American boil with anger, aroused by the stubborn defiance of the so-called intellectual elements of what was once a famous, but what is now a notorious, Heidelberg . . . [Bauer should be] told in definite and harsh terms that his attitude thus far has been one that practically justifies his hanging."[98]

On 27 February, two weeks after Penham's initial attack, Major Crum took action. In an understated and carefully documented report to the Commanding Officer, OMGUS, Stuttgart, he reported a raid by Penham on the Rektorat, Penham's flat refusal to give Crum a copy of his report, the Senate report of 22 February, the report on Penham from the UNRRA supervisors, a report from Bauer at Crum's request, and a statement by Crum himself regarding Penham's demeanor. He added a pointed remark that Penham's interference in university affairs was counterproductive.[99]

The two reports, Penham's and Crum's, led rapidly to the hearings in Berlin. On 16 March the overseas edition of the New York *Herald Tribune,* dateline 14 March, carried a headline: "U.S. Denies Ban on University of Heidelberg, Rejects Charge Numerous Nazis are in the Faculty and Student Body." On 17 March the U.S. edition bore a headline: "U.S. CIC Man Causes Furor at Heidelberg. American Military Government Acts to Curb Agent's Interference in Work of Ancient University." The story by John Elliott noted that: "Major Earl L. Crum, liaison officer of the American Military Government, with university authorities, defended the university's faculty and student body against accusations advanced by Mr. Penham at recent Berlin meetings attended by Maj. Gen. M. C. Stayer, Chief of the Public Health and Welfare Division; Col. John Taylor, Chief of the Education and Religious Affairs section in Berlin; and Maj. Steiner, head of that branch in Stuttgart." Elliott quoted Steiner: "We found [Penham's] evidence to be trivial and inconsequential. It seemed to us that it was a 'tempest in a teapot.'" Crum's remarks were also reported: "Heidelberg is not Nazi—neither as regards its faculty nor its student body. . . . Heidelberg is the only university in the American Zone that has never seen a nationalist outbreak nor witnessed a demonstration hostile to the Americans."[100]

Steiner's recommendations (which were honored) stipulated that "further disturbing action" cease and that Heidelberg remain open, that Major Crum, who had "ably taken care of" his duties, be retained, that the CIC refrain from making administrative recommendations (such as Bauer's removal) since such decisions "should more properly be made by the Military Government Education Officer."[101] Shortly thereafter Penham was transferred and the CIC offices in the Domus Wilhelmina were closed. The CIC continued to operate, however, from a preexisting base across the Neckar, the Bergius Haus, just off the Neuenheimer Landstrasse, near the Philosophenweg.[102]

The last episode in the war against Bauer and the university took place on 4 May, just before Major Crum's discharge. In the presence of Major Banks from Stuttgart and of Major Crum, Bauer denied in a deposition the still repeated charges that he wanted to nazify Heidelberg, and he requested that each of Penham's allegations be closely examined by an American military tribunal. But by this time Bauer's detractors had left the scene or did not relish another confrontation. With the exception of a few incidents, a dubious chapter in the history of American due process and fair play had ended. Ernst summed up the episode when he noted that "instead of showing the path toward democracy, Penham did everything he could, within his bailiwick, to make a democratic atmosphere impossible."[103] When Dr. Freudenberg was cleared of all charges on July 9, it was apparent that the witch hunt in Heidelberg had ended for the time being.[104] Another wave of denazification, however, would follow later that summer.

Two years later Dr. Crum told the following anecdote to John W. Taylor, who had been the ranking E & RA officer at the Berlin hearings and was then president of the University of Louisville. Martin Niemoeller, one of the most conspicuous victims of Nazi terror (eight years at Sachsenhausen and Dachau) had been brought to America by friends and well-wishers. When the time came for his flight home, Crum tried to get him a seat on an American military plane. Said Crum, "The statement of one of the G-2 men is classic: 'No German shall ever ride in one of our planes!'"[105]

The abiding significance of the Heidelberg experience lies first of all in its vivid exposure of the ambiguity of American postwar policy, illustrated by the yawning abyss between the objectives of Penham and those of Major Crum. Yet *both* goals were encompassed within JCS 1067. Penham's single-minded purpose, denazification, was utterly essential. Bona fide Nazis *had* to be exorcised from every influential sector before any meaningful democracy could flourish—exorcised from the media, from government, and especially from the schools.[106] But, to avoid doing violence to larger ends, an effective program—as time would prove—called for discretion and restraint, as once envisaged by the State Department. Denazification was no end in itself, but simply a means to an ultimate goal: the liberation of Germans from Nazi tyranny.and the creation of at least the opportunity for a brighter, freer future, which only the Germans themselves could fashion. Such a future presupposed, from the democratic point of view, that even German reactionaries would be brought back into the political process, "domesticated" as it were, however distasteful this may have been to many or however risky this might appear in the light of German history. That in the process "big fish got away while little fish were caught" has become a truism.

Another weakness of our policy was exposed in Heidelberg: jurisdictional conflict. The division and subdivision of OMGUS authority could have succeeded only if each level had fulfilled unambiguous and compatible directives with extra-ordinary prudence. But circumstances militated against that. Every level was understaffed and our policies were confusing and sometimes contradictory.

There is further significance to the Heidelberg story: it has a *Bell for Adano* ring about it. A humane and compassionate member of the occupying power put the legitimate needs of his wards above everything else. The perusal of history for moral lessons is no longer fashionable, but the Heidelberg people would draw such a lesson and fondly remember Major Crum. Fritz Ernst wrote in 1960, one year before Crum's death, that "with a heavy heart the university watched Crum's departure. As long as he was there she had always found help and encouragement. Now everything seemed uncertain"[107]

On 7 May, 1946, on the eve of his departure from Heidelberg, Major Crum was presented with a farewell message signed by every member of the Senate. It had been composed, for the most part, by Karl Jaspers, the very conscience of postwar Germany:

Today the painful moment of parting from you has come. You are returning home to America, but you will always belong to us. The touching goodbye letter which you sent us has established a bond that shall never be severed—neither by the ocean nor by barriers created by the war. The bond is firm, for through your guidance you have planted the seed of our new way of life. As a sign of our feeling for you we present the most precious thing we Heidelbergers are in a position to offer: a facsimile reproduction of the Manesse Manuscript, whose original, under your care, was returned to our library. We would wish that this work might accompany you throughout your lifetime as a memorial to your Heidelberg stewardship and that it might remind you of our deepest gratitude.[108]

In 1949 Dr. Crum returned to Heidelberg to teach the
classics during the summer semester. Before he left for Lehigh
in the fall, the Senate, in a poignant ceremony, made Dr.
Crum an honorary senator for life, bestowing upon him *Die Kette,* the
academic necklace of Ruperto-Carola bearing the appropriate
seal. At Villa Avita in Greenville, Virginia, there hangs today a
portrait of Dr. Crum in his academic gown, proudly wearing
that symbol of honor.

Notes

[1] James F. Tent, *Mission on the Rhine: Reeducation and Denazification in
American Occupied Germany* (Chicago, 1982), chap. 1, "Planning for
Reeducation."

[2] Ibid., p. 285.

[3] On 13 October 1981 the Earl L. Crum Papers (hereafter CP) were
presented to the George C. Marshall Research Foundation in Lexington, Va.,
by Mary Lyle Crum Baine of Oceanport, N.J., Dr. Crum's daughter.

[4] Fritz Ernst, *Die Wiederöffnung der Universität Heidelberg, 1945–46,
Aus Anlass des 70, Geburtstags von Karl Heinrich Bauer am 26. September 1960*
(Heidelberg, 1960), courtesy of Adolf Laufs, former rector of Heidelberg,
July 1982. This author's translations throughout.

[5] Fritz Ernst, *Ehrensenator Professor Earl Le Verne Crum,* a formal eulogy
bordered in black on the occasion of Dr. Crum's death (29 July 1961), 6
September 1961, Heidelberg University, CP.

[6] Lehigh University campus newspaper, *Brown and White,* 23 January
1946, CP.

[7] Earl L. Crum, *Der Wiederaufstieg der Universität Heidelberg seit 1945,*
Address to the students of Heidelberg, *Dies Academicus,* 15 June 1949, p. 4.

[8] Ibid., p. 12.

[9] Ibid., p. 5.

[10] Ernst, *Die Wiederöffnung,* p. 12.

[11] Earl L. Crum, "Address," Verdun, 27 January 1945, CP.

[12] Ibid., p. 11.

[13] Ernst, *Die Wiederöffnung,* p. 12.

[14] Crum, *Wiederaufstieg,* pp. 2, 5; Crum, "Heidelberg University Reopens," (undated manuscript), p. 5, CP.

[15] Robert Murphy, *Diplomat among Warriors* (Garden City, N.Y., 1964), p. 251.

[16] Lucius D. Clay, *Decision in Germany* (Garden City, N.Y., 1950), pp. 16–18.

[17] Murphy, *Diplomat,* p. 251; Crum, "Heidelberg Reopens," p. 32.

[18] Tent, *Mission,* chap. 4, *"Kulturkampf* in Bavaria."

[19] Crum to Col. D. P. Page, Hq. 12th Army Group, APO 655, 27 March 1945, CP.

[20] Harold Zink, *The United States in Germany: 1944–1955* (Princeton, 1956) p. 196; Zink, *American Military Government in Germany* (New York, 1947) pp. 151–53.

[21] Karl-Heinrich Bauer, *Rassenhygiene: Ihre Biologischen Grundlagen* (Leipzig, 1926). Cf., Bauer, *An die Militärregierung,* Office, Heidelberg University, 22 March 1946, CP; *Rassenhygiene,* p. 204: "jedes Kulturvolk ein hoffnungsloses Rassengemisch darstellt."

[22] The friendship between Jaspers and Bauer ended in 1968 because of Bauer's support of Kurt Georg Kiesinger (Ribbentrop's assistant) for president of the Republic (Renato de Rosa, ed., *Karl Jaspers, K. H. Bauer: Briefwechsel, 1945–1968* [Berlin-Heidelberg-New York, 1983], no. 70; Jaspers to Ernst, 7 March 1963: "Was ich damals [1945–46] galt, war nicht die Wirklichkeit meines Denkens, sondern eine für jenen Augenblick nützliche Puppe, die ich nicht mit mir identifizieren konnte," i.e., Jaspers felt that Bauer had used him; cf. Jaspers, "Erfahrung des Ausgestossenseins," *Der Spiegel,* 21, no. 41 [2 October 1967], pp. 40–54).

[23] Dr. R. Giessendorfer, Heidelberg, deposition, 16 November 1945; Dr. Bederke, Göttingen, deposition, 17 November 1945; Dr. Weil, Jewish orthopedist, Heidelberg, deposition, 7 March 1946; Dr. von Weizsaker, Heidelberg, deposition, 15 November 1945, CP.

[24] Ernst, *Die Wiederöffnung,* p. 2.

[25] De Rosa, *Briefwechsel,* no. 1; Tent, *Mission,* pp. 123, 312–18.

[26] Jaspers, "Erfahrung des Ausgestossenseins," pp. 42–46; Bauer, *Einige Daten über die Zeit vom 1.4. 45 . . . bis zum 1.8.45,* Documents from vol. 2, 1947, *Schriften der Universität Heidelberg* (Heidelberg 1947), courtesy of Adolf Laufs; Bauer to Major Crum, 9 October 1945, pp. 2–3, CP; Ernst, *Die Wiederöffnung,* pp. 3–12; de Rosa, *Briefwechsel,* nos. 10, 15, 16.

[27] John Gimbel, *The American Occupation of Germany: Politics and the Military, 1945–1949,* (Stanford, 1968), p. 2; Ernst, *Die Wiederöffnung,* pp. 3–4; Crum, "Heidelberg Reopens," p. 7.

[28] Gimbel, *American Occupation,* p. 2; Ernst, *Die Wiederöffnung,* p. 13; Crum, "Heidelberg Reopens," pp. 11, 23. "(Theodor) Heuss felt that, of all the persons hastily dismissed, only about 10 or 15 percent had been convinced Nazis" (Tent, *Mission,* p. 55).

[29] Karl Jaspers, "Philosophical Autobiography," in *The Philosophy of Karl Jaspers,* ed. Paul Arthur Schlep (New York, 1957), p. 62.

[30] Ernst, *Die Wiederöffnung,* p. 5 n. 5.

[31] Tent, *Mission,* pp. 58–59.

[32] Bauer to Crum, c. 20 February 1946, p. 3, CP.

[33] Ibid.; Crum, "Heidelberg Reopens," pp. 8–10.

[34] Jaspers: "Ernst kam die Entnazifizierung, bei der die höchsten Massstäbe angelegt und wirklich harmlose Leute schwer belastet wurden, dann aber die Freilassung der grossen, verderblichen Nazis zu öffentlicher Wirksamkeit" ("Erfahrung des Ausgestossenseins," p. 46); Ernst, *Wiederöffnung,* pp. 11, 14; Crum, "Heidelberg Reopens," pp. 15–19.

[35] Tent, *Mission,* p. 87.

[36] Ernst, *Die Wiederöffnung,* p. 7.

[37] De Rosa, *Briefwechsel,* no. 4.

[38] Bauer, *Einige Daten,* p. 2.

[39] Ernst, *Die Wiederöffnung*, p. 9; Crum, "Heidelberg Reopens," p. 29; Tent, *Mission*, p. 59.

[40] Bauer, *Einige Daten*, p. 4.

[41] Jaspers hastened the election, telling Hartshorne that Acting Rector Hoops, very old, was unlikely to denazify vigorously (Tent, *Mission*, p. 65; Ernst, *Die Wiederöffnung*, p. 9).

[42] Tent, *Mission*, p. 60.

[43] Bauer, *Einige Daten*, p. 15.

[44] Ernst, *Die Wiederöffnung*, p. 10; Crum, "Heidelberg Reopens," p. 18.

[45] Mr. William L. Brune, Crum's son-in-law, told this anecdote to the author, 7 June 1982.

[46] Bauer, *Einige Daten*, p. 9.

[47] Ernst, *Ehrensenator*, p. 2.

[48] Jaspers: "Die Amerikaner waren wohlwollend. Wir bewunderten die Freiheit und Ehrlichkeit ihres Denkens. . . . Aber wir vehehlten uns nicht die Züge von Naivität, die wir antrafen, den manchmal schnellen Wechsel ihrer Anordnungen" ("Erfahrung des Ausgestossenseins," pp. 45–46).

[49] Ernst, *Die Wiederöffnung*, p. 22.

[50] In the Crum Papers each Short Report appears "V-Mail" size. The following numbers, in order, correspond to the dates of discovery: 214, 137, 182, 183, 189, 141, 229, 223, 219, 281, 271, 336, 357, CP.

[51] Crum, "Wiederaufstieg, p. 9.

[52] Ernst, *Address by the Pro-Rector*, 7 May 1946, CP.

[53] Ernst, *Die Wiederöffnung*, p. 12; Bauer to Crum, c. 20 February 1946, p. 6, CP.

[54] Daniel F. Penham, *Memorandum for the Officer in Charge*, 307th CIC Corps, marked "Confidential," 23 February 1946, p. 9, par. 2, declassified 20 July 1982, CP.

[55] Ernst, *Die Wiederöffnung*, p. 12.

56 Lehigh University, *Brown and White*, 23 January 1946.

57 Bauer, *To Major Crum*, 9 October 1945, CP.

58 Ernst, *Die Wiederöffnung*, p. 60.

59 *Gemeinsame Sitzung des Senats von 1945/46 und 1948/49*, 31 May 1949, CP; Crum, "Heidelberg Reopens," p. 16.

60 Crum, *Wiederaufstieg*, p. 7; Crum, "Heidelberg Reopens," p. 3.

61 Jaspers: "Der Universitätsoffizier half uns gegen die CIC, natürlich stilschweigend" ("Erfahrung des Ausgestossenseins," p. 46).

62 Crum, *Wiederaufstieg*, p. 7; Crum, "Heidelberg Reopens," p. 24.

63 Ernst, *Die Wiederöffnung*, p. 16; Crum, *Wiederaufstieg*, p. 5; Bauer to Crum, *Report . . . January 1 . . . January 28, 1946*, CP; Crum, "Heidelberg Reopens," p. 26, CP.

64 Crum, *Wiederaufstieg*, p. 8.

65 Ernst, *Die Wiederöffnung*, p. 15.

66 Crum, *Weideraufsteig*, p. 10; Bauer to Crum, 18 January 1946, CP; Crum, "Heidelberg Reopens" p. 30.

67 *New York Herald Tribune*, European ed., Frankfurt, 8 January 1946; Crum, "Heidelberg Reopens," pp. 35–38; Ernst, *Die Wiederöffnung*, p. 18.

68 This tragedy occurred around Christmas 1963. Jaspers and Bauer were deeply distressed (de Rosa, *Briefwechsel*, no. 60).

69 Bauer to Crum, 28 January 1946, p. 6, CP.

70 Ibid.

71 Crum had taken great pains to document the case as he saw it, hence the fat folder.

72 Tent, *Mission*, p. 51.

73 Bauer to Crum, c. 20 February 1946, p. 4; Ernst, *Report of the Senate*, 22 February 1946, pp. 1–2, CP.

[74] Höpke, with a Jewish wife, had been expelled from Heidelberg in 1935. He then turned to private medical practice. His substantial income thereafter made him suspect.

[75] Penham, *Memorandum,* 23 February 1946, p. 1.

[76] Ibid., p. 2.

[77] Ibid., p. 3.

[78] *New York Herald Tribune,* European ed., 14 March 1946.

[79] De Rosa, *Briefwechsel,* p. 99, n. 19.

[80.] To Crum from Director William H. Sudduth and Student Supervisor Ruth E. Prager of the UNRRA D.P. Students, 5 March 1946, CP; Crum, "Heidelberg Reopens," p. 28.

[81] Senate report, 22 February 1946, p. 2, CP.

[82] Bauer to Crum, c. 20 February 1946.

[83] Senate Report, 22 February 1946, p. 3.

[84] Crum to Commanding Officer, OMGUS, Stuttgart, APO 154, 27 February 1946, p. 1, par. 3, CP.

[85] Senate report, 22 February 1946, p. 5.

[86] Bauer to Crum, c. 20 February 1946, p. 4; Crum, "Heidelberg Reopens," p. 17.

[87] Senate report, 22 February 1946, p. 2.

[88] Ernst, *Die Wiedereröffnung,* p. 19.

[89] Senate report, 22 February 1946, p. 2.

[90] Bauer to Crum, c. 20 February 1946, p. 6.

[91] Penham, *Memorandum,* 23 February 1946, p. 2.

[92] Bauer in a speech to his fraternity brothers, 1967, regarding the postwar policy at Heidelberg: "Wir 'Unbelasteten' handelten nach dem

Grundsatz: Wir belasteten keinen, aber entlasteten jeden, bei dem es vertretbar ist" (*Bubenreuther Zeitung,* no. 44 [1967], pp. 32–56).

[93] De Rosa to this author, 8 June 1983: "Diese Tage habe ich auch einen netten Brief vom Prof. Kristeller aus New York erhalten. Er war der Doktorvater von Penham und liebt ihn sehr. So hat er Genugtuung an der Art meiner Behandlung der Episode Penham-Bauer gefunden und fand meine Anmerkungen durchaus 'korrekt und distkret.' "

[94] Both persons perfer anonymity, but will defend this author *privately.*

[95] De Rosa, *Briefwechsel,* no. 70; also a private letter to this author 24 April 1983.

[96] Bauer to Crum, 22 March, p. 1, CP; Crum, "Heidelberg Reopens," p. 20.

[97] This book was lent to the author by a Military Government officer who retrieved it in 1946 from a stack of "Nazi literature" about to be macerated for recycling.

[98] Loran L. Elliott, Special Agent, CIC, Actg. Comdg. Officer, 307th CIC Detachment, APO 758, 25 February 1946, to A C of S, G-2 Hq. Seventh U.S. Army, APO 758, declassified, 20 July 1982, CP.

[99] Crum to OMGUS, Stuttgart, 27 February 1946, pp. 1–2, CP.

[100] *Herald Tribune,* European ed., 14 March 1946. *The New York Times* was more skeptical.

[101] John P. Steiner, Chief E & RA, APO 154, to Chief, I A & C Division, OMGUS, APO 742, pp. 1–3, CP.

[102] Ernst, *Die Wiederöffnung,* p. 21; de Rosa, *Briefwechsel,* p. 99.

[103] Ernst, *Die Wiederöffnung,* p. 19.

[104] Ibid., p. 22.

[105] Crum to Taylor, 7 May 1948, CP.

[106] Cf. Penham, *Memorandum,* 23 February 1946.

[107] Ernst, *Die Wiederöffnung,* p. 21.

[108] Karl Jaspers et al., *Hochverehrter Herr Major Crum!* Heidelberg, 7 May 1946, CP.

X

The Bibliography of
Oron James Hale

MARIE DONAGHAY

Books

Germany and the Diplomatic Revolution: A Study in Diplomacy and the Press, 1904–1906. Philadelphia: University of Pennsylvania Press, 1931; London: Oxford University Press, 1931; reprint New York: Octagon, 1971.

Publicity and Diplomacy, with Special Reference to England and Germany, 1890–1914 (University of Virginia, Institute for Research in the Social Sciences: Monograph No. 27) New York and London: D. Appleton-Century, 1940; reprint Gloucester, Mass.: Peter Smith, 1964.

The Captive Press in the Third Reich. Princeton: Princeton University Press, 1964; London: Oxford University Press, 1964; (German translation) *Presse in der Zwangsjacke, 1933–1945.* Düsseldorf: Droste, 1965.

The Great Illusion, 1900–1914 (William L. Langer, ed., *Rise of Modern Europe* series). New York and London: Harper and Row, 1971; Toronto: Fitzhenry and Whiteside, 1971.

Articles

"Prince von Bülow: His Memoirs and His German Critics," *Journal of Modern History*, 4 (June 1932): 261–77.

"The Way of Social Science and History Teaching in Hitler's Germany," *Social Forces*, 12 (December 1933): 187–90.

"Nationalism in Press, Films, and Radio," *Annals of the American Academy of Political and Social Science*, 175 (September 1934): 110–16.

"The Dignity of History in Times of War," *Journal of Modern History*, 15 (March 1943): 1–6.

"Adolf Hitler as Feldherr," *Virginia Quarterly Review*, 24 (Spring 1948): 198–213.

"The Fuehrer and the Field Marshal," *Virginia Quarterly Review*, 26 (Autumn 1950): 492–511.

"The American Experiment in Germany," *South Atlantic Quarterly*, 54 (July 1955): 229–311.

"Adolf Hitler: Taxpayer," *American Historical Review*, 60 (July 1955): 830–42.

"The Washington Meeting, 1955," *American Historical Review*, 61 (April 1956): 767–98.

"Adolf Hitler and the Post-War German Birthrate, an Unpublished Memorandum," *Journal of Central European Affairs*, 17 (July 1957): 166–73.

"Gottfried Feder Calls Hitler to Order: An Unpublished Letter on Nazi Party Affairs," *Journal of Modern History*, 30 (December 1958): 358–62.

"Bavaria," in Daniel H. Thomas and Lynn M. Case, eds. *Guide to the Diplomatic Archives of Western Europe* (Philadelphia: University of Pennsylvania Press, 1959): 311–20 (chapter 15).

"Europe, 1914: Was It Morning Light, High Noon, or Evening Twilight?" *Virginia Quarterly Review,* 41 (Summer 1965): 358–69.

"Retrospect and Prospect," in Dagmar Horna Perman, ed., *Bibliography and the Historian: The Conference at Belmont of the Joint Committee on Bibliographical Services to History, May 1967* (Santa Barbara, Calif.: Clio, 1968) pp. 167–71.

"Participant" in Donald R. McCoy and Benedict K. Zobrist, eds., *Conference of Scholars on the Administration of Occupied Areas: 1943–1955, April 1970* (Independence, Mo: Harry S. Truman Library Institute, 1970), pp. 24–103.

"World War II Documents and Interrogations," *Social Science,* 47 (Spring 1972): 75–81.

"Introduction to Session IV: Some specialized captured Records and their uses," in Robert Wolfe, ed., *Captured German and Related Records: a National Archives Conference, November 1968* (Athens, Ohio: Ohio University Press, 1974), pp. 155–56.

Reviews

André Siegfried, *France: A Study in Nationality. Annals of the American Academy of Political and Social Science,* 150 (July 1930): 298.

D. M. Ketelbey, *A History of Modern Times from 1789 to the Present Day. Annals of the American Academy of Political and Social Science,* 150 (July 1930): 299.

Morrison Beall Giffen, *Fashoda, the Incident and Its Diplomatic Setting. American Historical Review,* 36 (October 1930): 150–51.

Eugene N. Anderson, *The First Moroccan Crisis, 1904–1906. American Historical Review,* 36 (January 1931): 396–97.

Paul Cohen-Portheim, *England, the Unknown Isle. Annals of the American Academy of Political and Social Science,* 157 (September 1931): 248.

E. Malcolm Carroll, *French Public Opinion and Foreign Affairs, 1870–1914. American Historical Review,* 37 (January 1932): 328–29.

"The Memoirs of Prince von Bülow," *Virginia Quarterly Review,* 8 (October 1932): 624–29.

"Lloyd George at War," *Virginia Quarterly Review,* 10 (April 1934): 310–13.

Georges Weill, *Le Journal: Origines, Evolution, et Rôle de la Presse Périodique. American Historical Review,* 40 (July 1935): 717–18.

The History of "The Times." Volume I, *"The Thunderer" in the Making, 1785–1841;* William M. Clyde, *The Struggle for the Freedom of the Press from Caxton to Cromwell. American Historical Review,* 41 (January 1936): 338–40.

G. Bernard Noble, *Policies and Opinions at Paris, 1919. Annals of the American Academy of Political and Social Science,* 183 (January 1936): 293–94.

Lynn M. Case, *French Opinion on the United S.ates and Mexico, 1860–1867. Public Opinion Quarterly,* 1 (January 1937): 155–57.

Theodor Wolff, *The Eve of 1914. Journal of Modern History,* 9 (March 1937): 106–8.

Cyril Spencer Fox, ed. *This was Germany: An Observer at the Court of Berlin . . . 1908–1915. American Historical Review,* 43 (July 1938): 937–38.

Raymond James Sontag, *Germany and England: Background of Conflict, 1848–94;* E. Malcolm Carroll, *Germany and the Great Powers, 1866–1914: A Study in Public Opinion and Foreign Policy. Journal of Modern History,* 11 (September 1939): 405–7.

The History of "The Times." Volume II, *The Tradition Established, 1841–1884. American Historical Review,* 45 (January 1940): 388–89.

Ralph O. Nafziger, *International News and Press. Public Opinion Quarterly,* 5 (March 1941): 175.

"Turkey—Bridge or Bulwark," *Virginia Quarterly Review,* 17 (Autumn 1941): 629–30.

Frederick L. Schuman, *Design for Power: The Struggle for the World. Political Science Quarterly,* 57 (December 1942): 610–11.

Alan Moorehead, *Eclipse. Military Affairs,* 10, no. 2 (Summer 1946): 59–60.

John William de Forest, *A Volunteer's Adventures;* Edward W. Beattie, Jr., *Diary of a Kriegie. Annals of the American Academy of Political and Social Science,* 248 (November 1946): 304–5.

"International Relations: Facts and Fancies," *Virginia Quarterly Review*, 23 (Winter 1947): 145–52.

George Morgenstern, *Pearl Harbor: The Story of the Secret War.* *Annals of the American Academy of Political and Social Science*, 252 (July 1947): 130–31.

"Balance Sheet of the Third Reich," *Virginia Quarterly Review*, 23 (Summer 1947): 475–80.

Allen Welsh Dulles, *Germany's Underground. Annals of the American Academy of Political and Social Science*, 253 (September 1947): 214–15.

Kenneth Ingram, *Years of Crisis: An Outline of International History, 1919–1945. American Historical Review*, 53 (October 1947): 80–81.

The History of "The Times." Volume III, The Twentieth Century Test, 1884–1912. American Historical Review, 53 (July 1948): 806–8.

"Two Worlds in Conflict," *Virginia Quarterly Review*, 24 (Autumn 1948): 613–17.

Louis P. Lochner, ed. and trans., *The Goebbels Diaries, 1942–1943. The South Atlantic Quarterly*, 48 (January 1949): 134–36.

Wilheim Puschel, *Der Niedergang des Rechts im Dritten Reich;* Friedrich Buchwald, *Gerechts Recht;* Alexander Mitscherlich and Fred Mielke, *Das Diktat der Menschenverachtung. Journal of Central European Affairs*, 9 (April 1949): 101–3.

Ministère des Affaires Etrangères, *Documents Diplomatiques Français (1871–1914)*, Volume IX. *Journal of Modern History*, 21 (December 1949): 352–54.

Laing Gray Cowan, *France and the Saar, 1680–1948. Annals of the American Academy of Political and Social Science*, 272 (November 1950): 291.

Anglo-Jewish Association, *Germany's New Nazis. Annals of the American Academy of Political and Social Science*, 285 (January 1953): 225–26.

Wesley Frank Craven and James Lea Cate, eds. *The Army Air Forces in World War II*, Volume III. *Journal of Southern History*, 19 (May 1953): 261–62.

"Can We Trust the Germans?" *Virginia Quarterly Review*, 29 (Summer 1953): 476–80.

Walter Goerlitz, *History of the German General Staff, 1657–1945. Annals of the American Academy of Political and Social Science*, 291 (January 1954): 203–4.

Jacques Bardoux, *La Défaite de Bismarck: L'Expansion Coloniale Française et l'Alliance Russe. American Historical Review*, 59 (April 1954): 671.

"Germany, Past and Future," *Virginia Quarterly Review*, 30 (Spring 1954): 456–61.

John A. Lukacs, *The Great Powers and Eastern Europe. Annals of the American Academy of Political and Social Science*, 295 (September 1954): 202–3.

H. R. Trevor-Roper, ed. *The Bormann Letters. Annals of the American Academy of Political and Social Science*, 298 (March 1955): 227–28.

Hans W. Gatzke, *Stresemann and the Rearmament of Germany. American Historical Review*, 60 (April 1955): 668–69.

Paul Herre, *Kronprinz Wilhelm: Seine Rolle in der Deutschen Politik. Journal of Central European Affairs*, 15 (January 1956): 420–21.

Saul K. Padover, *French Institutions: Values and Politics. Journal of Modern History*, 28 (March 1956): 88–89.

Beate Ruhm von Oppen, ed. *Documents on Germany under Occupation, 1945–1954. American Historical Review*, 61 (July 1956): 1028–29.

Erich Eyck, *Geschichte der Weimarer Republik*, Volume I. *Journal of Modern History*, 28 (September 1956): 293–94.

Alistair Horne, *Return to Power: A Report on the New Germany. Annals of the American Academy of Political and Social Science*, 307 (September 1956): 169.

T. L. Jarman, *The Rise and Fall of Nazi Germany. American Historical Review*, 62 (April 1957): 621–22.

Minna R. Falk, *The History of Germany. Journal of Modern History*, 29 (December 1957): 364–65.

Friedrich Freiherr von Gaertringen, *Fürst Bülows Denkwürdigkeiten: Untersuchungen zu ihrer Entstehungsgeschichte und ihrer Kritik. Journal of Modern History*, 17 (January 1958): 427–28.

C. A. McCartney, *A History of Hungary, 1929–1945. Annals of the American Academy of Political and Social Science*, 316 (March 1958): 162–63.

Ernst Hanfstaengl, *Unheard Witness. Journal of Modern History*, 30 (September 1958): 284–85.

Peter Grothe, *To Win the Minds of Men. Annals of the American Academy of Political and Social Science*, 323 (May 1959): 192–93.

Eugene Davidson, *The Death and Life of Germany: An Account of the American Occupation. American Historical Review*, 65 (January 1960): 343–44.

Harry F. Young, *Maximilian Harden: Censor Germaniae. Journal of Central European Affairs*, 19 (January 1960): 427–28.

Arno J. Mayer, *Political Origins of the New Diplomacy, 1917–1918. Journal of Modern History*, 32 (March 1960): 89.

Boris Celovsky, *Das Münchener Abkommen von 1938. Journal of Modern History*, 32 (March 1960): 100–11.

Wenzel Jaksch, *Europas Weg Nach Potsdam: Schuld und Schicksal im Donauram. Journal of Modern History*, 32 (June 1960): 176–77.

Karl W. Deutsch and Lewis J. Edinger, *Germany Rejoins the Powers: Mass Opinion, Interest Groups, and Elites in Contemporary German Foreign Policy. American Historical Review*, 66 (October 1960) 157–59.

Louis P. Lochner, *Herbert Hoover and Germany. American Historical Review*, 332 (November 1960): 213–14.

Albert Krebs, *Tendenzen und Gestalten der NSDAP: Erinnerungen an die Frühzeit der Partei. Journal of Modern History*, 33 (March 1961): 91–92.

Hildemarie Dieckmann, *Johannes Popitz: Entwicklung und Wirksamkeit in der Zeit der Weimarer Republik. American Historical Review*, 66 (April 1961): 805.

Kurt Koszyk, *Zwischen Kaiserreich und Diktatur: Die Sozialdemokratische Press von 1914 bis 1933.* Journal of Central European Affairs, 21 (July 1961): 230–31.

James Donohoe, *Hitler's Conservative Opponents in Bavaria, 1930–1945.* American Historical Review, 67 (January 1962): 407–8.

Gerhardt L. Weinberg, *Hitlers Zweites Buch: Ein Dokument aus dem Jahr 1928. Journal of Central European Affairs,* 22 (July 1962): 240–42.

A. L. Rowse, *Appeasement: A Study in Political Decline, 1933–1939. American Historical Review,* 67 (July 1962): 1098.

"In a Place Called Armageddon," *Virginia Quarterly Review,* 38 (Summer 1962): 520–23.

Arthur J. Marder, *From the Dreadnought to Scapa Flow,* Volume I. *Journal of Modern History,* 34 (December 1962): 458–59.

Akten zur Deutschen Auswärtigen Politik, 1918–1945. Series D, 1937–1945, Volume III. *American Historical Review,* 68 (January 1963): 524.

Sherman David Spector. *Rumania at the Paris Peace Conference. American Historical Review,* 348 (July 1963): 211.

Jacques Willequet, *Le Congo Belge et la Weltpolitik (1894–1914). American Historical Review,* 69 (October 1963): 142–44.

"Love Affair with Germany," *Virginia Quarterly Review,* 39 (Autumn 1963): 660–64.

Henry Ashby Turner, Jr., *Stresemann and the Politics of the Weimar Republic. Annals of the American Academy of Political and Social Science*, 352 (March 1964): 193–94.

Erich Eyck, *A History of the Weimar Republic*, Volume II. *Annals of the American Academy of Political and Social Science*, 356 (November 1964): 223–24.

Allan Mitchell, *Revolution in Bavaria, 1918–1919: The Eisner Regime and the Soviet Republic. Annals of the American Academy of Political and Social Science*, 362 (November 1965): 205–6.

Ernest K. Bramsted, *Goebbels and National Socialist Propaganda, 1925–1945. American Historical Review*, 71 (January 1966): 612.

"On the Eve of Armageddon," *Virginia Quarterly Review*, 42 (Summer 1966): 476–79.

Adam Wandruszka, *Schicksalsjahr 1866. American Historical Review*, 72 (July 1967): 1381–82.

George F. Kennan, *From Prague after Munich: Diplomatic Papers, 1939–1940. Annals of the American Academy of Political and Social Science*, 380 (November 1968): 169.

"Germany Divided," *Virginia Quarterly Review*, 46 (Spring 1970): 349–52.

P. J. V. Rolo, *Entente Cordiale: The Origins and Negotiations of the Anglo-French Agreements of 8 April 1904. American Historical Review*, 75 (December 1970): 2039.

Frank G. Weber, *Eagles on the Crescent: Germany, Austria, and the Turkish Alliance, 1914–1918. American Historical Review*, 77 (February 1972): 131–32.

Richard C. Cobb, *Reactions to the French Revolution. Annals of the American Academy of Political and Social Science,* 405 (January 1973): 188–89.

"The German Secret Service," *Virginia Quarterly Review,* 49 (Winter 1973): 126–31.

Ernst Feder, *Heute Sprach Ich Mit . . .: Tagebücher eines Berliner Publizisten, 1926–1932. Journal of Modern History,* 45 (June 1973): 347–48.

Josef Hofmann, *Journalist in Republik, Diktatur und Besatzungszeit: Erinnerungen, 1916–1947. American Historical Review,* 83 (June 1978): 752.

Contributors

ROBERT D. COAKLEY received his master's degree in 1940 as a student of Professor Hale and completed his Ph.D. at Virginia in 1949. He served as Deputy Chief Historian, U.S. Army Center of Military History, until his retirement in 1980. Dr. Coakley is coauthor of two volumes in the *U.S. Army in World War II* series on *Global Logistics and Strategy.*

MARIE DONAGHAY, one of Professor Hale's graders between 1965 and 1968, received her doctorate from the University of Virginia in 1970. She is the author of more than a dozen articles, papers, and reviews concerning late eighteenth-century France and Anglo-French diplomacy. Dr. Donaghay is presently teaching at Villanova University.

DOUGLAS W. FOARD is a professor of history at Ferrum College, Ferrum, Va., where he has taught since 1965 after having completed his master's degree at Virginia under Professor Hale's direction. Professor Foard took his Ph.D. in history at Washington University and has since continued his research in the field of modern Spain.

F. X. J. HOMER (Coeditor) received his M.A. and Ph.D. at Virginia under Professor Hale. In 1968 he returned to his undergraduate alma mater, the University of Scranton, where he now serves as professor of history. The recipient of NEH grants for advanced study at Vanderbilt and Yale universities, Professor Homer has focused his research on twentieth-century Germany and Britain.

LEE KENNETT received his doctorate in history from the University of Virginia in 1962, and in that same year began teaching at the University of Georgia, where he now holds the rank of professor of history. A specialist in military history, Professor Kennett is the author of *A*

History of Strategic Bombing (New York: Charles Scribner's Sons, 1982).

ENNO E. KRAEHE is Oron J. Hale's successor as the William W. Corcoran Professor of History at the University of Virginia and was a fascinated bystander at many of Professor Hale's undertakings. He is the author of *Metternich's German Policy,* 2 vols. (Princeton: Princeton University Press, 1963, 1983).

JAMES A. MUMPER was with the U.S. Seventh Army in the spring of 1945. A graduate of Swarthmore College, he was a John Hay Fellow at Yale and then a Jefferson Fellow at Virginia where he completed his dissertation under Dumas Malone. Professor Hale supervised his master's thesis. A member of the Raven Society, Professor Mumper served as chairman of the Department of History and Political Science at Bridgewater College from 1969 until his death in late 1984.

EUGENE L. RASOR completed his M.A. and Ph.D. at the University of Virginia where Professor Hale directed his master's thesis and served as a reader for his dissertation. Since 1965 he has been professor of history at Emory and Henry College, Emory, Va., where he presently serves as chairman of the Division of Social Science. Professor Rasor has on three occasions been a research fellow at the Institute of Historical Research in London and is the author of *Reform in the Royal Navy: A Social History of the Lower Deck, 1850–80* (Hamden, Conn.: Shoe Tree Press, 1975).

HARRY RITTER is associate professor of history at Western Washington University, Bellingham, Wa. He is the author of several articles on Central and East European history and is presently completing a *Dictionary of Concepts in History.* Professor Ritter received his doctorate under Professor Hale's direction at the University of Virginia in 1969.

LARRY D. WILCOX (Coeditor) completed his M.A. and Ph.D. degrees under Professor Hale at the University of Virginia. Since 1968 he has taught modern German and European history at the University of Toledo where he is now professor of history. His major research interests are interwar Germany and Anglo-German relations. Professor Wilcox's reviews and articles have appeared in several scholarly journals.

Index